MERSEYPRIDE
Essays in Liverpool exceptionalism

JOHN BELCHEM

LIVERPOOL UNIVERSITY PRESS

First published 2000
Revised second edition published 2006 by
LIVERPOOL UNIVERSITY PRESS
4 Cambridge Street
Liverpool L69 7ZU

British Library Cataloguing-in-Publication Data
A British Library CIP Record is available

ISBN 1-84631-010-5

Design and production: Janet Allan

Typeset in 10/13 Century Schoolbook by
Koinonia, Bury
Printed and bound in Great Britain by
Bell and Bain, Glasgow

Contents

Illustrations

(after page 92)

1. Liverpool Shipperies Exhibition plate, 1886, from the International Exhibition of Navigation, Commerce and Industry held at Wavertree.
2. J.A. Picton, architect, local historian and 'annalist' of Liverpool, from the *Liverpool Leader Album*, 1874.
3. Letters Patent of King John, founding the Town of Liverpool, 28 August, 1207.
4. Postcard celebrating the 700th anniversary of the granting of letters patent to Liverpool, 1907.
5. Programme of the concert to celebrate the 750th anniversary of the granting of letters patent to Liverpool, 1957.
6. Liverpool and Africa exhibition at Liverpool Library, 1957.
7. Multi-racial Community exhibition, Toxteth Library, 1979.
8. Programme of the Scouser Songs concert at Philharmonic Hall, Liverpool, 3 March 1962.
9. Map of the most unhealthy district in Liverpool, by Nathaniel Smyth, c. 1875.
10. Father Nugent, from the *Liverpool Leader Album*, 1874.
11. The 'Martyr Priests'
12. Photograph by T. Burke of the 'Dandy' Patrick Byrne memorial drinking fountain, Scotland Road, late nineteenth century.
13. Samuel Holme, Mayor of Liverpool 1852-3, by E. Patten.
14. Wood engraving by Edward Carter-Preston, one of a series on Liverpool Cathedral themes produced in the 1930s.

Illustration Acknowledgements

Plates 1, 5 and 8 courtesy Fritz Spiegl, 2, 4, 6, 7, 9, 10, and 12 courtesy Liverpool Record Office, plate 11 reprinted from J.O. Bennett, *Father Nugent* (Liverpool, 1949), plate 13 courtesy the Board of Trustees of the National Museums and Galleries on Merseyside (Walker Art Gallery, Liverpool), plate 14 courtesy Dean and Chapter of Liverpool Cathedral. Plate 3, Courtesy of School of History, Unversity of Liverpool. We are grateful to Ian Qualtrough, of the Department of Geography, University of Liverpool, for his help in photographing the illustrations in the Liverpool Record Office.

FRONT COVER

The front cover reproduces Roger McGough's nine-line double acrostic poem on his home city of Liverpool. The poem, commissioned by Channel Five as part of its Five Arts Cities initiative, also marked Liverpool being named as European Capital of Culture. Liverpool was the first city to feature in the Five Arts Initiative, developed in association with Arts Council England to encourage enjoyment of the arts, and as part of it Roger McGough and fellow Liverpool poet Brian Patten took viewers on a poetic tour of the city in a programme entitled 'Liverpool: A Lyrical City' to demonstrate Liverpool's unique artistic, social and cultural heritage.

Celebrated poet Roger McGough first became internationally well-known alongside Adrian Henri and Brian Patten as one of the original 1960s Liverpool poets; their collection *The Mersey Sound*, first published in 1967, became the best selling poetry anthology of all time. Roger continues to enjoy an international career as poet, writer and performer and, although he now lives in London, he remains very closely associated with Liverpool.

Tables

Acknowledgements

I owe a considerable debt of gratitude to librarians and archivists in various locations in Liverpool (in particular the Athenaeum and the City Record Office) and elsewhere (most notably in London, Dublin and Belfast). My thanks, too, to seminar and conference organisers in Amsterdam, Bochum and Paris for allowing me to try out ideas and encouraging me into the comparative frameworks within which Liverpool's exceptionalism is best appreciated. Ingrid and Fritz Spiegl, doyens of local history and 'scouse' heritage, provided every encouragement and assistance, as well as several of the illustrations. Robin Bloxsidge of Liverpool University Press has offered expert advice throughout. Mary Belchem, my partner and fellow southerner, has shared the joy of living in Liverpool and learning of its past – as well as the agonies and anxieties of the historian trying to do it justice in print. I hope the final product does not disappoint.

Introduction:
the new 'Livercool'

A reflection of its time, *Merseypride: essays in Liverpool exceptionalism* grappled with the stigma, doom and gloom which kept late twentieth-century Liverpool apart, an internal 'other' within enterprise Britain. Written in the context of seemingly irreversible economic and demographic decline, the essays sought to re-evaluate Liverpool's history of difference and apartness – and to offer some limited optimism for the future. Liverpool's 'exceptional' past, it was suggested, offered the last best hope in the city's 'urban asset audit':[1] repackaged as heritage, 'Merseypride' history might facilitate regeneration through conservation and cultural tourism. How circumspect and unambitious this now seems. In the space of a few short years, the 'reborn' city (as the former leader of the council, Mike Storey, described it) has reinvented itself, moving beyond regeneration towards urban renaissance.[2] Population loss has been halted and employment prospects improved. Like its re-named and re-branded 'John Lennon' airport, among the fastest growing in Europe, the city has taken off, outstripping other major cities in the latest surveys of new business start-ups.[3] Once considered a hindrance, its distinctive accent is now a marketing asset, placing Liverpool at the top of the league for call centres, including the

1] The terminology derives from Charles Landry, *The Creative City: a toolkit for urban innovators* (London, 2000), 7, essential reading for those of us involved in the working groups which helped to prepare Liverpool's Capital of Culture bid.
2] 'A city matured – a city reborn', *Guardian 2*, 20 Oct. 2004.
3] See the Liverpool Business Centre website, itself part of the mission to establish Liverpool as '*the* business friendly city', at *www.liverpoolbusinesscentre.co.uk*. At the time of writing there is talk not only of extending the budget airline European destinations but of establishing a direct link to New York, one of Liverpool's twin cities.

European reservations centre for US Airways.[4] From just one entry in the *Good Food Guide* in 1995, the city, picked out for special mention in the introduction to the 2005 edition, now boasts six entries.[5] Forward-looking self-promotion, not self-pitying nostalgia, prevails in the new 'Livercool', incipient European Capital of Culture. Alongside courses on social exclusion, the Department of Sociology at the University of Liverpool now offers a flagship MA programme on 'Cities, Culture and Regeneration' with Liverpool as exemplary case study, the 'ideal environment' (the brochure asserts) in which to study and contribute to key policy and academic debates about the relationship between culture and regeneration.[6]

The Toxteth riots of 1981, an indictment of exclusion, deprivation and discrimination, brought Liverpool, the shock city of post-colonial, post-industrial Britain, to the forefront of political attention, hastening a major policy shift from regional development to urban regeneration. Thereafter a kind of experimental test-bed for a large number of ill-fated initiatives, Liverpool for example had one of the first Enterprise Zones, the first Task Force, one of the first City Action Teams, and one of the two first-generation Urban Development Corporations. Regeneration, however, was a pious and cruel irony: throughout the 1980s employment and population fell by 23 and 12 per cent respectively. Pioneer attempts at cultural tourism, the International Garden Festival of 1984 and refurbishment of the Albert Dock (despite the successful establishment of Tate Liverpool), failed to turn the tide. Seemingly irreversible decline spiralled Liverpool down into European Union Objective One status in 1993, the first major 'industrial' conurbation to be so defined, the level of GDP per head having fallen to only 73 per cent of the European Union average. Although at the time it seemed a badge of failure, the 'award' of Objective One funding to the Merseyside 'sub-region' may come to be seen in historical perspective as a decisive turning-point for the city. Subsequent political factors added to the impetus: under the Liberal Democrats since 1998, the city has adopted a style of urban entrepreneurialism, partnership governance and civic boosterism, anathema to the Militant politics of the 1980s, the legacy of which (budgetary and otherwise) kept Liverpool (the third-worst performing council in Britain with the highest council tax when the Liberal

4] 'Scousers put the accent on success', *Guardian*, 22 Sept. 2000. There must be doubt, however, as to whether Liverpool call centres will be able to withstand competition from further afield than the United Kingdom and the European Union.
5] *The Good Food Guide 2005* (London, 2004), 15, and 331–34.
6] For further details, see the Department's website, *www.liv.ac.uk/sspsw*

Democrats took over) for some while behind other northern cities in urban transformation.[7]

A latecomer to successful implementation of the process, Liverpool now applies state of the art regeneration procedures (as befits what the architect Will Alsop has envisaged as the western gateway to the northern 'super-city' spanning the M62 motorway corridor from Liverpool via Manchester and Leeds across to Hull). Inspired by the 1999 Rogers Report, *Towards an Urban Renaissance*, Liverpool Vision, the nation's first Urban Regeneration Company, bridges key public and private agencies in promotion of a 'Strategic Regeneration Framework' (based on seven 'action areas'), with partnership funding from English Partnerships, the North West Development Agency and the city council. Having waited so long, Liverpool is comparatively well-placed to benefit from regeneration. While badly damaged by the Second World War blitz, the remarkable waterfront and public architecture of England's finest Victorian city (recently celebrated in a highly successful new version of Pevsner's guide)[8] subsequently escaped some of the worst excesses of late twentieth–century 'planning' vandalism, perhaps the one advantage of the city's declining fortunes at the time (and an interesting parallel with Providence, Rhode Island, America's 'renaissance city').[9] Established in 2002, HELP – the Historic Environment of Liverpool Project – brought the now obligatory partnership approach (embracing English Heritage, the North West Development Agency, Liverpool Vision, National Museums Liverpool, Liverpool Culture Company and the city council) to the promotion of the rich architectural heritage, now valued as 'a unique asset that can help provide a sustainable future for the city as it continues to change and develop'.[10] Then in July 2004 came UNESCO

7] Richard Meegan, 'Urban Regeneration, Politics and Social Cohesion: The Liverpool Case', and Gideon Ben-Tovim, 'Futures for Liverpool', in R. Munck (ed.), *Reinventing the City: Liverpool in Comparative Perspective* (Liverpool, 2003), 53–79 and 227–46. See also Peter Batey, 'Merseyside', in P. Roberts, K. Thomas and G. Williams (eds), *Metropolitan planning in Britain: a comparative study* (London, 1999), 97–111.

8] Joseph Sharples, *Liverpool: Pevsner Architectural Guides* (New Haven and London, 2004).

9] Francis J. Leazes, Jr, and Mark T. Motte, *Providence: The Renaissance City* (Boston, 2004). In June 2005, the Royal Society of Arts (RSA) in the United States organised a major international symposium at the Rhode Island School of Design, 'Transforming Urban Communities: Lessons from Providence, Rhode Island, and Liverpool, England'.

10] Sir Neil Cossons, *HELP* newsletter, Oct. 2003.

inscription for the Liverpool Maritime Mercantile City World Heritage Site which covers far more than the Pier Head with its iconic 'three graces' (and new cruise liner terminal currently under construction): the site embraces the Albert Dock Conservation Area (now one of the leading visitor attractions in the north west); the Stanley Dock Conservation Area (where the sheer scale but pinched interior construction of the gargantuan tobacco warehouse, closed since 1980, seemingly defy any re-use or regeneration); the 'commercial' centre around Castle Street, Dale Street and Old Hall Street (now increasingly residential and 'desirable' as commercial palaces are transformed into luxury apartments); the William Brown Street 'Cultural Quarter' (where Victorian civic pride reached its acme, a heritage preserved with requisite commercial acumen by National Museums Liverpool and soon to be enhanced by major renovation schemes for the City Central Libraries); and the warehouses and merchants' houses of Lower Duke Street, historic buildings which contribute much to the character of the 'Rope Walks', the parallel narrow streets which now provide the main focus of the city's thriving night life and creative industries sector. Yet another partnership scheme, the Townscape Heritage Initiative, was launched in 2005, aided by Heritage Lottery Funding, to bring properties back into a good state of repair, adapt them for new uses and restore historic details.

World Heritage Site inscription should have considerable long-term benefit for Liverpool. Will the same apply to the award of European Capital of Culture status in 2008? Announced in June 2003, this was an unexpected (but most welcome) success, overshadowing tentative plans (following the publication of *Merseypride*) for civic commemoration of the 800th anniversary in 2007 of the granting of letters patent. The local authorities have openly acknowledged that expectations extended no further than the initial boost simply of bidding for the coveted and prestigious award, of establishing the city's credentials to be judged alongside more favoured (and less denigrated) locations. To its surprise (and delight), the council's 'Culture Company' is now transforming its role (no easy task) from civic boosterism to major project delivery. Thanks to World Heritage inscription and Capital of Culture status, Liverpool has a brace of glittering prizes (with attendant benefits in tourism, inward investment and employment), more than adequate compensation for the end of the second round of Objective One funding in 2006.

Given this impressive record, it was only fitting that Liverpool F.C.

should return to European winning ways. The victory against the odds in the Champions League final in 2005 instantly served as metaphor for the city's revival and rehabilitation. Here for once was a Liverpool story with which the tabloid press wished to identify, hence headlines proclaiming 'We're all scousers now'. Adorned in fake wigs, breakfast television presenters somewhat guilelessly adapted Harry Enfield's 'scouse git' routine for the joyous celebration, part of a national 'freak show' in which 'everybody from Natasha Kaplinsky to Tony Blair appeared to transmogrify into plastic Scousers overnight'. Amidst the euphoria, only the most dyspeptic were concerned about the psychological impact on scousers themselves, so well attuned to 'wallowing in mawkish laments about their defeats': success, it was feared, 'could seriously damage their self-image of put-upon miserablist isolationism'.[11]

At the top end of the market, 'posh' publications (with one notorious exception) were already taking note of Liverpool's make-over, a transformation which belied external perceptions and the old scouse stereotypes. In March 2003, *Tatler* dedicated 23 pages of fashion shoots to locations in what it described (quite without irony) as 'Livercool', the 'jewel of the north ... the place where tradition meets cutting edge'.[12] It was perhaps no coincidence that the leading model was Lady Eloise Anson, niece of the Duke of Westminster whose company Grosvenor Henderson were beginning work on the Paradise Project, a 42-acre city-centre regeneration programme on an immense scale to provide 'world-class shopping, leisure and living at the heart of a world-class city', due for completion in 2008, capital of culture year.[13] In November 2004, *Country Life* drew attention to 'The Quality of Mersey', concentrating on the 'Georgian quarter' (a term rapidly familiarised by estate agents and property developers) to chart the 'extraordinary revival of fortunes of Liverpool's under-celebrated streets and squares'. Under the heading 'A City Reborn', the *RSA Journal* charted the resurgence of creative and cultural activity, noting that Liverpool in 2004 was 'a city whose hour has come'. Oblivious of such transformation, the hapless *Spectator* caused a furore (for which the penitent editor, then the shadow minister for the arts, was compelled to make humble public apology) when it regurgitated the

11] Mick Hume, 'We're all Scousers now? Count me out', *Times*, 27 May 2005.
12] 'Livercool', *Tatler*, March 2003
13] Promotional literature is available from the Paradise Project Information Centre, 76–78 Lord Street, Liverpool, and the website: *www.liverpoolpsda.co.uk*

old tropes about self-pitying 'tribal' Liverpudlians wallowing in economic misfortune, excessive sentimentality and victim status, in its infamous commentary on local response to the tragic fate of Ken Bigley, an engineer from Liverpool kidnapped, humiliated and murdered in Iraq.[14]

As *Merseypride* noted, scally scousers are still lovingly reconstructed in heritage publications, while economic adversity remains the unchanging context for the ever-popular 'saga' fiction of Helen Forrester and followers (with its valuable insights into previously unrecorded women's history and survival strategies).[15] However, there is no place for such nostalgic anachronisms in the new life-style magazines. Trinity Mirror, owners of the *Liverpool Daily Post* and *Echo*, now offer *Space*, a glossy magazine dedicated to 'stylish living in Liverpool', distributed selectively along 'geodemographic' lines, an upmarket application of the postcode analysis pioneered in the city in the 1970s to help explain 'certain nuances of geographical deprivation'.[16] Designer chic prevails in a city henceforth propelled by cultural and creative industries, tourism, consumption and city-centre living. Although regularly handling over 30 million tonnes of cargo a year, the docks are now far distant with a workforce reduced to under 500: scrap metal has replaced manufactured goods as the main export trade, a change of greater economic and symbolic significance than the metamorphosis of Ford into Jaguar out at Halewood at the opposite outskirts of the city.

As readers of *Merseypride* will appreciate, there is an interesting historical irony to observe here. There is nothing new about Liverpool's image problem. In early exercises in urban promotion, however, culture was deployed as a counterweight to provide legitimacy and pride, to counteract the otherwise philistine, mercenary and squalid aspects of the great seaport's commercial success, 'to redeem Liverpool from the reproach of an exclusive devotion to commercial pursuits and the acquisition of wealth'.[17] Nowadays by contrast, culture itself is hailed as the commercial driver – with initial (over-optimistic?) predictions of 14,000 new jobs, 1.7 million extra visitors and up to £2 billion in investment, the Capital of

14] 'Bigley's fate', *Spectator*, 16 Oct. 2004.
15] Val Williamson, 'Regional identity: a gendered heritage? Reading women in 1990s fiction', in S. Caunce, E. Mazierska, S. Sydney-Smith and J. K. Walton (eds), *Relocating Britishness* (Manchester, 2004), 183–95.
16] See the interview with Professor Richard Webber, 'the father of geodemographics' in *Guardian Weekly*, 16 July 2005.
17] 'Festival of the Literary and Philosophical Society', *Daily Post*, 22 Feb. 1862.

Culture nomination has been described as 'rocket fuel' for the local economy – the best hope for sustained economic prosperity.

In an effort to purge memories of the slave trade, Liverpool underwent a second stage of the 'urban renaissance' which had earlier established the infrastructures and organisations of polite society throughout Georgian Britain.[18] While deeply imbued with classical references and legitimacy, the new 'Liverpolis', dedicated to commerce, culture and civilisation, went beyond the Hellenism which boosted civic pride elsewhere in urban Victorian Britain. Inspired by the Roscoe circle, Liverpool scholar-merchants (Liverpool gentlemen not Manchester men) stood forward as the new Medici, looking beyond ancient Greece to renaissance Florence as what Tristram Hunt has described as the idealised urban model: 'a society that made its money from cotton and finance, combined democracy with civic leadership, and exercised an even more impressive aesthetic patronage'.[19] Combined with the 'improving' civic duties undertaken by the council, following municipal reform in 1835, this new cultural mission in the would-be 'Florence of the north' did much to make good previous deficiencies: the absence of 'historic' cultural, educational and charitable endowments; and the inattention to social problems in the single-minded pursuit of commercial advantage. Much applauded by Ramsay Muir, the city's foremost historian, the 'new spirit of civic pride' reached a high-point in the construction of St George's Hall, 'that noble building, one of the noblest in the modern world, which is to-day the supreme architectural boast of the city'.[20] However, the cost of the building scandalised sanitary reformers who were concerned less about reversing Liverpool's philistine image than eradicating its reputation as 'the black spot on the Mersey', an early instance of a recurrent controversy in urban promotion between public display and basic infrastructure. 'There is in course of expenditure, for splendour, on one single edifice, St George's Hall, upwards of £100,000', Sir Edwin Chadwick expostulated: 'a sum which would, if so applied, serve to sweep and cleanse in perpetuity, and make decent, the filthy by-streets of upwards of 23,000 houses, out of the 45,000 houses which are under the corporation jurisdiction.'[21] Liverpool was the first to appoint a Medical

18] Jon Stobart, 'Culture versus commerce: societies and spaces for elites in eighteenth-century Liverpool', *Journal of Historical Geography*, 28 (2002), 471–85.
19] Tristram Hunt, *Building Jerusalem: The Rise and Fall of the Victorian City* (London, 2004), ch. 5.
20] Ramsay Muir, *A History of Liverpool* (London, 1907), ch. 15.
21] Quoted in Hunt, *Building Jerusalem*, 191–92.

Officer of Health, Dr Duncan, but his advocacy of heavy expenditure on sanitary works (which he believed the corporation could well afford with its vast income from dock dues) was accompanied less by materialist understanding of the poverty at the bottom of the residential and social hierarchy with its vast casual labour market than by 'racist' condemnation of 'reckless' Irish migrants and the 'peculiar habits' they brought with them.[22] Prompted by continued denigration of the Irish, social reform became a priority in Liverpool, local Tories leading the way to 'municipal socialism', but a cultured elite continued to advocate 'the political value of art to municipal life'. In 1875 Philip Rathbone called upon his fellow Liverpolitans to 'decide whether we will take advantage of our almost unequalled opportunities for the cultivation of Art, or whether we shall be content to rot away, as Carthage, Antioch and Tyre have rotted away, leaving not a trace to show here a population of more than half a million souls once lived, loved, felt and thought. Surely the home of Roscoe is worthy of a better fate?'[23]

Viewed from this perspective, the current priority accorded to culture may well lead to further forms of tension and fracture. Sociologists are warning of 'culture wars' between cultural policy as a tool for economic growth and cultural policy as an expression of grassroots and community-based activity – the kind of 'scouse' culture that has been so creative in dialectic reaction to recent economic adversity.[24] There is an important spatial dimension behind such concerns. In its official conception, cultural re-branding is reinforcing (perhaps rather too dramatically) the city-centre focus of the regeneration agenda, markedly different from interwar attempts at redefining (and reviving) Liverpool through a policy of out-lying industrial diversification in Speke, Aintree and Kirkby. As part of the new marketing strategy, National Museums and Galleries on Merseyside has been renamed National Museums Liverpool (and duly admitted to the

22] G. Kearns and P. Laxton, 'Ethnic Groups as Public Health Hazards: the Famine Irish in Liverpool and Lazaretto Politics', in E. Rodriguez-Ocana (ed.), *The Politics of the Healthy Life: An International Perspective* (Sheffield, 2002), 13–40.

23] P. H. Rathbone, *The Political Value of Art to Municipal Life* (Liverpool, 1875), 45, quoted in Matthew Vickers, 'Civic Image and Civic Patriotism in Liverpool 1880–1914', unpublished DPhil thesis, University of Oxford, 2000, 187. This important thesis was not available until after *Merseypride* was published.

24] Paul Jones and Stuart Wilks-Heeg, 'Capitalising Culture: Liverpool 2008', *Local Economy*, 19 (2004), 341–60, a special edition on 'Cultural Policy and Urban Regeneration'. See also the free magazine, *Nerve: promoting grassroots arts and culture on Merseyside*.

city's Freedom Roll of Associations and Institutions). No longer stigmatised, Liverpool itself is the region's 'unique selling point', its cultural and 'historic' core.[25] The rich legacy of vacated warehouses, lofts and old office buildings is being converted into stunning apartments, the latest exercise in re-cycling of city-centre space – a century ago, when commercial space was at a premium, the iconic three graces, the epicentre of the World Heritage site, were built upon land reclaimed from a redundant central dock. The population of the city centre has increased some fourfold in the 1990s with bijou accommodation for affluent young professionals, miles away in every sense from the deprived outer estates. Liverpool it seems is following the pattern of Glasgow, the last British city to enjoy European City of Culture status in 1990: a rapidly regenerating and gentrifying urban core surrounded by a ring of intensely disadvantaged residential areas.[26]

Within the city centre itself, 'official' culture is being prioritised in self-defeating manner, denying space to the alternative, diverse and challenging cultural forms of expression which have contributed so much to the city's cultural creativity and distinctive identity. As culture is commodified into corporate blandness, alternative and individual outlets cannot afford the regenerated rents, while public spaces in the city centre are being privatised and sanitised by developers (and their attendant security staff and cctv cameras), again at the expense of a diverse and vibrant street culture. For the historian there are echoes here of the 'clean-up' ahead of the 750th anniversary celebrations in 1957 with the closure of the original site of Paddy's Market, 'the coloured seamen's bazaar'; the removal of Codman's Punch and Judy show from its time-honoured Lime Street location to the windswept plateau where business soon hit 'rock bottom'; and a concerted but abortive attempt to rid city-centre streets of barrow boys 'called a variety of things from spivs to archaic anachronisms'. It was

25] As geographers have recognised, there has always been a disproportionately high concentration of activity in the central area of Liverpool, a distinctive feature of the Merseyside conurbation within which there is 'no equivalent of Wolverhampton or Bolton'; see F. I. Masser, 'The Analysis and Prediction of Physical Change in the Central Area of Liverpool', in R. Lawton and C. M. Cunningham (eds), *Merseyside: Social and Economic Studies* (London, 1970), 455–56.
26] Beatriz Garcia, 'Cultural policy and urban regeneration in Western European cities: lessons from experience, prospects for the future', *Local Economy*, 19 (2004), 312–26. Dr Garcia is leading research into the long-term legacies of Glasgow 1990 European City of Culture for 'The Cities and Culture Project' at the Centre for Cultural Policy Research, University of Glasgow, details on the website: *www.culturalpolicy.arts.gla.ac.uk*

also the year when decisions were taken to abandon both the overhead railway, the 'dockers' umbrella', and the tramway system (a lottery was held for tickets on the last ride).[27] With a thoroughness beyond the 1957 exercise, Liverpool city centre is currently being improved in appearance (the festival of litter, noted by Bill Bryson, however, still continues if on a less spectacular scale)[28] but is this at the cost of its distinct identity, that 'otherness' so cherished in its past? In chronicling the city's popular music from the Cavern to the Coral, Paul Du Noyer describes Liverpool (designated as the United Kingdom's number one music city in 2002 with 53 number one chart hits by 23 different bands and soloists over the previous 50 years) as 'a sort of sunless Marseille', defiantly non-provincial, the capital of itself.[29] Will it be able to retain that 'edge' city creative excitement characteristic of de-centred major ports like Naples and Marseille with similar 'second city' pretensions and picaresque reputations?

Notwithstanding these concerns that in gentrified and commercial format Liverpool might be regenerated into yet another 'franchise' city, there has been much to commend in the manner by which the city secured Capital of Culture status. The city council did not abdicate cultural leadership to private-sector culture and heritage consultants, but took a close interest in the Capital of Culture bid, ensuring in the process the winning formula – a wider public engagement with the project than was achieved in any of the competing cities. Somewhat earlier, Liverpool Organisation, a pioneer exercise in partnership urban 'visioning', had recognised the importance of engaging the local citizenry in civic boosterism. Established to attract inward investment and industrial diversification in the 1920s, Liverpool Organisation was premised on the understanding that 'if we were going to meet with any success in our efforts to interest people in the possibilities of Liverpool as an industrial centre, we had first to interest them in Liverpool'. As well as running extensive advertising campaigns in national and overseas newspapers, Liverpool Organisation sought to enlist local residents though the promotion of an annual Civic Week. As Lord Woolton noted in his *Memoirs*, 'this event brought large numbers of people into the city, where they spent money, but – most important of all – it told

27] See the Town Clerk's Press Cuttings for 1957 in Liverpool Record Office, 352CLE/CUT1/95.
28] Bill Bryson, *Notes from a Small Island* (London, 1996), 235.
29] Paul Du Noyer, *Liverpool: Wondrous Place: Music from the Cavern to the Coral* (London, 2002), 5.

the citizens of Liverpool something about their own city that helped to create a feeling of civic pride, and these self-same people wrote to their friends in different parts of the country, carrying on in the most effective manner the advertising of Liverpool'.[30] In similar manner, the promotion of the Capital of Culture bid and its (unexpected) success has done much to boost pride and morale throughout the city. However, this again is where potential 'culture wars' might come into play. Obviously the cultural pro-gramme should promote community participation and empowerment, but attention must also be accorded to the expectations of a wider audience. As European Capital of Culture, Liverpool will have a unique opportunity not only to showcase its remarkable local talent but also to disabuse (once and for all) external misperception and residual media misrepresentation of the city (alas not confined to the columns of the *Spectator*). Having fallen so far down the urban hierarchy, Liverpool needs to re-establish itself as a major European venue in 2008, able to attract, stage and afford the very best national and international talent.

Here it is instructive to look back not only to Rathbone's apostrophe on the civic value of ('high') art but also to the controversy following the 700th anniversary celebrations in 1907 (which figure prominently in the opening essay of *Merseypride*) when the proceeds from the Pageant were used to finance frescoes in the Town Hall, a commission accorded to London artists, much to the dismay of local practitioners. Shortly before its demise in 1895, local artists had succeeded in infiltrating the Liverpool Art Club dominated by the Rathbone clique – 'essentially a gentlemen's club for those who loved art, or who pretended to be art-lovers'[31] – but they bemoaned their lack of influence over municipal policy towards the arts: 'It is as ridiculous in our view that the destiny of Liverpool Art should be at the mercy of "the butcher, the baker, and candlestick maker", as it would be to place in the hands of an artist the control of the tramway system'. Seen from their perspective, it was 'more important that such culture as is native in any city should be tended, developed, and ultimately employed than that a hundred masterpieces adorn the walls of the public gallery'. Despite vociferous protest, the city council remained resolute in its

30] Lord Woolton, *The Memoirs of the Rt. Hon. The Earl of Woolton* (London, 1959), 112–14.
31] Dongho Chun, 'Collecting collectors: The Liverpool Art Club and its exhibitions 1872–1895', *Transactions of the Historic Society of Lancashire and Cheshire*, 151 (2002), 127–49.

determination to eschew any suggestion of parochial provincialism at a time when Liverpool's pretensions as 'second city of empire' were open to question, the recent failure to incorporate contiguous Bootle marking the end of plans for a 'Greater Liverpool' to keep pace with Glaswegian expansion.[32]

As demographic (and other) statistics turned against it in subsequent decades, Liverpool looked to culture to reaffirm its civic credentials as being 'second only to London'. In preparing for 'three joyous weeks' of escape from the 'dull monotony and austerity' of everyday life in post-war Britain, Liverpool discovered the winning formula for cultural celebration during the Festival of Britain of 1951:

> Companies such as Covent Garden, Sadler's Wells, the Old Vic, the English Opera Group, ensure that our artistic standards shall compare with any in the whole Festival of Britain. Names like Flagstad, Beecham and Barbirolli will guarantee that the Liverpool Festival attracts national and even international attention. But it is interesting to compare the Liverpool plans with the programmes announced by the largest Festival Centres. For while one town places all the emphasis on exhibitions, and another spotlights the best executants of music and the arts of theatre, Liverpool has a great deal of both, and throws in for good measure, the principle of mass participation.[33]

Around the theme of 'To-morrow's Tide', Liverpool enjoyed 'a Festival of the people for the people', offering spectacular street processions and pageants (initially under the direction of Tyrone Guthrie) and lavish firework displays on the Mersey, special treats for 'Everyman' who 'may not be at home at the opera, may be bored by the ballet, and may sit out orchestral concerts with clenched fists'. Free open-air concerts held on bomb sites or in the central courtyards of the new council housing blocks attracted vast crowds, and the enthusiasm on display at impromptu street parties proved infectious.[34] The *Manchester Evening News*, dismayed by Manchester's failure to 'capture the Festival spirit' was full of praise, acknowledging that 'Liverpool had done magnificent justice to an historic occasion':

32] *The Sport of Civic Life, or Art and the Municipality* (Liverpool, 1909), 4 and *passim*. See also the introduction, 'Let Glasgow Flourish', in W. Hamish Fraser and I. Maver, *Glasgow volume ii: 1830 to 1912* (Manchester, 1996).
33] 'Liverpool Festival 1951', *Liverpolitan*, Jan. 1951
34] There are three volumes of press cuttings on the 1951 Festival, see 352CLE/ CUT3/8-10. Tyrone Guthrie was called back to the Old Vic shortly before the Festival began.

Liverpool spent £25,000 on street decorations alone during the celebrations and twice as much on the river pageant and fire-works. Hundreds of thousands of people flocked to enjoy themselves. Great concerts with world-famous conductors were held night after night and bands played throughout the day. And apart from the official efforts the Festival has entered the side-streets and the humblest back gardens. The result has been the finest show outside London and one which has attracted visitors from all over the world.[35]

A few years, later, however, the Manchester press was the one voice of criticism in commentary on Liverpool's 750th celebrations in 1957:

It was widely felt that the anniversary was celebrated by the Liverpool Corporation rather than by the citizens of Liverpool ... It may be a sign of the times, this concept of local government as provider and the citizen as consumer ... the sense of participation by the ordinary citizen, that so distinguished the Festival of Britain celebrations in 1951, was conspicuously lacking'[36]

Much enjoyed at the time, these short-lived cultural festivities followed the earlier efforts of Liverpool Organisation in promoting product recognition, a process described by the *Liverpolitan* as 're-dressing our shop window'.[37] A kind of loss leader, their purpose was to 'sell' the area, to attract further industrial investment in Merseyside. No longer a civilising counterweight to commerce, culture was the handmaiden of manufacturing industry, providing the opportunity to display the 'new' Liverpool with its state of the art industrial estates. One of the main visitor attractions in 1951 was the futuristic Skylon towering above the 'Daylight on Industry' exhibition, while in 1957 the Cleveland Square–Paradise Street area was transformed from a bomb site into a 'white tent town' with

35] *Manchester Evening News*, 13 Aug. 1951
36] *Manchester Guardian*, 18 Apr. 1958. At the time, the only note of criticism in the correspondence columns of the Liverpool press concerned the 1,000 guinea fee charged by the great pianist Arthur Rubinstein. The *Evening Echo*, 20 May 1957, refused to endorse localist and populist protest: 'Such world-renowned artistry rightly commands a high price. Liverpool cannot, and should not try to bring it here very often. Equally, however, Merseysiders should not be denied ever enjoying such memorable occasions as only a Rubinstein or a Menuhin can create – and when better than in this memorable year? By all means, let our local societies organise their own charter-year celebrations, but if I have to choose between one such festival for each of Liverpool's 750 years and a single Rubinstein, I'll still choose Rubinstein.'
37] 'Merseyside Industry', *Liverpolitan*, July 1951.

75,000 square feet of display space for the 'Industry Advances' exhibition.[38]

The boosterism notwithstanding, the festivities of the 1950s lack the assured confidence which resonated throughout the 700th anniversary celebrations in 1907, following in the wake of the dual success of Liverpool in the League and Everton in the F.A. Cup in the previous year.[39] Looking to a bright economic future, Muir's *History* ended on a note of high optimism as he enumerated a range of major projects recently completed or under construction: commercial palaces such as the domed dock office (destined to be the first of the three graces) and the stately pillared cotton exchange (one of the buildings which was alas to fall victim to 1960s vandalism); and the 'twin citadels of the ideal', a citadel of faith (the Anglican cathedral, Sir Giles Gilbert Scott's masterpiece, nearly a century in the making) and a citadel of knowledge (the University of Liverpool which rapidly outgrew its original Waterhouse 'redbrick' premises).[40] For all the cranes that now dominate the skyline (the city's former Chief Executive apparently counted them every morning), there seems nothing to match the scale and ambition of a century ago. There is a profusion of new apartment blocks (some to the detriment of the coherence and site lines of the World Heritage site), but a distinct lack of *grands projets*. The one notable exception is the Foundation for Art and Creative Technology (FACT) in the Rope Walks, the first purpose-built arts project in the city for over 60 years: a major boost to the Capital of Culture bid, it has already attracted high visitor numbers (500,000 by November 2004) while reinforcing Liverpool's pre-eminence (aided by local specialisation in digitisation) in new media and contemporary visual arts (celebrated in the Liverpool Biennial). FACT apart, there is a growing catalogue of curtailment and delay which, as Downtown Liverpool, a business-led pressure group, has observed, questions the ability of partnership governance (hindered by 'local politicians and officials

38] There is a separate volume of cuttings and other material for 1957 in the Liverpool Record Office, see 'Liverpool Charter Celebrations: 750th Anniversary, 1957' at Hf394.5.SEV

39] Some reviewers expressed surprise at the lack of references to football in *Merseypride*. Here it should be remembered that the Saturday half-holiday came late to Liverpool with its casual labour market, hence the city was not to the fore in the development of league competition; see Douglas A. Reid, 'Playing and praying', in M. Daunton (ed.), *Cambridge Urban History of Britain, vol iii, 1840–1950* (Cambridge, 2000), 751.

40] There is some evidence, however, of donor fatigue given the competing claims for funding, as indicated by the initial poor support for the Victoria memorial, erected on the site of the medieval castle; see 'Talk in Town', *Liverpool Review*, 1 June 1901.

arguing among themselves') to deliver on 'prestigious, strategic priorities':[41] the lack of any major millennium memorial; the collapse of plans for a mega football stadium at King's Dock (work has now started on a concert and sports arena and conference centre); the cancellation of Will Alsop's controversial 'Fourth Grace' (possibly to be replaced by a Danish-designed museum building, funding permitting); and set-backs and hold-ups over the proposed reintroduction of a tram system. In the absence of a world-class new landmark building will Liverpool be able to match the benefits enjoyed by Bilbao (another 'edge' city) through lucrative architectural tourism? As already noted, the city possesses a rich archi-tectural heritage (often incorporating ground-breaking construction technology) but it lacks an iconic style figure – such as Mackintosh for Glasgow or Gaudi for Barcelona – around whom to package the Liverpool visitor 'experience'. It is an unfortunate irony that Waterhouse, son of a local cotton-broker, is best known not for his native Liverpool buildings but for his great work in Manchester and London. There is always of course the Beatles Magical Mystery Tour (with associated National Trust properties and prospective specialist accommodation, the Hard Day's Night Hotel) to guide the visitor though the city, although this may have to be modified when the Salvation Army closes Strawberry Fields in Woolton in 2007.[42]

The absence of prestige projects notwithstanding, the transformation of the city centre and the adjacent Rope Walks area has been a considerable achievement, although not without its critics (prompting some unfavour-able comparisons between Liverpool and 'authentic' café-bar Milan on the eve of the Champions League final).[43] Helen Walsh, the latest literary voice to uphold the Liverpool 8 bohemian tradition, has written disap-provingly of the new-look city centre and its pretensions:

> There are new bars, coffee shops and restaurants cropping up all over the place. I don't like it. The city is starting to take on the guise of a salesman who lacks faith in what he is selling. Artificial. Insincere. A barrage of plush eateries bought by drug money and pseudo gangsters who lack the erudition to pull it off.[44]

41] Downtown Liverpool in Business, website release 14 June 2005. See also, 'Culture clash threatens Liverpool's capital year', *Independent*, 18 June 2005.
42] Tourism associated with the Beatles is estimated to account for 600,000 visits to Liverpool a year, bringing in some £20 million to the local economy.
43] 'A Tale of Two Cities', *Observer Review*, 22 May 2005.
44] Helen Walsh, *Brass* (Edinburgh, 2004), 70.

Others have questioned the sustainability of the city-centre boom given Liverpool's continuing 'relative deprivation', although the statistics they cite lag somewhat behind the cranes and the developers, the latest dating back to 2001 when the average household income throughout Liverpool was just 79 per cent of the national figure. Perhaps this is why Harvey Nichols have yet to consider Liverpool a suitable site for their upmarket operations in the north – significantly, Harrods dropped their plans for a Liverpool store in 1920 as the brief post-war boom came to an end, a symbolic precursor of the city's downward spiral in the interwar decades.[45] For a future premised on consumption, the statistics from 2001 fail to register any urban renaissance: judged against the national average, levels of health, qualifications, home and car ownership are comparatively low in Liverpool, while those of unemployment, lone parenting and house rentals are comparatively high.[46] However, these figures fail to take account of the high levels of disposable income of visitors attracted to the city, whether rich Dubliners visiting their weekend second apartments in Liverpool (a staggering reversal of former migrant flows[47]) or affluent 'cultural' tourists whose ever-increasing numbers are fuelling a hotel boom. The city is soon to acquire its first five-star hotel, 'Layla' in Sir Thomas Street, and work has begun on a Liverpool branch of the upmarket boutique hotel chain Malmaison at a waterfront site alongside the Crowne Plaza, hopefully to enhance the otherwise 'instantly forgettable corporate architecture' of the redevelopment of Prince's Dock.[48] This 'business park' site, however, has attracted significant inward commercial investment, encouraged by the efforts of yet another partnership, the Mersey Partnership, a 'catalyst' for economic development, representing some 400 businesses and organisations. Coutts, the royal bankers, have set up an office in Prince's Dock for clients with a minimum £500,000 of disposable cash or assets worth £5 million. Within its first year, it had generated more than £100 million of business from football players, pop stars, lottery winners and business people, prompting the rival J.P. Morgan to enter this apparently lucrative local market.[49]

45] *Daily Post*, 9 Feb. 1920.
46] The figures, available from the National Statistics website, *www.statistics gov.uk*, are given prominence in the *Visitor Management Plan* drawn up by PLB Consulting Ltd in April 2005 for the Liverpool World Heritage Site.
47] 'Dublin's rich add twist to tale of two cities', *Guardian*, 5 Feb. 2001.
48] Sharples, *Liverpool: Pevsner Architectural Guides*, 122.
49] 'Financier opens city office', *Daily Post*, 18 May 2005.

Retail rental growth in Liverpool in 2001 was over twice the national average,[50] the statistical evidence of relative deprivation notwithstanding. Consumption aside, perhaps the most noteworthy aspect of statistics drawn from the 2001 census relates to Liverpool's ethnic composition. Once so proud of its cosmopolitanism as *Merseypride* amply attests, Liverpool is now one of the least ethnically diverse of British cities with small numbers of post-1945 'new Commonwealth' migrants. Those categorised as Asian or Asian British in the 2001 census constituted only 1.1% of the city's population against a national average of 4.6%, while the Black British registered 1.2% against a national average of 2.1%. In this respect, the strapline of the successful capital of culture bid, 'The world in once city', drew upon Liverpool's historical legacy rather than its contemporary complexion. A startling historical reversal, it may indeed be open to question as to whether Liverpool, the most multi-cultural and un-English of Victorian provincial cities, now has a sufficiently cosmopolitan and bohemian complexion to attract the highly mobile 'creative classes' regarded by Richard Florida as the key drivers of economic growth in the post-industrial city.[51] In applying Florida's approach to the United Kingdom context, the think-tank Demos constructed a 'Boho Britain Creativity Index' headed not by Liverpool but by Manchester, Leicester and London.[52]

Once hailed as 'the New York of Europe, a world-city rather than merely British provincial',[53] polyglot Liverpool stood proudly above the 'Coketown' monoculture of adjacent Lancastrian textile and industrial towns. Gateway to the empire and the new world, Victorian Liverpool was what historical geographers term a 'diaspora space', a contact zone between different ethnic groups with differing needs and intentions as transients, sojourners or settlers (categories, which as Linda Grant's parents attest, were by no means mutually exclusive).[54] However, cosmopolitan interaction in this human entrepôt was not to persist. Where there was a pronounced gender imbalance, as in the male seafaring presence (whether 'alien' Chinese or 'black' British subjects – Kru, Lascar and West Indian), inter-ethnic

---

50] This figure features as a headline on the Liverpool Business Centre website.
51] Richard Florida, *The Rise of the Creative Class* (New York, 2002).
52] See the editorial by Wilks-Heeg and North in *Local Economy*, 19 (2004), 305–11.
53] 'Liverpool: Port, Docks and City', *Illustrated London News*, 15 May 1886.
54] See Linda Grant's article. 'History broke Liverpool, and it broke my heart', *Guardian*, 5 June 2003, on how her parents, transients turned settlers, mistook Liverpool for their intended destination, New York; see also her novel, *Still Here* (London, 2002).

relations were soon refracted and racialised through masculine competition and sexual jealousy. Studies of sectarian violence (a feature of Liverpool historiography) have highlighted disputed borders between 'green' and 'orange', but the inviolable boundary which came to keep 'black' distant and apart awaits investigation.[55] It was these 'racialised' relations, stemming from the early twentieth century, as much as the city's declining economic fortunes in subsequent decades, which made Liverpool an unattractive destination for later generations of immigrants, a troubled legacy still readily apparent to visiting black commentators such as the writer Caryl Phillips and the anthropologist Jacqueline Nassy Brown. Phillips, indeed, was glad to leave Liverpool, 'a place where history is physically so present, yet so glaringly absent from people's consciousness'.[56] Brown's fieldwork, conducted in the 1990s, took her into an invisible and embattled Black Liverpool, as apart in its history as in its geography. She found little left of a shared pan-racial affection in popular imaginings of 'the Liverpool That Was', an ever more distant and irretrievable past before global trade declined, the empire disintegrated, and racial tensions increased (despite high levels of mixed dating, marriages and parentage). Histories and narratives had diverged in a polarising process of 'localisation as racialisation'. Those denigrated as 'half-caste' acquired racial pride as Liverpool-born blacks, the collective place-birth lineage of those descended from seafaring founding fathers. Not always welcoming to new arrivals from the Caribbean and post-colonial Africa (or recent refugees from Somalia), this local essentialism gave a 'black' (and alternative) inflexion to Merseypride, the insistence on exceptionalism and apartness, through which the city mediated its descent into marginality and 'renegade outsiderism'.[57] The critical commentary of Phillips and Brown, although recent, stems like *Merseypride* from a previous era, written at a time of depression, decline and despair. In the new 'Livercool', multi-culturalism (as the Capital of Culture strapline attests) is at a premium, at least in civic rhetoric and in the transformed city centre. Tragically, racism still persists further out.[58]

55] John Belchem, 'Whiteness and the Liverpool-Irish', *Journal of British Studies*, 44 (2005), 146–52.
56] Caryl Phillips, *The Atlantic Sound* (London, 2000)
57] Jacqueline Nassy Brown, *Dropping Anchor, Setting Sail: Geographies of Race in Black Liverpool* (Princeton and Oxford, 2005).
58] Travelling people have also fallen foul of such prejudice as in the horrific murder of Johnny Delaney in the middle of a playing field in Ellesmere Port; 'Brutal death of a travelling child', *Guardian*, 10 June 2003.

Outrage at the brutal and sickening murder of Anthony Walker in Huyton may prove a decisive turning-point.

Given the pace of change since the publication of *Merseypride*, it would be unwise to comment further on Liverpool's present or likely future. The essential purpose of *Merseypride* was to revisit the past, to arouse interest in Liverpool's history ahead of the octocentenary in 2007, now labelled the 'year of heritage' by the Culture Company. Thus it is only fitting to conclude by acknowledging the generosity of the City Council, the University of Liverpool and the Leverhulme Trust in providing funding for a major new history for 2007, *Liverpool 800: Culture, Character and History*, to be written by a team of experts whom I have the honour of leading, and to be published by Liverpool University Press in September 2006. Here there should be scope for full-scale engagement with the undulating fortunes and contested images, representations and perceptions of what Muir described a century ago as 'no mean city'.

Liverpool
September 2005

Preface to the first edition

O utside the main narrative frameworks of modern British history, Liverpool's past has been characterised as different, the exception which proved the rule.[1] These essays critically address and interrogate this proverbial exceptionalism, a 'difference' which extends far beyond historiographical discourse. Liverpool's apartness, indeed, is crucial to its identity. Although repudiated by some as an external imposition, an unmerited stigma, Liverpudlian 'otherness' has been upheld (and inflated) in self-referential myth, a 'Merseypride' that has shown considerable ingenuity in adjusting to the city's changing fortunes. The purpose of these essays is to deconstruct some of these representations, projections and portrayals in the period covering Liverpool's exponential growth to become the second city of the empire to its recent (seemingly irreversible) economic and demographic decline into European Union Objective One status.[2]

Located at the intersection of competing cultural, economic and geopolitical formations, Liverpool defies ready historical categorisation. In its Victorian heyday a kind of 'city state' dedicated to commerce, culture and civilisation – the would-be 'Florence of the north' – Liverpool defined itself against industrial Manchester and in rivalry with commercial London. In the north of England but not of it, Liverpool (and its 'sub-region' of Merseyside) was (and has continued to be) highly distinctive, differing sharply in

1] 'Liverpool says much that is unrepeatable ... [a] warning to anyone wishing to paint a national picture by enlarging local tints', Michael Bentley *The Climax of Liberal Politics* (London, 1987), 30.
2] In the period 1701–1851, the population of Liverpool grew at the rate of three-and-a-half times every fifty years, leading Abraham Hume to predict a population of over 1 250 000 by 1900, Abraham Hume, *Condition of Liverpool, Religious and Social* (Liverpool, 1858), 31–32.

socio-economic structure, cultural image and expression, political affiliation, health, diet and speech from the adjacent industrial districts. Vaunting its status as 'second metropolis' – the first after London to introduce a
system of postal districts[3] – this northern outpost of 'gentlemanly
capitalism' was the least 'English' of the great Victorian provincial cities.
The industrial conurbations of the north grew out of conglomerations of
small towns and villages, augmented by short-distance rural in-migration
which tended to reinforce their culture, character and status as regional
centres. Long-distance in-migration – the multi-ethnic, mainly celtic inflow
– transformed Liverpool and its 'scouse' culture, setting it apart from its
environs. In Liverpool, competing and conflicting inflexions of celticism
(Irish, Welsh, Manx and Scottish) have been particularly pronounced,
tensions (awaiting full scholarly investigation) at the very centre of the
multi-national United Kingdom. Beyond the 'inland' Irish Sea, Liverpool's
private celtic empire, the great seaport looked to the oceans, adding an
external dimension to the city's cultural life and its migrant mix. The
'community' mentality of the Scottie-Road 'slummy' – the 'scouse' identity
cherished by those clustered around the main artery of Scotland Road – co-
existed with a broader culture, a seafaring cosmopolitanism which made
Liverpool, the gateway of empire, particularly receptive to (unEnglish)
foreign ideas (syndicalism, for example) and to American popular music. A
cultural intersection on the geographical margin, Liverpool is thus a
critical site for investigation of northerness, Englishness, Britishness and
the (pre-devolved) United Kingdom.

Recently, geography has worked against Liverpool, ill-placed for trade
with European partners. However, new twinning arrangements with
Dublin, and the resurgence of the Irish 'tiger' economy, should secure some
future for the port, a bridgehead on a northern pathway across the
European Union. But the great days have gone, an absolute decline
rendered more painful by relative comparison. Manchester has usurped
regional capital and second metropolis status. Other 'Atlantic' cities like
Glasgow and Bristol have successfully 're-branded' themselves. Liverpool
is left with its past. Packaged as heritage, history is becoming its main
'trade' and source of attraction, the last hope of regeneration for the shock
city of post-industrial Britain.

While focused on Liverpool, these essays should thus not be considered
as local or antiquarian. Drawing upon current historiographical and

3] 'The Post Office in Liverpool', *Daily Post* 22 Nov. 1861.

sociological debates in areas such as ethnicity, migration, labour and urban history, several essays look beyond Britain – the final section, indeed, offers comparative perspectives embracing Europe, North America and Australia. The collection opens with cultural studies of how Liverpool projected itself (a task that required the elaboration of a suitable history, and thence its reproduction as heritage) and how it has been portrayed and perceived externally (not least in media 'mis'-representation). The 1907 celebration of the 700th anniversary of the granting of the letters patent to the borough, the focus of the first essay, was a defining moment – in historical retrospect the city's climacteric. While confident of its future (as its remarkable architecture proclaimed), Edwardian Liverpool was less sure about its past. Rather than inflate its history (or invent something factitiously venerable), Ramsay Muir encouraged his fellow citizens to accept their city's former insignificance and obscurity, to take an inverse pride, as it were, in Liverpool's inauspicious past. Here, indeed, was the benchmark by which to appreciate (and celebrate) the remarkable progress of modern Liverpool to 'world city' status – 'the New York of Europe, a world-city rather than merely British provincial'.[4] In its abbreviated but prodigious historical narrative, Edwardian Liverpool, 'no mean city', stood proudly apart. As it developed from Muir's foundation texts, however, Merseypride history was characterised by exclusion and closure. While the rise of the port dictated the narrative, the contribution of the slave trade was hastily glossed over: indeed, it was in its rapid adaptation to abolition of the trade that Liverpool displayed its true acumen, enterprise and commercial pre-eminence. But in its history (as in its civic life) there was to be no place for settlers from overseas, 'black scousers' – Kru, Lascar, Chinese and other sea-faring communities – drawn to Liverpool by the opening up of new markets and routes after abolition.[5] Cosmopolitanism was a point of Merseypride, a factor that raised Liverpool above provincialism, but it was seldom given an inclusive (or 'melting-pot') inflexion. What made Liverpool different was not its precocious multi-cultural demographic profile (a pattern not found in other British cities until the later twentieth century), but the disproportionate celtic presence in an English city.

4] 'Liverpool: Port, Docks and City', *Illustrated London News* 15 May 1886.
5] I am grateful to Diane Frost for letting me read her essay, 'Ambiguous Identities: Constructing and De-constructing Black and White "Scouse" Identities in 20th Century Liverpool' prior to its publication in N. Kirk (ed.), *Northern Identities* (Aldershot, 2000) 195–217.

The Scots and the Welsh in Liverpool – generally of a higher socio-economic status than the locally born – await full scholarly investigation (as does the Liverpool Manx community). Attention has focused on the Liverpool Irish, irremovably located at the bottom of the social, occupational and residential hierarchy. They now have no place, however, in the revisionist narrative of the Irish in Britain, a celebration of widespread distribution, successful socio-economic integration and 'ethnic fade'. Labelled as 'the dregs' by Father Nugent (an Irish-Liverpudlian himself), those who remained in the port of entry have been dismissed as the *caput mortuum*, a kind of under-class, as it were, unable, unwilling or unsuited to take advantage of opportunities elsewhere in Britain or the new world. The image has endured. It is 'Irishness' of this order – immobile, inadequate and irresponsible – that has purportedly set Liverpool and its notorious social problems apart. The Liverpool-Irish (of whom Heathcliff, the great other/outsider of Victorian literature, brought starving and houseless from the streets of Liverpool, may well have been one)[6] have always suffered the prejudice and negative reputation which now blight the city itself.

With characteristic inverted pride, Liverpudlians have chosen to adopt not to contest this crude stereotype. Inspired by Nugent, the Catholic church claimed the depraved Irish as their essential concern, their special mission for spiritual salvation and welfare protection, saintly tasks beyond their Protestant rivals. The unadulterated image of the lowly Irish 'slummy', reckless and feckless, has been adopted as the foundation character in recent writings in popular history and working-class autobiography, a symbolic figure of inverse snobbery and pride in the evolution of the true Scottie Road scouser. Heritage publications have valorised the character. The distinctive local accent – the register of the true scouser (and the subject of the second essay) – has been traced back to the assumed laziness and casualism of its Irish originators. The fugitives from the Potato Famine, Fritz Spiegl contends, 'gave the Liverpudlian (whose speech was formerly Lancastrian rustic) not only his accent but also his celtic belligerence'.[7]

Out of place in studies of the Irish in Britain, the Liverpool-Irish 'colony' is perhaps best approached through comparison with large migrant communities overseas, enclaves within which 'ethnic' culture was not only

6] Terry Eagleton, *Heathcliff and the Great Hunger* (London, 1995), 1–26.
7] Fritz Spiegl, 'Preface' to 1984 reprinted edition of *Lern Yerself Scouse* (Liverpool), iv.

retained but rewarded. Drawing upon the sociology of ethnicity and migration (in particular the social constructionist perspectives of recent American studies discussed in the final section),[8] the essays in section two explore the sites – most notably the Irish pub and the Catholic parish – where a distinctive (and exclusive) sense of 'ethnic' Irishness was constructed, implanted and upheld (with considerable success and longevity) against competing and alternative identities and affiliations. While taking due (post-modernist) account of dissonance, multiplicity and fracture, these essays seek to apply the ethnic functionalism displayed by urban Irish-Americans (under the control of middle-class culture brokers) to their compatriots in Liverpool. In so doing, they move beyond spatial geography (a strength of Liverpool historiography) to reconstruct social and cultural space where ethnic affiliation spanned socio-economic boundaries.

Inspired by the methods and paradigms of historical geography and urban sociology, studies of Liverpool have tended to concentrate on spatial and socio-economic factors, ignoring cultural and associational aspects of ethnic identity and collective mutuality. Census statistics have been deployed as 'hard' evidence for a positivist case study in the paradigmatic 'urban transition'. Liverpool was ahead of other cities in its 'modern' spatial segregation, a pattern already established on Merseyside by 1871. Distinct areas took their character and identity from the socio-economic status of the residents, although choice of residence was influenced by subsidiary variables such as position in the family life cycle, and ethnic affiliation.[9] In this model, Irishness was reduced to the lowest socio-economic level, an ethnic stigma that clung to the worst housing areas adjacent to waterfront casual labour markets, recourse of the impoverished famine migrants. Considerably smaller in numbers, the Irish middle class, a longer-established and mainly Protestant mercantile presence, rapidly distanced themselves from these 'core' areas, abandoning any

8] For a useful introduction to social constructionist analysis which acknowledges the constructed and invented nature of ethnicity within 'real life context and social experience', see K.N Conzen, D.A. Gerber, E. Morawska, G.E. Pozzetta and R.J. Vecoli, 'The Invention of Ethnicity: A Perspective from the USA', *Journal of American Ethnic History*, Vol. 12 (1992), 3–41.
9] R. Lawton and C.G. Pooley, 'The Social Geography of Merseyside in the Nineteenth Century', Final report to the Social Science Research Council, July 1976 (Dept of Geography, University of Liverpool); See also J.D. Papworth, 'The Irish in Liverpool 1835–71: Segregation and Dispersal' (unpublished PhD thesis, University of Liverpool, 1982).

identification with such Irishness to seek socio-economic integration in the more desirable residential location of outer suburban Merseyside. Isolated and segregated in the city, the Liverpool-Irish poor were simply assumed to lack the resources for associational culture – other than the 'muscle' to defend disputed residential boundaries.[10] The essays here argue otherwise, pointing to an infrastructure of ethno-sectarian solidarity and social security – constructed around parish, pub and the leadership of middle-class Catholic 'Micks on the make' – which made the Irish reluctant to leave Liverpool and its culture of poverty. Seen in these terms, continued 'ghetto' residence in the 'black spot on the Mersey' was quite as rational as the peripatetic and uncertain quest for 'success' elsewhere.

The political resonance of Liverpool's ethno-sectarian formations – from the outset, parties of social inclusion not merely parties of individual representation – has long been acknowledged, placing the city outside the conventional national narrative of party development.[11] Contrary to present-day assumption, Liverpool was not to the fore in the forward march of Labour. 'Liverpool is rotten and we had better recognize it', Ramsay MacDonald rued in 1910.[12] By adjusting its programme to local concerns, the Irish National Party retained the support of second- and third-generation (i.e. Liverpool-born) Irish. A cross-class exercise, this 'Nat-Labism' reached lower down the social scale and proved more enduring than conventional Lib-Labism elsewhere. Protestant workers, the majority of the electorate, looked to the well-oiled Tory machine, the nearest equivalent to American 'boss' politics in the British system, to protect their 'marginal privilege'. Section three examines the origins – cultural, economic and sectarian – of what John Vincent has described as the deepest and most enduring Tory 'deviation' among Victorian workers.[13] A compound of populism, protectionism and Protestantism, Tory political hegemony was to persist – albeit with occasional riotous fracture[14] – well into the

10] Frank Neal, *Sectarian Violence: The Liverpool Experience 1819–1914* (Manchester, 1988).
11] John Garrard, 'Parties, Members and Voters after 1867', in T.R. Gourvish and A. O'Day (eds), *Later Victorian Britain 1867–1900* (Basingstoke, 1988), 127–50.
12] Quoted in Sam Davies, *Liverpool Labour: Social and Political Influences on the Development of the Labour Party in Liverpool, 1900–1939* (Keele, 1996).
13] J.R. Vincent, *Pollbooks: How Victorians Voted* (Cambridge, 1967), 61.
14] See, for example, John Bohstedt, 'More than One Working Class: Protestant and Catholic Riots in Edwardian Liverpool' in John Belchem (ed.), *Popular Politics, Riot and Labour: Essays in Liverpool History 1790–1940* (Liverpool, 1992), 173–216.

xxxviMERSEYPRIDE

twentieth century, continuing to confound external critics and observers. As P.J. Waller notes, it seemed 'paradoxical that the Conservatives could be so successful, without being dishonest, in Liverpool, given the grim circumstances in which much of the population lived and worked'.[15]

The collection ends, as noted above, with some theoretical, methodological and comparative reflections, offering non-British benchmarks by which to assess Liverpool's difference, exceptionalism and 'pride'. As preparations begin for the celebration of Liverpool's 800th 'birthday' in 2007, it is essential to adopt a comparative perspective and an inclusive historical agenda. In locating its difference, Liverpool must acknowledge the diversity within its history and heritage. Merseypride should not sell itself short.

*   *   *   *   *

With the exception of the paper on scouse (reprinted here in slightly amended and updated form), all the essays are either published for the first time or have been specially and extensively adapted for this collection. I am grateful to publishers for allowing me to draw upon some previously published material.

15] P.J. Waller, *Democracy and Sectarianism: a political and social History of Liverpool 1868–1939* (Liverpool, 1981), xix.

Part One
MERSEYPRIDE

1
'Liverpool's story is the world's glory'

Merseypride was at its height in the Edwardian years, a confidence embodied in the imposing architecture (and attendant public sculpture) of the new Pier Head: the Mersey Docks and Harbour Building (1907), the Royal Liver Building (1911) and the Cunard Building (1913), the photogenic sea-facing skyline by which Liverpool remains instantly recognisable.[1] Immune to the blandishments of Westminster, local 'boss' politicians revelled (American-style) in the bustle and manipulation of the municipal 'machine'. Jealously upholding Liverpool's provincial pre-eminence, they defended its prized status as the 'second city of the Empire' against Glaswegian pretension.[2] Some Liverpolitans, indeed, cherished the hope of overtaking London, although the 'future supremacy of Liverpool' would, alas, necessitate merger with Manchester. Lancastrian rivalries were to be set aside in exploitation of the commercial potential of the new ship canal:

> From Liverpool to Manchester will run continuous quays, on which will be discharged and loaded merchandise from all parts of the world.

1] Terry Cavanagh, *Public Sculpture of Liverpool* (Liverpool, 1997), xi–xii. Liverpool, Cavanagh notes, 'possesses an abundance of monuments and sculpture in its public places, unsurpassed by any other city in England, excepting London'.
2] Stanley Salvidge, *Salvidge of Liverpool: Behind the Political Scene 1890–1928* (London, 1928), 9, 55, 106 and 306. The demise of Archibald Salvidge, who '"bossed" Liverpool more efficiently and far more clearly than anything Irish-America ever accomplished', marked the end of an epoch: 'The whole modern trend is towards a concentration, amounting almost to a monopoly, of talent and responsibility within the Metropolis. To-day the provincial centres seem content to become mere appendages of London. To that conception of the British system of commerce and government Salvidge never subscribed.'

Table 1.1 Population of Liverpool and Merseyside; Manchester; and Glasgow, 1801–1981 (in thousands)

Year	Liverpool	Merseyside	Manchester	Glasgow
1801	78	100	75	77
1811	95	124	89	101
1821	119	165	126	147
1831	165	240	182	202
1841	286*	354	235	275
1851	376	499	303	345
1861	444	575	339	420
1871	493	684	351	522
1881	553	818	341	587
1891	518	900	505	658
1901	685*	1023	544	762
1911	746*	1150	714	784
1921	803	1263	730	1034
1931	856	1347	766	1088
1951	789	1382	703	1090
1961	746	1338	662	1055
1971	610	1267	544	898
1981	510	1127	449	766

Sources: Figures for Liverpool and Merseyside, 1801–1911 are taken from R. Lawton and C.G. Pooley, 'The Social Geography of Merseyside in the 19th Century', final report to the SSRC, Department of Geography, University of Liverpool, July 1976. Their definition of Merseyside incorporates the whole of Liverpool (* denotes borough boundary change in previous decade); West Derby, Birkenhead and Wirral registration districts (as defined in 1861); and the Huyton, Much Woolton and Hale sub-districts of Prescot registration district. All other figures derived from B.R. Mitchell, *British Historical Statistics*, Cambridge, 1988, pp. 25–28.

Around these quays will spring up streets, squares, manufactories, mills, offices – all that goes to make a great city … This vast city will be the greatest and richest ever known to the world … London, compared to it, is out of the way … London will be our historic city – the city of culture, fashion and intellect. But whoever lives long enough will find the great city on the banks of the Mersey will be the commercial city of the future.[3]

3] 'The Future Supremacy of Liverpool', *Tit-Bits*, quoted in *The Liverpool Magazine* May 1890.

The city of the new century, Edwardian Liverpool continued confidently along the path celebrated by royal presence at the International Exhibition of Navigation, Commerce and Industry in 1886, held on a site in Wavertree 'exceeding by thirteen acres that occupied by the great Exhibitions at South Kensington, London':

> Liverpool, thanks to modern science and commercial enterprise, to the spirit and intelligence of the townsmen, and to the administration of the Mersey Docks and Harbour Board, has become a wonder of the world. It is the New York of Europe, a world-city rather than merely British provincial.[4]

While confident of its future, Liverpool – one of Lancashire's four medieval royal boroughs – was less sure about its past. The problem was not a lack of documents or of antiquarian interest,[5] but the absence of historical significance in the municipal records. The year 1907 marked the 700th anniversary of the granting of letters patent to the borough, an occasion which required due historical commemoration. Given the 'precipitancy of her uprising', to use Dixon Scott's grandiloquent Edwardian prose, Liverpool lacked a past commensurate with its contemporary 'world city' status. In short, it was 'a city without ancestors'.[6] Thanks largely to Ramsay Muir,

4] 'Liverpool: Port, Docks and City', *Illustrated London News* 15 May 1886. *All About the Liverpool Exhibition together with a Concise Guide to Liverpool* (Liverpool 1886). Divided into three sections, Navigation, Travelling, and Commerce and Manufacture, the exhibition gave pride of place to 'the history and development of travelling by land, sea and air'. After the closure of the exhibition, there was concern about the future commercial use of the site, which it was feared might 'take the form of a huge untaxed bazaar in disguise, to the serious annoyance and detriment of the tradesmen of the City', 'To Be or Not to Be', *Liverpool Review* 8 Jan. 1887. The Victorian 'exhibition' presented a problem for Liverpool, given the priority normally accorded to industrial exhibits. 'Liverpool was not like any great centre of manufacturing industry, and therefore there had not been as yet any great demand for space from this town', Lieutenant-Colonel Shadwell noted when despatched north by organisers of the International Exhibition in London in 1862. Prompted by his visit, the council appointed a special committee to ensure that Liverpool achieved due prominence in an exhibition whose 'range included every branch of trade and commerce', *Daily Post* 12 July and 16 Sept. 1861.
5] 'Liverpool owes much to its antiquarians, who have contributed more to the preservation and development of the Liverpool tradition than any other group. There is no other large city, except possibly London, whose history is continuously better documented from its foundation than that of Liverpool'; George Chandler, *Liverpool* (London, 1957), 449.
6] Walter Dixon Scott, *Liverpool* (London, 1907), 6 and 24. Muir was an admirer of Dixon Scott, who died on active service in the First World War, 'a brilliant if sometimes too florid writer, who died too young to win the fame he would have deserved'; Stuart Hodgson (ed.), *Ramsay Muir: An Autobiography and Some Essays* (London, 1943), 81.

lecturer (subsequently professor) in modern history at the University
(which received its charter only in 1903), a 'history' emerged that met the
needs of various constituencies – scholarly, official and popular – for a sense
of the past. A professional historian with a sense of national perspective,
Muir was dismissive of earlier efforts, not least Picton's antiquarian
'Memorials' published in 1875, to disabuse the external perception of
Liverpool as 'something akin to the parvenu who never had a grand-
father'.[7] While recognising that modern Liverpool was unintelligible without awareness of its 'long story of development', he refused to upgrade its
past or invent a venerable history. Muir encouraged his fellow citizens to
accept their city's former insignificance and obscurity, to take an inverse
pride, as it were, in its inauspicious past. Here, indeed, was the benchmark
by which to appreciate (and celebrate) the remarkable progress and achievements of modern Liverpool. In its abbreviated historical narrative, Edwardian Liverpool, 'no mean city', stood proudly apart.[8] The more ardent exponents of Merseypride, however, required more of their past: the desideratum
was 'a complete history of our phenominally [sic] wonderful city'.[9]

7] J.A. Picton, *Memorials of Liverpool* (London: 2 vols, 1875), i, 1. See the Appendix:
Notes on Authorities in Ramsay Muir, *A History of Liverpool* (London, 1907: rpt.
Wakefield, 1970 with a new foreword by J.J. Bagley), 341–49. Muir acknowledged
that Picton's second volume on topography was 'full and interesting'. Significantly,
there was one history that impressed him: Thomas Baines, *The History of the
Commerce and Town of Liverpool, and of the Rise of the Manufacturing Industry
in the Adjoining Counties* (London, 1852), 'distinguished by a conscientious
endeavour to relate the growth of the town to the general growth of English
commerce' 348.
8] Muir, *Autobiography*, 44–81. In the 'Preface' to his commercial prosopography,
compiled in the previous decade, Orchard had used the same phrase: 'Liverpool is
no mean city … it is one of the most interesting places in the world to a thoughtful
observer, especially if, as in my case, he honours and loves commerce, regards a
merchant as a benefactor to humanity and believes that on the whole no occupation
is more beneficial than trade in stimulating the mental powers, bracing conscience,
and producing content'; B.G. Orchard, *Liverpool's Legion of Honour* (Birkenhead,
1893), ix.
9] James Touzeau, *The Rise and Progress of Liverpool* (Liverpool, 1910), 884. Aided
by the Finance Committee, Touzeau, a local government officer in the Town Clerk's
office, published a hefty tome (nearly 900 pages) based on records in the Corporation's
possession from 1551 until municipal reform in 1835. Viewed from this uncritical
antiquarian perspective, what Liverpool lacked was not history, but an historian:
'And so it must remain until some young genius comes forward who can afford to
devote the number of years of earnest and concentrated energy, labour and skilful
attention necessary to produce such a work (even with the materials already at hand)
before we can hope for or expect a really authentic and complete history of Liverpool'.

In readiness for the 700th celebrations, Muir set to work on three projects which were to occupy all his 'leisure for seven years ... the hardest-working and happiest years of my life'.[10] First, a general *History of Liverpool* – 'an attempt to present the life-story of the community of Liverpool in a concise and consecutive narrative, designed rather for the citizen than for the professed historical student' – deliberately devoid of footnotes and other scholarly apparatus which might deter the general reader.[11] Second, an unashamedly dry and scholarly study of Liverpool for the *Victoria County History of Lancashire*: 50 000 words of dense text accompanied by 932 footnotes, a definitive reference chronicle of developments since 1207 when the letters patent brought Liverpool into historical existence:

> Liverpool is distinguished from most other boroughs by the fact that it owes its foundation absolutely to an exercise of the royal will; there is no evidence that the place was a centre of any trade before the date when John fixed upon its sheltered Pool as a convenient place of embarkation for men and supplies from his Lancashire lands for his Irish campaigns.[12]

Finally, supervision of an archival exercise (purportedly the responsibility of the redoubtable and resentful Professor Mackay, Muir's head of department).[13] True to the historian's responsibilities, Muir ensured the publication of the collection of Fee-Farm leases transcribed, translated and edited by Edith Platt, adding a 'long narrative introduction' of his own. Written for 'ordinary readers who are not historical specialists, and are apt to be baffled by the technical terms which abound especially in the realm of municipal history', the introduction provided a 'logical and coherent account of the history of the development of municipal government in Liverpool', a path-breaking survey down to the Municipal Reform Act of 1835.[14] While

10] Muir, *Autobiography*, 44–52.
11] Muir, *History*, vii.
12] *The Victoria History of the County of Lancaster: Vol. iv* (London, 1911), 1–57. Muir had hoped for publication in 1907.
13] Muir claimed that a malicious and envious Mackay 'talked down' his Liverpool publications, but a more sympathetic assessment of the Rathbone Professor of History emerges in P.E.H. Hair, 'The Real Mackay' in idem (ed.), *Arts, Letters, Society: A Miscellany Commemorating the Centenary of the Faculty of Arts at the University of Liverpool* (Liverpool, 1996), 183–211.
14] See the 'Preface' to R. Muir and E.M. Platt, *A History of Municipal Government in Liverpool from Earliest Times to the Municipal Reform Act of 1835* (Liverpool, 1906).

working on these projects, the indefatigable Muir found time to engage in discussions with Edward Pickmere, the town clerk, to prepare for civic celebration of the anniversary. The high spot was to be the historical pageant at which Muir, cast as King John, had the only speaking part.[15]

The narrative structure of the *History*, the work that has endured best, divided Liverpool's past into two phases: the gradual removal of obstacles to its development, and the modern exploitation of its advantageous position. It was truly a story of human geography, of the interaction between physical location and human endeavour. For centuries, Liverpool's 'natural advantages' had been 'nullified' by 'a combination of adverse circumstances': 'a poor and thinly peopled surrounding country; isolation; great physical obstacles to inland communication; a lack of natural waterways; a successful rival long established and close at hand'. Liverpool was no match for 'historic' (and pre-silted) Chester, but its early history, Muir insisted, 'has more than a mere antiquarian interest...the real beginning of Liverpool as a town of any importance belongs to a late period yet it is in no small degree to be placed to the credit of the humble and in most cases nameless townsmen who fought for freedom in the long centuries of small things'. This independent spirit was a portent of great things to come, the 'splendid progress of the later ages' when Liverpool – having shaken off its old connections, feuds and overlords – quickly surpassed Chester, Bristol and all other rivals. Liverpool's success owed much to the enterprise, vision and commercial acumen of its corporate body, reformulated by the charter of 1695. Council investment in an innovatory wet-docks system in the early eighteenth century – followed by improvements in internal communication – enabled Liverpool to assert comparative advantage. Over the next decades, it reaped the commercial dividends of a remarkable conjuncture: development of the Americas; British naval supremacy secured in the 'second hundred years' war'; and industrial revolution in the adjacent 'manufacturing districts'. Once established as the 'gateway to the west', Liverpool eschewed commercial complacency. Corporate enterprise and investment expanded to facilitate greater command of the Mersey and its thirty-foot tidal range. While maintaining its 'rigidly exclusive oligarchy', the municipality of Liverpool, the Webbs acknowledged, 'showed itself, generation after generation, markedly superior in energy, dignity, integrity and public spirit to any other Municipal

15] Muir, *Autobiography*, 67.

Corporation'.[16] Single-minded in pursuit of commercial advantage – and hence of maximum returns on the 'town dues' and the corporate estate – the council continued to improve and enlarge the dock system. Following criticism from dues-paying customers in the industrial hinterland, responsibility for the docks eventually passed to the Mersey Docks and Harbour Board, but the enterprising spirit persisted. With characteristic Liverpudlian foresight, large sections of the system were reconstructed in readiness for fundamental changes in late nineteenth-century maritime architecture. The dock system, Muir proudly recorded in 1907, 'has no rival anywhere in the world':

> For seven miles and a quarter, on the Lancashire side of the river alone, the monumental granite, quarried from the Board's own quarries in Scotland, front the river in a vast sea wall as solid and enduring as the Pyramids, the most stupendous work of its kind that the will and power of man have ever created ... It is here, beside the docks, that the citizen of Liverpool can best feel the opulent romance of the city, and the miracle of transformation which has been wrought since the not distant days when, where the docks now stand, the untainted tides of the Mersey raced past a cluster of mud hovels amid fields and untilled pastures.[17]

In charting Liverpool's 'stupendous development', Muir did not minimise the contribution (or horrors) of the slave trade, the 'amazingly lucrative' triangular traffic by which 'a treble profit was made on every voyage'. 'Beyond a doubt', Muir acknowledged, 'it was the slave trade which raised Liverpool from a struggling port to be one of the richest and most prosperous trading centres in the world.'[18] Muir's unconcealed liberal discomfiture at the undeniable inhumanity of the middle passage and other aspects of the trade was in marked contrast to contemporary eighteenth-century studies, pioneer essays 'towards the history of Liverpool'. In these early guides to the town, the lucrative slave trade, assessed in the same quantitative terms as other traffic, exemplified Liverpudlian enterprise *par excellence*.[19] At the expense of any moderate or neutral

16] Quoted in F. Vigier, *Change and Apathy: Liverpool and Manchester during the Industrial Revolution* (Cambridge, Mass., 1970), 47. Vigier is harshly critical of the council's inattention to social, health and environmental problems.
17] Muir, *History*, 301–2.
18] Ibid., ch.12, 'The Slave Trade, 1709–1807', 190–206.
19] See, for example, William Enfield, *An Essay towards the History of Liverpool* (Warrington, 1773), ch. vi. This is an important foundation text, attesting to

position, the attitude hardened into what was perhaps the first expression of Liverpool's self-declared 'otherness'. The slaving capital of the world, Georgian Liverpool extolled its commercial acumen and success – an 'efficiency dynamic' that matched the entrepreneurial achievements of the industrial revolution – against the meddlesome moralism of 'outside' abolitionist opinion. Having cut itself off from the mainstream of changing British ideology, Liverpool, Seymour Drescher notes, 'was faced with a threat not just to its economic base but to its cultural identity'.[20] As abolitionists claimed the high ground, materialist Liverpool stood condemned for barbarism, philistinism and lack of civilised culture, charges which Muir was to reiterate with force.[21]

Before the trade was abolished in 1807, Liverpool guidebooks had already withdrawn from the ideological barricades, relegating the trade (and hence discussion of its morality) to no more than peripheral importance to the town's prosperity – a defence eschewed by Muir, but rehearsed by more recent 'revisionist' historians. After abolition, the moral and social distancing continued apace. Henceforth, the register of Liverpool enterprise was no longer the slave trade, but the remarkable rapidity and success with which it adapted to abolition, opening lucrative new markets and trade to Africa and elsewhere. Faced with economic adversity, Liverpool had shown itself at its best, thereafter a recurrent (and reassuring) trope in the articulation of Merseypride. There were other adjustments, including a cultural reassessment of the past which henceforth privileged the 'Humanity' men, the minority of local merchants who had opposed the trade against the odds. Reviled at the time, William Roscoe and his circle were rehabilitated as role models, the foundation figures of Liverpool's post-abolitionist pre-eminence in the civilised culture of commerce. Through study of renaissance Florence, Roscoe had found 'refreshment

---

Liverpool's surpassing of Bristol, its non-manufacturing commercial character and lack of antiquity: 'The history of a place which has lately emerged from obscurity, and which owes, if not its being, at least its consequence to the commercial and enterprizing spirit of modern times, cannot be supposed to afford many materials for the entertainment of the curious antiquarian', p. 8.
20] Seymour Drescher, 'The Slaving Capital of the World: Liverpool and National Opinion in the Age of Abolition', *Slavery and Abolition*, Vol. 9 (1988), 128–43. See also, B.K. Drake, 'The Liverpool-African voyage *c*.1790–1807: commercial problems' in R. Anstey and P.E.H. Hair (eds), *Liverpool, the African Slave Trade and Abolition* (enlarged edition, 1989, n.p.), 126.
21] Muir, *History*, 270–84.

from the brutal materialism of his native town, and inspiration for the attempt to breathe into it a new spirit'. These were themes which Muir was to embellish, not only in his *History* but also in his inaugural lecture on Roscoe and his circle, 'the glory of Liverpool', on election to the Geddes and Rankin chair of Modern History at the University in 1906. Roscoe, indeed, was Muir's ideal, a model of liberal scholarship in which 'the historian and citizen are never dissociated'.[22]

Roscoe's life-story – from humble, self-taught origins to mercantile success, distinguished scholarship and civic responsibility – provided the framework for the urban biography of Liverpool which Muir wished to write. There was considerable progress to record. Taken together, the new cultural mission of Roscoe-inspired gentlemanly capitalists and the 'improving' civic duties undertaken by the council, following municipal reform in 1835, did much to make good previous deficiencies: the absence of 'historic' cultural, educational and charitable endowments; and the inattention to social problems in the single-minded pursuit of commercial advantage. A plethora of learned societies attended to the promotion of literature and the arts – science and technology were at a discount in the culture of commerce – supplemented by a number of voluntary associations specifically geared to the education and recreation of young clerks, 'Liverpool gentlemen' (not 'Manchester men') in the making.[23] Conscious of 'the vast responsibilities and the magnificent opportunities that lay before it', the new council initiated programmes of educational, sanitary and health reform, and was among the first to establish a public library and museum. Much applauded by Muir, the 'new spirit of civic pride' reached a high-point in the 'great Athenian period' (to use C.H. Reilly's subsequent architectural classification), symbolised by construction of St George's

22] Ibid., 291–94; and idem, *William Roscoe: An Inaugural Lecture* (Liverpool, 1906). See also Arline Wilson, 'Culture and Commerce: Liverpool's merchant elite c.1790–1850', unpublished PhD thesis, University of Liverpool, 1997, ch.2.

23] See the essays marking the 150th anniversary of the Historic Society of Lancashire and Cheshire, by John Belchem ('Liverpool in 1848: Image, Identity and Issues'), Arline Wilson, ('The Cultural Identity of Liverpool, 1790–1850: The Early Learned Societies'), and Edward Morris ('Provincial Internationalism: Contemporary Foreign Art in nineteenth-century Liverpool and Manchester') in *Transactions of the Historic Society of Lancashire and Cheshire*, Vol. 147 (1998), 1–26, 55–80 and 81–114. Although commercial Liverpool was the first to feel the adverse effects of the American civil war, the money expended on art sales in Liverpool was nearly four times that in Manchester, 'The Fine Arts in Liverpool and Manchester', *Daily Post* 7 Dec. 1861.

Hall, 'that noble building, one of the noblest in the modern world, which is to-day the supreme architectural boast of the city'.[24]

Muir's account of Victorian Liverpool, however, was not uncritical. He found the last chapter difficult to write, and sent drafts to a number of experts in the field, including the town clerk, the medical officer of health and the vice-chancellor of the University. Despite ongoing civic improvement and further pioneering exercises (more 'Liverpool firsts') in public health reform to eradicate its reputation as 'the black spot on the Mersey', Liverpool failed to fulfil Roscoe's vision of a 'Florence of the north'. [25] To Muir's dismay, the Roscoe ideal – the practice of commerce, culture and civilisation – was not hegemonic. The culture of civilised commerce remained restricted to a Liberal minority, a socially exclusive (predominantly Unitarian) elite – an aristocracy of wealth and letters, as Hazlitt had initially designated them[26] – lacking in political influence and popular resonance.

In their brief exercise of power after municipal reform, the Liberal elite purged the carnival and corruption of traditional electoral politics without offering an alternative forum for popular participation, leaving the field free for Tory (and Orange) organisational initiatives. George Melly, 'a Liberal of the most advanced principles of social science', was characteristically incredulous of the subsequent electoral consequences. He bemoaned the hegemony of Tory populist-paternalism in 'the largest commercial port in the world - and commerce is another word for free trade - commerce is another word for radicalism - commerce is another word for free and enlightened opinion'.[27] Liverpool was, indeed, disappointing territory for the Liberals (as it was later to be for Labour). As 'second metropolis' – the

24] Muir, *History*, ch. 15. Muir and Platt, *History of Municipal Government*, 150. C.H. Reilly, 'The Changing Face of Liverpool' in *The Book of Liverpool* (Liverpool, 1928), 12.

25] Iteration of Liverpool's pioneer achievements has always been a feature of Merseypride. For the latest example, designed to counter contemporary denigration of the city ('God's Own Country'), see Jack Cooper, *Liverpool Firsts: Great Merseyside Geniuses* (Wilmslow, 1997). However, there have always been internal critics, as in the 1880s, when the *Daily Post* castigated the 'shilly-shallying neglectfulness of the Health Authorities of Liverpool', see *Squalid Liverpool. By a Special Commission* (Liverpool, 1883), 27.

26] Cited in P.J. Waller, *Democracy and Sectarianism: A Political and Social History of Liverpool 1868–1939* (Liverpool, 1981), 13.

27] *Northern Daily Times* 28 Oct. 1857, newspaper cutting in Danson Archive, National Museums and Galleries on Merseyside.

only municipality which had a London Office[28] – it should have been at the forefront of provincial progressivism, but as the *Liverpool Leader in Politics, Literature, Science and Art* acknowledged, there was no centre for 'higher thought' – no 'Liverpool school' – to set the standard:

> We are obliged to confess that in Liverpool this higher thought is not common ... and the fact that the wealthiest and the most fashionable society is not the most educated, make difficulties in the way of reform not inconsiderable; but it is also true that there is no small amount of intellectual life scattered here and there which only requires the necessary machinery to utilise it, and though Liverpool has not been conspicuous as a school of political thought, there is no reason why she should not become so.[29]

The American Civil War – when many local merchants supported the Confederate South – was a dispiriting experience for the gentlemanly capitalists of the Liverpool liberal elite. In the intense speculation created by the cotton famine, it seemed that little had changed since the philistine commercialism of the slave trade, other than a further decline in conduct and manners on the Exchange where the Tories set the tone for a brash new breed of traders. As practised in Liverpool, commerce was no guarantee of character or of enlightened views:

> There are a number of young rowdy snobs who infest the Liverpool Exchange, and who take every opportunity of showing how unfit they are to consort with gentlemen. These men, in many cases the spawn of limited liability banks, have forced themselves into business without character, without capital, and without credit, except in the most con-fiding of bank directors, are the curse of Liverpool. It is with no feelings of disrespect to the Tory party that we say that the majority are Tories, because this class of men have been forced into existence by the gambling spirit induced by the American war, and the Tories having

28] W.O. Henderson, 'The Liverpool Office in London', *Economica*, Vol. xiii (1933), 473–79.
29] 'Intellectual Centralization', *Liverpool Leader* 29 Aug. 1868. The publication was launched on 1 Aug. 1868 in the conviction that 'the prominent position of Liverpool distinctly entitles it to the complete production and publication of a high-class newspaper and review, which shall be, as far as practicable, local, but in no sense, as to their contributors and their opinions, provincial', i.

identified themselves with the South, these young fellows naturally incline to that side.[30]

Dismayed and disgusted, some Liberals abandoned faith in Liverpool commerce and enterprise, questioning its prized provincial pre-eminence. Liverpool remained geographically isolated and apart, 'Vindex' averred in a lecture to the Junior Reform Club, its exponential growth notwithstanding. At a distance from the high-roads of national life and public opinion, Liverpool faced outwards to the sea: hence, it tended to adopt 'a *semi-colonial* method of looking at State questions'. Where liberalism flourished in other provincial cities, Liverpool displayed a 'landlord instinct', reliant upon a privileged and parasitic 'toll-bar' conservatism alien to progress and reform:

> The rise of Manchester and Birmingham have been in the fullest sense instances of 'a clear stage and no favour' and 'letting the best man win'. Such towns are in their nature Liberal in politics; enterprise, energy, ingenuity, novelty, free trade, 'are the breath of their nostrils' ... There is nothing of the 'clear stage and no favour' principle displayed in the rise of Liverpool. On the contrary, it is her geographical position which gives her the advantage and privilege of the business she does, with but a certain amount of assistance from any merit of her inhabitants. She is in fact gaining by the energy and industry of the manufacturing districts at her back, who crowd goods on to her wharves for shipment; and to the energy and industry of the American planters and farmers who pour grain and cotton into her warehouses. The fact that business has always, so to speak, been thrust upon her rather than created by her, has developed what may be called a sort of *landlord instinct* here. She is in possession of a fine river, and she bargains for the use of it. She builds fine docks – but she has also levied town-dues – she has claimed a sort of landlord right to stipulate terms for the use of her advantages – and such landlord right is of the essential nature of privilege.[31]

30] 'Blackguardism on "Change"', *Liverpool Leader* 28 Nov. 1868. Some Tories were themselves critical of the speculative mania and its demoralising influence upon Liverpool's commercial life; see Sir William B. Forwood, *Recollections of a Busy Life* (London, 1910), 52–55.
31] 'Vindex' (Col. W.W. Biggs), *Some Reasons for the Conservatism of Liverpool. A Lecture* (Liverpool, n.d., 1880?) 17.

His political sympathies notwithstanding, Muir eschewed such Liberal disenchantment. As the concluding pages of the *History* attest, he took considerable heart from late-Victorian and Edwardian developments when Liverpool responded positively to adverse change in the terms of trade – and to the challenge of the new Manchester Ship Canal, built to evade Liverpool 'tolls'. The era of international free trade and Britain's economic ascendancy was at an end, but – as in the past – Liverpool enterprise and resourcefulness was to flourish in adversity. While the port reached new peaks of prosperity, Liverpool acquired city, diocesan and university status, a fitting climax to Muir's narrative. Despite growing competition and international protectionism, addition to the tonnage of Liverpool after 1870 was 'more than twice as great as the actual addition made during the period of unquestioned ascendancy':

> The result is, that at the end of her seventh century as a chartered borough, Liverpool finds herself amongst the three or four greatest ports of the world. She conducts one-third of the export trade, and one-fourth of the import trade, of the United Kingdom. She owns one-third of the total shipping of the kingdom, and one-seventh of the total registered shipping of the world ... In the midst of a fiercer competition than she has hitherto known, the port proclaims her confidence in the future by erecting for the new century a domed dock office at the gateway of the town, and a stately pillared cotton exchange near by; two such palaces of trade as fifty years ago could scarcely have been dreamed of.[32]

As an historian, Muir's enthusiasm for the new commercial palaces at the Pier Head and adjacent (rather cramped) business district was tempered by a due sense of time and space. (His final project on Liverpool before he left in 1913 for a post at Manchester, away from Mackay, was to be another 'narrative introduction' – an account of 'the topographical growth of the city' – for a large collection of prints and drawings of 'Old Liverpool'.[33]) To his dismay, these qualities were sadly absent in the new discipline of 'town planning', pioneered at his own University. Planners, he rued, either abandoned the city centre to concentrate on soulless suburban develop-

32] Muir, *History*, 297–98.
33] *Bygone Liverpool Illustrated by ninety-seven plates reproduced from original paintings, drawings, manuscripts and prints* (Liverpool, 1913).

ment[34] or, as in the case of Professor Adshead, first holder of the Lever chair, advocated shifting the centre 'to some new and less costly region'. Outraged at the suggestion, Muir undertook a detailed analysis of central Liverpool with its 'clearly-marked areas or zones already existing'. His purpose was 'to show that circumstances which the town-planner might be tempted to overlook have already determined the geographical distribution of the main civic functions, and determined it, if blindly, on the whole wisely and well'. Liverpool lacked antiquity, but it should continue on its familiar path to progress, eschewing ahistorical modernism: 'Just as we win power over Nature, not by opposing her, but by understanding her, so we shall make the best of our problem of Town Planning by understanding as fully as we may the forces which have already been blindly at work in shaping the arrangement of the city, and by regulating them rather than attempting to reverse them'.[35]

Muir's historical sensitivity was all the more forceful as two new building projects, architectural embodiments of urbane civilisation, were taking shape appropriately on ground immediately above the commercial centre, new 'crowns' of the city's identity and pride, the ideal ending to his *History*. First, the plans for an Anglican cathedral:

And now, to crown the so recent ecclesiastical reorganisation, comes the magnificent and daring proposal to erect, in the midst of a busy modern trading city, a vast cathedral like those of the Middle Ages, whose tall towers and soaring roofs, raised on the hill above the river, shall stand forth above the roar of the traffic as a perpetual reminder that 'man does not live by bread alone'.[36]

34] In fear of such development, the newly-formed Liverpool City Guild, a middle-class inflexion of Merseypride, concentrated its energies on the district of Wavertree, Woolton and Allerton, 'the only remaining opportunity for the preservation in or near the city of a region suitable for the larger kind of house and garden, with a pleasant approach through the existing parks to the heart of the city', *Town Planning Review*, Vol. I (1910), 84–86 and 268.
35] Ramsay Muir, 'Liverpool: An Analysis of the Geographical Distribution of Civic Functions', *Town Planning Review*, Vol. I (1910), 235–45, and 303–311, followed by Adshead's reply, 312–15. See also, D.K. Stenhouse, 'Liverpool's office district 1875–1905', *Transactions of the Historic Society of Lancashire and Cheshire*, Vol. 133 (1984), 71–87.
36] Muir, *History*, 329–30. For the protracted process of completing the project, illustrated with great detail, see Peter Kennerley, *The Building of Liverpool Cathedral* (Preston, 1991): 'Though Liverpool Cathedral cannot boast that it is the last resting place of the bones of some Anglo-Saxon saint, or that the stonework of

Second, the rapid expansion of the University from federal beginnings in January 1882 'in a disused lunatic asylum, in the midst of a slum district' to its new independence and impressive precinct, 'a remarkable group of big buildings, equipped for the most advanced work':

> Beginning almost last of all English cities in the provision of higher education, Liverpool has, in twenty-five years, surpassed all but the oldest of her compeers ... in the midst of a community necessarily engrossed in the pursuit of gain, a fastness has been erected for the support and maintenance of the disinterested love of knowledge and of pure thought.

> This is perhaps the crown of the achievements of a wonderful period: a period which has witnessed a transformation in the character of the town, and in the spirit in which civic obligations are regarded, still more remarkable than the growth of its wealth and population.[37]

Not surprisingly, Muir's *History* concluded in a mood of high optimism:

> The city which, at the opening of a new age, is simultaneously engaged in erecting a great cathedral and a great university, is surely no mean city. It is building for itself twin citadels of the ideal, a citadel of faith and a citadel of knowledge; and from the hill which once looked down on an obscure hamlet, and which later saw ships begin to crowd the river, and streets to spread over the fields, their towers will look across the

---

the Chancel reveals the ravages of Reformation or Civil War, it is justifiably proud of its rich archive record', p. 7. There is now, of course, a cathedral 'to spare' in 'our Liverpool home': the Roman Catholic Cathedral, begun in 1933, was finally completed in very different ultra-modern form for consecration in 1967. For 'the secret in the foundation stone' of the Anglican Cathedral, see Fred Bower, *Rolling Stonemason* (London, 1936), ch. 9. Wrapped between copies of the *Clarion* and the *Labour Leader* (provided by his schoolboy sectarian sparring partner, Jim Larkin), Bower allegedly placed a socialist address on behalf of the 'wage slaves' building the cathedral, to remind posterity that 'within a stone's throw from here, human beings are housed in slums not fit for swine'.

37] Muir, *History*, 334–37. Muir was a leading advocate of independence for the University, see Ramsay Muir, *The Plea for a Liverpool University* (Liverpool, 1901). At the vice-chancellor's request, he wrote 'a little book on the past development and future hopes of the University' to mark the double celebration of 1907, as 'the twenty-fifth anniversary of the foundation of University College happened to coincide with the seven-hundredth anniversary of the city'; see Ramsay Muir, *The University of Liverpool: its Present State* (Liverpool, 1907). For a general history of the University, see Thomas Kelly, *For Advancement of Learning: the University College and University of Liverpool 1881–1981* (Liverpool, 1981).

ship-thronged estuary, monuments of a new and more generous aspiration.[38]

Exhilarated by the energy and intellectual vitality of Edwardian Liverpool, Muir encouraged the city council to celebrate the 700th anniversary of the granting of borough status, an occasion for popular enjoyment, civic promotion and instruction in citizenship. Following discussions with Muir, Pickmere, the town clerk, presented a series of proposals to the Finance Committee to mark the anniversary in ways which 'would stimulate civic pride and patriotism and (especially in the young) encourage the growth of a higher citizenship, and they would bring Liverpool more prominently to the notice of other countries, and be the means of inducing visitors to the British Isle to spend some time in the City'.[39] The Walker Art Gallery mounted an Historical Exhibition of Liverpool Antiquities, designed to show that 'the materialism of a great commercial city and seaport is not necessarily inimical to the pursuit of learning, research and analysis'.[40] The exhibition was accompanied by a catalogue, available in special limited edition on hand-made paper, an epitome of Merseypride: 'for the first time, we believe, in the history of modern municipalities, has been compiled an elaborately comprehensive catalogue of practically everything that bears on or illustrates in any way the rise and development of a great city'. In fact, the catalogue exposed the paucity of Liverpool's ancient past while it chose to conceal controversial aspects of its recent commercial growth. 'Undoubtedly the fact that we have no reliable view of the town dated earlier than the latter half of the seventeenth century is deplorable', the curator of views and prints admitted: 'it was not until the town was well on the way to ultimate commercial prosperity that there was any serious attempt on the part of a painter to record its outward appearance.' Even the shipping section had 'but few relics of the quaint old craft and of the sturdy old sea-dogs in which, and by whom, the foundations of our present supremacy in the world of shipping were so well and truly laid'. The emphasis was perforce on more recent examples of Liverpool's 'traditional' adaptability and progress. Modern exhibits, the curator opined, 'will serve to show that, while the picturesque days and the romance of sail are

---

38] Muir, *History*, 340. His study of central Liverpool, however, regretted the lack of 'a civic opera-house, such as every continental city of any importance possesses'.
39] *City of Liverpool: Proposed Celebration of the 700th Anniversary of the Foundation of Liverpool: Report of the Town Clerk* (Liverpool, 1907).
40] *Pageant News*, no. 5, 12 July 1907.

silently slipping away, the era of steam, with its many great changes and
sudden developments, still finds our ship-owners and merchants filled
with the old spirit of progress and ready at all times to maintain the
modern City of Liverpool – in worthy succession to the "Old Town" – *a
Seaport second to none'*. It was the manuscript section, however, which
provoked controversy, prompted by Robert Gladstone's exposure of excision
of slave trade material from the published catalogue:

> I was unable to give in my section of it a complete collection of the
> materials for the history of the Liverpool slave trade. The catalogue does
> not contain any mention of two most important manuscript volumes
> known by the name of 'The Log of the Slave Ship Boom' covering the
> period from 1779 to 1792.
>
> The fault is not mine. The authorities in charge of the Public Library
> flatly refused me permission to include these volumes in our Exhibition,
> on the ground (so I understand) that it was desirable to suppress and
> conceal the evidence of the important part taken by Liverpool in the
> slave trade ... I would suggest that those who are keeping our catalogue
> as a book of reference should cut out this letter and insert it at page 156.

'The charge that our authorities have such a parochial outlook in matters
of this kind', the *Liverpool Courier* noted, 'must appear damaging to the
disinterested outsider'. [41] Undaunted by the controversy, James Touzeau's
history, published in 1910, insisted that Liverpool had 'borne more than its
share of stigma attaching to this trade': 'The Slave Trade has been held by
many as the source or foundation of Liverpool's wealth and prosperity, but
we venture to think that this view is exaggerated ... if this traffic had not
entered into the commercial life of Liverpool, the ultimate success of the
port would not have been prejudiced or impaired, although perhaps to
some extent retarded'. Such views (along with downward reassessment of
the profit margins of the trade) have continued to fuel historiographical
controversy, as in the recent claim by Anstey and Hair that 'Liverpool was
more important for the slave trade than the slave trade for Liverpool'. The
debate seems not to have enhanced 'race relations' in the city. [42]

41] *Foundation of Liverpool 700th Anniversary: Historical Exhibition of Liverpool
Antiquities at the Walker Art Gallery* (Liverpool, 1907). The copy in the Athenaeum
Library contains cuttings from the *Liverpool Courier* 4 Oct. 1907, and Robert Glad-
stone's letter, 23 Sept. 1907, inserted at the appropriate page.
42] Touzeau, *Rise and Progress of Liverpool*, 688 and 745. Anstey and Hair,
Liverpool, the African Slave Trade and Abolition. For a very different perspective

The historical pageant at which Muir, adorned in King John's robes, crown and beard, read a paragraph of the original 'Charter', proved less contentious and far more popular – but it was not a fully inclusive celebration. There was some initial doubt as to whether Liverpool could match the commemorations already planned for summer 1907 in such 'historic' towns as St Albans, Bury St Edmunds and Oxford. However, a representative of the new world, J.L. Griffiths, the American Consul, offered the requisite sense of perspective, promptly dismissing any suggestion that Liverpool's history was too commonplace and prosaic for public celebration:

> Not even Oxford, with its thousand years and more of hallowed life, its historical associations, its religious traditions and its academic influence, has had a more romantic history than this sentinel of the Mersey, which has been transformed through the enterprise and faith and courage of its people from a cluster of mud hovels into an opulent city whose ships sail every ocean and whose trade has spread to every land.[43]

Thus encouraged, the city proceeded with plans for a great pageant – 'a series of living and moving pictures, the continuous story of Liverpool's growth through these seven hundred years, from a humble fishing hamlet to the mightiest seaport of the world'[44] – to be held in Edge Lane Hall Gardens and Wavertree Park, an appropriate Liverpudlian venue, 'as unromantic a spot', the *Morning Post* noted, 'as could possibly have been selected'.[45]

The promotional literature echoed the themes and motifs of Muir's *History*. Although fancy dress from bygone times was the order of the day, the pageant, an exercise in Edwardian citizenship, culminated in celebration of present achievement:

(published under the auspices of the Libraries and Arts Department of the City Council), see G. Cameron and S. Crooke, *Liverpool – Capital of the Slave Trade* (Liverpool, 1992). Note the importance attached to slave trade historiography in Lord Gifford, Wally Brown and Ruth Bundey, *Loosen the Shackles. First Report of the Liverpool 8 Inquiry into Race Relations in Liverpool* (London, 1989). For developments after abolition, see Martin Lynn, 'Liverpool and Africa in the Nineteenth Century: the Continuing Connection' *Transactions of the Historic Society of Lancashire and Cheshire*, Vol. 147 (1998), 27–54.
43] *Pageant News*, no. 3, 4 July 1907.
44] 'Foreword', *700th Anniversary of the Foundation of Liverpool: Programme of the Pageant* (Liverpool, 1907), 3–4.
45] Quoted in *Pageant News*, no. 14, 6 Aug. 1907.

The ambition of every true citizen must surely be to leave the dignity and worth of the City higher than he found it, and to aid him in this a knowledge of the past is essential ... We shall see how our City – learning wisdom from her mistakes, fortitude from her trials, courage from her disasters – has ever moved onward and upward. As in the thirteenth century, around her grim old feudal castle, she fought for liberty; as in her medieval Town Hall and Exchange she set the foundations of her Corporate power and wealth; so in the twentieth century her University that is, and her Cathedral that is to be, tell us how, in her wider vision, freedom and wealth and power are but the means to a nobler end, and that in the perfecting of her moral and intellectual life she sees her best ideals.[46]

The success of the event, however, owed much to Liverpudlian commercial resources, coordinated through the columns of *Pageant News*, a specially-launched newspaper edited by Percy Corkhill, the master of ceremonies. Lorries and floats for the twelve historical periods in the great procession were provided gratis by the Cart Owners' Association – including a car entitled 'The Slave Trade' in the 'Wealth and Charity' period; banners and props were supplied by local artists under the direction of F.V. Burridge, head of the School of Art; local musicians were enlisted to write melodies to accompany the six 'historical episodes', the centre-piece of the pageant; a committee of five hundred ladies, headed by local dignitaries and Pickmere's wife, took free possession of the old Cotton Exchange to make the costumes for the cast of nearly 1200; unemployed men from the Distress Committee were brought in to level the ground and prepare the stage (some 8000 square yards) under the direction of the City Engineer; and staff from the Bank of Liverpool took charge of the admissions receipts. In a shrewd commercial move, the pageant was held in early August rather than on the actual anniversary of the 28th of the month, to 'cause the least possible interference with business' by making use of the bank holiday weekend. Along with a thanksgiving service, a special visit by fourteen battleships and cruisers of the Channel Fleet was also arranged, attracting large crowds to the city – tramway receipts, perhaps the best indicator of success, were up over £2000 on the week.[47] Some employers – most notably pawnbrokers and hairdressers – agreed to early closure on

46] *Programme*, 4.
47] C.W. Mallins, traffic manager (tramways) was included in *Liverpool's Men of Mark*, a specially produced collection of photographic portraits of the leading dignitaries and worthies in 1907.

the fourth and final afternoon of the scheduled programme to enable their assistants to attend the pageant. An additional 'free display for the benefit of the poorer classes' was arranged for the following Sunday. In all, some 200 000 people witnessed the event. To the delight of the Council, it returned a small profit (boosted by souvenir sales) and had 'very greatly benefited the trade of the City, as well as given healthy amusement and recreation to so many thousands'. As entertainment, history was good not only for citizenship but also for business.[48]

Modelled on celebrations at Ripon, Sherborne, Warwick and Shrewsbury, the pageant was a very English affair with tableaux more appropriate to the 'historic' boroughs of 'merrie England'. There were few celtic references despite the considerable influx into Liverpool over the centuries from Ireland, Wales and Scotland (Muir's ancestral homeland). The 'Grand Car of Liverpool' which brought the procession to an end symbolised the city's essential Britishness: 'In the front of the Car is a figure of *Britannia*, with Trident, and at the back a figure of *Erin*, with Harp'. Other identities were unacknowledged, despite the presence (floating and permanent) of Kru, Lascar, Chinese and other seafaring communities, drawn to Liverpool as routes and markets had diversified.[49] Although a number of black children, sons and daughters of African merchants and slavers, had been sent to Liverpool for primary education in the eighteenth century, the 'black presence' in Liverpool – much of which defied or eluded census and other forms of registration, enumeration and civic participation[50] – dates

---

48] *Pageant News*, nos 1–17, 24 June–17 Oct. 1907. F.J. Leslie's letter, *Liverpool Courier* 23 Aug. 1907. *City of Liverpool: 700th Anniversary of the Foundation of Liverpool: Report of the General Committee to the City Council* (Liverpool, 1907, and other pageant material in Athenaeum Library: Miscellaneous Pamphlets, Box 33. The twelve periods were: Ancient Britons, Norsemen and Saxons; Normans and Plantagenets; Days of the Barons; Early Days of Trade; Stanleys and Molyneuxs; the Tudors; Midsummer's eve pageant in Elizabeth's time; the Stuarts and the Civil War; Wealth and Charity; the Age of War, 1756 to 1815; the Age of Commerce and Industry, Roadways, Waterways, Steam; and 1907. The six historical episodes were Granting of the Charter, 1207; Birkenhead Priory, 1276; the Stanleys and Molyneuxs, 15th century; Midsummer's eve, AD 1580; the Surrender of Liverpool, 1644; and Liverpool, 1907.
49] The Kru have attracted most attention, see Diane Frost, *Work and Community among West African Migrant Workers since the Nineteenth Century* (Liverpool, 1999). Maria Lin Wong, *Chinese Liverpudlians* (Birkenhead, 1989) provides an introduction to the history of the Chinese in Liverpool.
50] Andrea Murphy, *From the Empire to the Rialto: Racism and Reaction in Liverpool 1918–1948* (Birkenhead, 1995), Appendix B, concludes cautiously that

from the decades after abolition of the slave trade, with a distinct expansion after 1870. Pat O'Mara, a Liverpool-Irish 'slummy', grew up in the dire poverty of the Edwardian south end alongside 'Negroes, Chinese, Mulattoes, Filipinos, almost every nationality under the sun, most of them boasting white wives and large half-caste families ... each color laying claim to a certain street'.[51] Significantly, there is no reference to the 700th anniversary celebrations in his autobiography.[52] As a 'world city', Edwardian Liverpool was proud of its cosmopolitan importance, but, as Muir made clear, it had no wish to acquire a multi-ethnic 'melting-pot' identity:

> There is no city in the world, not even London itself, in which so many foreign governments find it necessary to maintain consular offices for the safeguarding of their exiled subjects. It should, however, be noted that this amazingly polyglot and cosmopolitan population, consisting to a considerable extent of races which are backward in many ways, and maintaining itself largely by unskilled labour, vastly increases the difficulty of securing and maintaining the decencies of life.[53]

Cosmopolitanism, indeed, hindered social progress to the detriment of Liverpool's reputation in attaining national minima and efficiency in the 'Land of Hope and Glory' – with which refrain the pageant concluded.[54]

For all the confidence in the future – not least as expressed in the 700th

---

until after the Second World War *resident* Blacks comprised no more than between one and two per cent of the population. Racism and black settlement are portrayed as 'integral parts of Liverpool's history' in Ian Law and June Henfrey, *A History of Race and Racism in Liverpool, 1660–1950* (Liverpool, 1981).

51] Pat O'Mara, *The Autobiography of a Liverpool Irish Slummy* (London, 1934), 11.
52] Colin Wilkinson registers (undue) surprise at this omission in his 'Introduction' to the recent (undated) Bluecoat Press reprint of the autobiography which unaccountably drops the term 'Irish' from the title.
53] Muir, *History*, 305.
54] Edwardian socialists in Liverpool were more positive about cosmopolitanism but their language fell short of today's political correctness. The International Club in Liverpool included a 'pleasant-faced Chinaman'; an 'Egyptian interpreter, employed at a large Liverpool café, sphinx-like in look, action or inaction, and speech'; a 'Hindoo ... acquired from somewhere'; a 'Jap who had imbibed Socialistic doctrines'; but no black African: "'Couldn't you give the platform a little more colour?" our secretary asked me. "How so?" I replied. "Why," he said, "you've got no coon." Off I set, jumped on the first tram car, got down to the purlieus of the docks, and soon ran up against a son of Africa. "Say, have a drink?" I called to him. Sure, he would. "Would he like to come to a meeting?" "Anything for a shilling"', *Rolling Stonemason*, Bower, 184–85.

anniversary celebrations and the 'new' history – the Edwardian years were
to prove Liverpool's climacteric. Technically speaking, the zenith had long
since passed: however, as economic historians acknowledge, the port
remained in sound health from the apogee of the 1850s through to the First
World War.[55] Thenceforth in spiralling economic decline, Merseypride
required reformulation. History was called upon to fulfil different functions.
Two groups established in the 1920s demonstrate the range: the Society of
the Lovers of Old Liverpool relapsed into nostalgic consolation for the
(recent) good old days, while Liverpool Organization Limited re-packaged
Muir's chronicle of enterprise and adaptability in the hope of attracting
inward investment and economic rejuvenation.

Established in 1925 for 'the promotion of the study of the history,
traditions and development of Liverpool', the Society of Lovers of Old
Liverpool was an exercise in social and political unity, an indication of the
need to rally to the defence of the city in unwonted decline.[56] The
committee, for whom C.A. Healy of the *Daily Post* served as secretary,
embraced all shades of political opinion, including T.P. O'Connor, long-
serving Irish Nationalist MP for the Scotland division; Sir Leslie Scott,
distinguished lawyer and Tory MP for Exchange; and Jack Hayes, the city's
first Labour MP (Edge Hill). Robert Gladstone – city councillor, member of
the Docks Board, the last of the businessman-scholars – was closely involved
in preliminary discussions which led to the appointment of George
Milligan, dockers' leader in the north end, as the first president of the
society. A talented autodidact – he had previously edited and published his
own *Mersey Magazine* – Milligan was a true Liverpool 'character': a devout
Catholic, anti-socialist but militant and fearless in defence of his fellow
dockers' rights.[57]

Merseypride united these disparate men, an attitude enshrined in the
Society's epigraph, 'Liverpool's story is the world's glory':

> For over a century Liverpool has been the advance agent of Civilization;
> our record as a pioneer of thought, of national, nay of world-service, is
> so splendid that any cultivated man who knows the history of the great
> cities of Old Time – Athens, Rome, Bagdad, Constantinople, Paris, and

55] Lynn, 'Liverpool and Africa in the Nineteenth Century', 27–8.
56] See C.A. Healy's typescript account, Sept. 1927 in Athenaeum Library: Robert
Gladstone Miscellaneous pamphlets, 139.
57] See the entry on Milligan by Eric Taplin in *Dictionary of Labour Biography:
Volume 5* (London, 1979), 152–57 (but this contains no reference to the Society).

London, and measures our effort against theirs, then this city, the pioneer of railways, nursing, lending libraries, blind asylums, ocean liners, cold storage, the city through which the virile life of the old world has flowed to fertilise the new, this, the chief city of New Time can inspire its sons and daughters to be worthy of the nobility, sacrifice, and endeavour of their fathers, and our Society can play its part by keeping alive the story of our city's past glories, of the wonders of the present, and so prepare the way for the wonders of the future.[58]

Here was a celebratory record of recent progress, unsullied by its immediate antecedents in the slave trade, the topic of a lecture by J.M. Dow, the society's treasurer:

Dame Liverpool has, swathed in flowing white robe and candle in hand cried *Mea Maxima Culpa*! The penance has been protracted, and not only in absolution long over-due, but I suggest that instead of wearing the penitent's garb any longer she, on the other hand, might well don the wreath of victory; for, thanks to the Liverpool School of Tropical Medicine, the lives of millions of negroes have been saved. Dame Liverpool sinned, suffered, and in our own day has made ample and generous restitution.[59]

In his lectures, Robert Gladstone offered a longer chronology, insisting that Liverpool 'of world-fame as a sea-port, is also a place of very considerable antiquity – though it must be admitted that there are no visible evidences of that antiquity now remaining'.[60] For most members of the society, however, 'old' Liverpool was not antique but within living memory: above all, it signified the good times that were now slipping away.

Most lectures reminisced about the practices and characters of yesteryear in commerce, professions and on the docks – there was even a talk on the 'romance' of the meat trade in the nineteenth century. Until his untimely death, Milligan was a popular and racy lecturer, recounting the sartorial eccentricities and the old work and drink habits – not least the

58] Healy's report, Sept. 1927.
59] Dow typescript, 25 Feb.1927, Gladstone Miscellaneous Pamphlets, 23.
60] One of Gladstone's lectures to the Society became standard issue for conference delegates in Liverpool. *Notes on the History and Antiquities of Liverpool* (3rd impression, 1932) first appeared in *Merseyside*, the handbook of the meeting of the British Association in 1923 and was reprinted in the handbook of the Chemical Industry Society, 1924, and the British Hospitals Association, 1932.

formerly obligatory 'three tides' of Saturday indulgence – of the north-end dockers. Encouraged by Milligan, the society engaged in oral history interviews, 'collecting the story of the Liverpool men and women whose memories went back four decades, or half a century or more back, which were not recorded either in books or newspapers'. Driven by nostalgia, history was being transmuted into heritage, intended for internal reassurance.[61]

Liverpool Organization Limited, established by local businessmen in 1923, aimed at a different audience. An 'ambassador of commerce' aided by grants from the Merseyside local authorities, it sought to attract new businesses and industries into the area, a practical approach to diversification based on local manufacture for local distribution.[62] History was a useful marketing ploy, attesting to the enterprise, civic responsibility and cultural provision – put on special display in 'Civic Weeks' in the late 1920s – which placed Liverpool ahead of other provincial cities, able to resist 'the bribes of London, the vampire that lives on the best blood of the provinces'.[63] Not simply a matter of luck or geographical good fortune, Liverpool's pre-eminence, the *Book of Liverpool* (specially published for the 1928 'Civic Week') asserted, was hard won through toughness and struggle, inherent qualities in the local fibre which incoming manufacturing employers would quickly appreciate. Traced back to medieval struggle against the Moores, Molyneuxs and other overlords, the Liverpool 'spirit' had subsequently shown its worth in securing commercial supremacy:

61] 'Dockers in Toppers', *Liverpool Weekly Post* 6 June 1925, and other cuttings, including material on Milligan's requiem mass, in Gladstone Miscellaneous Pamphlets, 139.

62] See the lavish supplement to the *Daily Post* 21 Feb. 1927, *The Ambassador of Commerce. Merseyside's Industrial and Commercial Potentialities*.

63] London, however, attracted an undue share of inward foreign industrial investment: 'A foreigner coming to England thinks of London. He prefers to live in London. His wife prefers to live in London… it will require all the force that the most active organisation can secure and the fullest co-operation of the Mersey Docks and Harbour Board, and of all the councils, if we are not to see repeated again and again the instances of Pirelli Tyres, the Ford Motor Works, and, now, of Mr Thomas Barta, the Czech boot manufacturer, who has just decided to take a square mile in Essex and build colossal boot factories there. I believe that all of these firms would have found in Liverpool a cheaper centre of production, a greater supply of cheap labour, and at least as good facilities for distribution'. Speech by Mr Marquis at the annual meeting of the Liverpool Organization, Adelphi Hotel, reported in *Liverpool Echo* 14 Jan. 1932.

It must be remembered that it was our superior skill and industry which beat Bristol and London out of the slave trade, then a perfectly legitimate and praiseworthy occupation in everybody's estimation, and it was the greater hardihood and courage of our privateers and the commercial adventurousness of our people at home that turned to our particular profit the general misfortune of a hundred years of war.

True to this spirit, current massive investment in public works – to complete the dock system, the tunnel under the Mersey and the East Lancashire arterial road – affirmed Liverpool's commitment to remain the 'gateway of the west'. Other traditions, not least the city's pioneer role in social and environmental reform, were still proudly upheld, while the Cathedral, 'as yet but a fragment', bore witness to 'that union of practical achievement and high idealism which is the true basis of Liverpool's claim to be reckoned the "Second City of the Empire"'. Without a mention of economic decline, the *Book* – having 'painted a vision of the City Perfect at the top of well-nigh unscaleable height' – concluded in confident Muir-like expectation of 'a still livelier civic consciousness, a new dignity and a philosophy in which the more intensive cultivation of the graces will be a feature of the Liverpool of to-morrow'.[64]

The efforts of Liverpool Organization notwithstanding, the run-down of Liverpool gathered pace in the inter-war period, as surveys by Carradog Jones and others attested, aggravated by world-wide depression in which trade declined more rapidly than production.[65] History, however, continued to offer hope. *The Story of Liverpool* (1935), a specially commissioned text-book for schools (approved by Robert Gladstone and members of the local branch of the Historical Association), rehearsed Muir's main theme: Liverpudlian adaptability in the face of adversity. Liverpool, its school children were assured, had responded with characteristic enterprise to the economic problems at the end of the First World War:

64] See, in particular, 'Foreword' and 'Liverpool by the Editor', *Book of Liverpool* 6–10. D. Carradog Jones, *Social Survey of Merseyside* (3 vols: Liverpool, 1934), Vol. ii, 198, approved of its 'niche-marketing' approach. The Organization's publicity officer was Christopher Murray Grive, better known as the poet Hugh MacDiarmid.
65] 'Merseyside has most to hope from a high standard of living combined with freedom of trade. These denied, Britain will be compelled to take a lesser share of the world's commerce and the Port of Liverpool to accept a marked restriction in the scale of its activities', Carradog Jones, *Social Survey*, Vol. i, 39–40.

The city that a century earlier had believed itself faced with ruin over the loss of the slave trade, only to become greater than ever, again confronted its difficulties in a spirit of enterprise ... Just as the city in the nineteenth century had found substitutes for the slave trade, so in the twentieth she set to work to make good the loss of that passenger traffic that had passed to Southampton by the encouragement of new manufactures, such as those of artificial silk and electrical apparatus.[66]

The claim was reasserted with triumphalist fervour – a mood, alas, soon to be dispelled – in George Chandler's *Liverpool*, a publication sponsored by the City Council in 1957 to celebrate the 750th anniversary of the charter. Hailing the Liverpool of the late 1950s as 'an industrial boom town', Chandler, the city librarian, accorded the credit to the inter-war City Council which had shown 'a vision comparable to that which had inspired the old borough Council in the early eighteenth century'.[67]

With its space-age imagery, welfare statism and industrial optimism, Chandler's history has not worn well – not to mention its cursory discussion and complacent defence of the slave trade.[68] Based on a social tapestry of 'kings, barons, lords of the manor, mayors, village workers, port workers, industrial workers and the poor', it aimed to extend the chronological and social boundaries of Merseypride:

> ... these groups are now knit together by common patriotism although their economic and political interests may in the past have led to conflicts in which the more humble classes have progressively become stronger at the expense of the rich.
>
> Civic pride in Liverpool is enormously strong to-day and its citizens often prefer to serve the interest of the town rather than those of their political, economic, religious or class loyalties ... is it not a political

66] C.L. Lamb and E. Smallpage, *The Story of Liverpool* (Liverpool, 1935), 74.
67] Chandler, *Liverpool*, 354–64. For details of other celebrations of the 750th anniversary, see Athenaeum Library, Miscellaneous pamphlets, 47. The main event was a series of recitals in St George's Hall to mark the re-opening of the world-famous organ. The Liverpool Music Group under Fritz Spiegl presented a special concert of Liverpool music including the first English performance of Donizetti's 'Emilia Di Liverpool'. Associated British Pathe produced a documentary, *This in our Time*, covering the more significant events since the 1907 celebrations.
68] 'In the long run, the triangular operation based on Liverpool was to bring benefits to all, not least to the transplanted slaves, whose descendants have subsequently achieved in the New World standards of education and civilisation far ahead of their compatriots whom they left behind', Chandler, *Liverpool*, 306.

example for all the world that the descendants of the Normans, Anglo-Saxons, Irish, Welsh, Scots and Vikings who have peopled Liverpool are now united in a common pride in being Liverpolitans.

Although broader than Muir's *History*, there were limits to Chandler's investigation of Liverpool's distinct and 'cosmopolitan' identity as 'the provincial metropolis of the United Kingdom: it is not English, like London, nor Lancashire, like Manchester'. There was no place in Liverpolitana – still viewed in the high cultural framework set by Roscoe – for 'scousers' (a provincialism that Chandler deplored) or for blacks.[69]

Despite their long presence in the city, Liverpool blacks remained apart. Classified as aliens, although often subjects of British colonies, they suffered institutionalised racism (augmented by the notorious Elder Dempster agreements) in inter-war employment practices in the merchant marine.[70] Concentrated (if not marooned) in parts of Toxteth, the 'new Harlem of Liverpool', they lacked the public funds and assistance that were later to be made available to post-Second World War immigrants from the commonwealth. So far from a register of integration, inter-marriage was condemned as miscegenation, the 'social problem' which, having pre-occupied inter-war academics and eugenicists, continued to compound what the Gifford Inquiry described as Liverpool's 'uniquely horrific' racism.[71]

It is to be hoped that Liverpool's imminent 800th anniversary will produce a comprehensive history of the city and its inhabitants. The need is urgent. Packaged as heritage, history itself has become Liverpool's main

69] Ibid., 9, 13, and 421–23. The Library, however, mounted an exhibition in 1957 on Liverpool and Africa.

70] Laura Tabili, *'We ask for British Justice': Workers and Racial Difference in Late Imperial Britain* (Ithaca, 1994), 68–77.

71] Ali Rattansi, 'Race, Class and the State: from Marxism to "Post-Modernism"', *Labour History Review*, Vol. 60 (1995), 23–36. D. Carradog Jones, *Social Survey*, Vol. I, 74–5, 205–6, Vol. II, 102, and Vol. III, 515–46. M.E. Fletcher, *Report on an Investigation into the Colour Problem in Liverpool and other Ports* (Liverpool, 1930). Gifford et al., *Loosen the Shackles*, 27–45. Lord Gifford's inquiry recommended that 'Liverpool's museums and public institutions, when they present Liverpool's history, give a full and honest account of the involvement of Black people in the city'. There is now a growing historiographical awareness; see, for example, Mark Christian, 'Black Struggle for Historical Recognition in Liverpool', *North West Labour History*, Vol. 20 (1995–96), 58–66; Marika Sherwood, *Pastor Daniels Ekarte and the African Churches Mission Liverpool 1931–1964* (London, 1994); and Diane Frost, 'Ambiguous Identities: Constructing and De-constructing Black and White "Scouse" Identity in Twentieth-Century Liverpool' in Neville Kirk (ed.), *Northern Identities* (forthcoming).

'trade' and source of attraction, the last hope of regeneration for a city blighted by post-industrial collapse and now ill-placed geographically (one of history's ironies) for trade with European partners. History, indeed, may be all that is left of Merseypride as Liverpool has collapsed into European Union Objective One status, a deprived city in which resourcefulness and enterprise, once the hallmarks of its merchant princes and corporate elite, survive residually in the ploys and devices of the street-wise scally scouser.[72] Whether as the story it tells itself, or the image it projects for others, Liverpool history must extend its narrative beyond the constituencies addressed with such confident and high-minded assurance by Ramsay Muir in 1907.

72] See my essay, '"An Accent Exceedingly Rare": Scouse and the Inflexion of Class', reprinted in this volume. See also Frank Boyce, 'From Victorian "Little Ireland" to Heritage Trail: Catholicism, Community and Change in Liverpool's Docklands', in R. Swift and S. Gilley (eds), *The Irish in Victorian Britain: the Local Dimension* (Dublin, 1999), 277–97.

2
'An accent exceedingly rare': Scouse and the inflexion of class*

Although instantly recognisable today, the Liverpudlian accent and identity pose considerable problems of historical reconstruction. Liverpool's apartness has not always taken a 'scouse' inflexion. With characteristic Merseypride, George Chandler's *Liverpool*, the official celebration of the 750th anniversary of the charter, eschewed any suggestion of provincialism in speech or character:

> ... the Liverpool dialect has no strong regional feature at all. It tends, as befits a cosmopolitan town with many Irish, Welsh and Scots, to be neutral phonetically ... And although the speaker of the Liverpool dialect is through Music Hall fame widely known as a scouser, a second nomenclature had to be found for the Liverpolitan born within the sound of St Nicholas's church – a Dicky Sam, which has etymologically no trace of provincialism.[1]

In seeking the origins of 'scouse' – not just a pattern of speech but a micro-culture in historical formation – my essay has an important historiographical purpose. It seeks to expose some limitations of the fashionable 'linguistic turn' in historical studies and to raise questions about Liverpool's proverbial exceptionalism, its incompatibility with the main

* This is an amended and updated version of a paper published with the same title in John Belchem and Neville Kirk (eds), *Languages of Labour* (Aldershot, 1997), 99–130. I would like to thank Andrew Hamer, Fritz Spiegl, Jonathan Bate, Tony Lane, Jim Dillon, Eric Taplin, Nick Hardy, Arline Wilson, John Davies, Frank Boyce, Mike Power and Jon Lawrence for their comments on earlier drafts of this paper.
1] George Chandler, *Liverpool* (London, 1957), 423.

narrative frameworks of modern British history.[2] As a social historian, my purpose is not to engage with the complexities of semiotics and linguistic theory, but to explore the ambivalence and tension between cultural representation and socio-economic materialism. I intend simply to offer some historical commentary on linguistic studies of Liverpool vernacular speech, the unmistakable accent upon which the various cultural representations of the 'scouser' have been constructed.

The study of 'scouse' stands outside the linguistic turn in historical studies. While now exalting its importance, historians still tend to view language in narrow and restricted manner. The ideas and idioms of public language – rhetoric, discourse and text – retain pre-eminence.[3] Demotic or vernacular speech is seldom considered, even though it is speech patterns which tend to express and encode critical differences of power and status in modern Britain.[4] Concentrated for the most part on public political language – on the means by which political formations deploy rhetoric, narrative and other discursive practices to construct identities and create constituencies of support – the linguistic turn has marked a backward step, re-affirming the traditional historical agenda. Analysis of the 'representational' is restricted to a narrow and often readily accessible range of public 'texts'.[5]

An accent not a dialect, 'scouse' does not lend itself to such textual deconstruction. In the virtual absence of a distinctive grammar or extensive vocabulary, the peculiarities of scouse are almost entirely phonological,

---

2] See my essay on 'The Peculiarities of Liverpool' in *Popular Politics, Riot and Labour: Essays in Liverpool History 1790–1940*, Belchem (Liverpool, 1992), 1–20.

3] Here the pattern was set by the foundation text of the 'linguistic turn', Gareth Stedman Jones 'Rethinking Chartism' in his *Languages of Class: Studies in English Working Class History, 1832–1982* (Cambridge, 1983). For a significant broadening of the understanding of 'political' language, see James Epstein, *Radical Expression: Political Language, Ritual and Symbol in England, 1790–1850* (New York, 1994). See also Raphael Samuel's two-part essay, 'Reading the Signs', *History Workshop Journal*, Vol. 32 (1991), 88–109 and Vol. 33 (1992), 220–51.

4] There are considerable problems for the historian in recapturing demotic speech, compounded by the tendency for all social groups to move towards an RP accent in formal contexts, see Andrew Hamer, 'Non-Standard Accents and the Classroom', *Proceedings of the English Association North*, Vol. 6 (1992), 56–64.

5] Patrick Joyce, *Visions of the People: Industrial England and the Question of Class, 1840–1914* (Cambridge, 1991); *Democratic Subjects: The Self and the Social in Nineteenth-Century England* (Cambridge, 1994); and 'The End of Social History', *Social History*, Vol. 20 (1995), 73–91. James Vernon, *Politics and the People: a Study in English Political Culture, c. 1815–1867* (Cambridge, 1993).

comprising (as detailed linguistic study has shown) the preferred position of speech organs, the way plosives and nasals are produced, and the distribution of prominence in diphthongs and pitch patterns.[6] Velarisation, the accompaniment of other articulations by the raising of the back of the tongue towards the soft palate, produces the famous Merseyside sound which suggests to outsiders some congestion in the upper respiratory tract. Scousers articulate a constant stream of prosodic patterns and segmental features which distinguish them unmistakably as Liverpudlians.[7] Their identity is constructed, indeed it is immediately established, by how they speak rather than by what they say. Instantly recognisable, the accent is the essential medium for the projection and representation of the local micro-culture, the 'scouse' blend of truculent defiance, collective solidarity, scallywaggery and fatalist humour which sets Liverpool and its inhabitants apart.

The scouse accent announces a cherished otherness which not all visitors appreciate. 'There is a rising inflection in it, particularly at the end of a sentence that gives even the most formal exchange a built-in air of grievance', Alan Bennett noted in his recent critical account of Liverpudlian self-dramatisation: 'They all have the chat, and it laces every casual encounter ... They are more like Cockneys than Lancashire people and it gets me down.'[8] Unlike cockney, however, scouse lacks a long and changing history: there is no 'sequence of representations' to reconstruct.[9] As an accent (and much more), scouse is a recently invented tradition, a cultural response to the city's decline.

As accent and/or identity label, scouse does not figure in nineteenth-century accounts of Liverpool. Until the late 1880s, indeed, serious phonetic studies made no distinction between the town and the surrounding countryside: apparently Liverpool spoke like the rest of south

6] The definitive linguistic study is Gerald O. Knowles, 'Scouse: the Urban Dialect of Liverpool', unpublished PhD thesis, University of Leeds, 1973. See also Hilary B. De Lyon, 'A Sociolinguistic Study of Aspects of the Liverpool Accent', unpublished MPhil thesis, University of Liverpool, 1981; and Mark Newbrook, *Sociolinguistic Reflexes of Dialect Interference in West Wirral* (Frankfurt, 1986). The study of Merseyside in J.C. Wells, *Accents of English* (Cambridge, 3 vols, 1982),Vol. ii, 371–73 draws heavily on Knowles.

7] A. Hughes and P. Trudgill, *English Accents and Dialects* (London, 1979), 62.

8] Alan Bennett, *Writing Home* (London, 1994) 144 and 289.

9] See Gareth Stedman Jones' marvellous study of 'The "Cockney" and the Nation, 1780–1988' in *Metropolis London: Histories and representations since 1800*, ed. D. Feldman and G.S. Jones (London, 1989), 272–324.

Lancashire.[10] Liverpudlians – or Liverpolitans, to use the genteel inflexion which (as Chandler exemplified) remained in fashionable use throughout the nineteenth century and beyond – deployed a variety of names to identify themselves, but scouse did not feature among them. One common practice in the early nineteenth century was to add some forename (usually Dick) to that of the town's emblem, the mythical liver bird,[11] guardian of 'shipping and sailors, commerce and counting-houses, mud and merchandise, tar and traffic, pitch and prosperity, and all other ingredients that contribute to the filling up of his "pool"'.[12] For reasons which remain obscure (but hint at the growing importance of American influences in the town), Dick Liver was replaced by Dick(e)y Sam, the preferred nomenclature throughout the nineteenth century.[13] 'I am myself a Liverpool man, or Dicky Sam, as we love to call our native-born inhabitants', J.A. Picton, the distinguished architect and local historian, introduced himself when drawn into the controversy in *Notes and Queries* in 1888: 'Does Mr Gladstone speak with a provincial accent?' Where previous contributors had detected a 'northern' or 'Lancashire' edge to the grand old man's accent, Picton, a fellow-Liverpudlian, insisted that Gladstone's 'tones and mode of utterance are decidedly of Liverpool origin. We bring out our words "ore rotundo", without the mincing word-clipping of the cockney, and equally distant from the rough Tim Bobbin Lancashire dialect.' Picton offered no further elucidation of the Liverpool accent, other than to insist on its distinct difference from nearby Manchester urban dialect.[14]

Dicky Sam gradually fell out of use, leaving Liverpudlians without an eponym until the advent of radio when various local characters were introduced to a national audience by a succession of Merseyside comedians.

10] According to Knowles, 'Scouse', 17, the first reference is to be found in A.J. Ellis, *On Early English Pronunciation. Part V: the Existing Phonology of English Dialects* (1889). By this time, the accent had apparently already crossed the river to Birkenhead and 'Merseyside Wirral', as Ellis disregarded the area north of Bebington in his discussion of West Cheshire usage, see Newbrook, *Sociolinguistic Reflexes*, 53.
11] See, for example, *The True and Wonderful History of Dick Liver* (Liverpool, 1824), in which 'Timothy Touchstone', alias the Revd William Shepherd, condemned the old Corporation and championed Dick Liver, the Liverpool commonalty.
12] *Liverpool Lion*, 14 Aug. 1847, 132.
13] Peter Aughton, *Liverpool: a People's History* (Preston, 1990), 214. For the importance of the American connection, see Peter Howell Williams, *Liverpolitana* (Liverpool, 1971), ch. 7.
14] *Notes and Queries*, 7th series, Vol. 6 (1888), 124–25, 153, 178 and 210.

'Frisby Dyke', named after the town's leading drapers and outfitters, was probably the most memorable, a 'truly Scouse character' according to Frank Shaw, pioneer revivalist of Liverpool's cultural heritage.[15] By this time, however, 'whacker' or 'wacker' – probably derived from army slang – was the emerging generic term for Liverpudlians and was the common form of address within the town (hence its prominence in the first volume of *Lern Yerself Scouse* published by the newly-established Scouse Press in 1966). After a brief period of interchangeability – during which Liverpudlians were known as scousers to outsiders but continued to converse with each other as wackers[16] – scouse has now firmly established its supremacy. Frank Shaw's *My Liverpool*, a celebration of 'Scousetown', stands as the foundation text. The totemic slogan, 'Scouse Power', adorns the football supporter's coat in the exhibit in the Liverpool Life Museum commemorating the Hillsborough disaster. As memories prompted by the recent fiftieth anniversary of VE Day have recently confirmed – in letters sent to the local press from around the world – 'Scousers: They're the "salt of the earth"'.[17]

In its origins, scouse refers to a type of cheap food, to the sailor's dish of stewed meat, biscuits and vegetables similar to Scandinavian lobscouse.[18] Food, of course, is often an essential ingredient of identity: along with dress and religion, diet is the main badge of ethnicity, hence the proliferation of 'ethnic' restaurants. It figures prominently too in the construction of

15] Frank Shaw, *My Liverpool* (Parkgate, 1971: rpt, 1988), 163.

16] This distinction applies throughout Jack Robinson's autobiography, *Teardrops on my Drum* (London, 1986). Writing of the 1930s and 1940s, by which time Dicky Sam had 'lost its provenance', Ron Garnett claimed that 'Scouse is a generic term applied to Liverpudlian seamen or members of H.M. forces. Whacker is used mainly as a form of greeting between fellow scousers', *Liverpool in the 1930s and the Blitz* (Preston, 1995), 124.

17] *Liverpool Echo*, 5 May 1995, 30. Another instance of the affection for scouse is in the term 'scouse mouse'. First coined by George Melly as the title of his autobiography (1984), 'Scouse Mouse' is now a loveable comic character occupying the centrepiece of the world's largest continuous mural, over a quarter of a mile long, painted in a corridor at Alder Hey Children's Hospital. P. Young and J. Bellew, *The Whitbread Book of Scouseology: an Anthology of Merseyside* (Liverpool, n.d.), 95.

18] There is no reference to food (or to Liverpool), however, in the entry on scouse in Joseph Wright (ed.), *The English Dialect Dictionary* (London, 1904), Vol. v, 264. Here scouse/skouce/skouse is west country dialect for to frolic, frisk about, to run fast; to cause to gallop, to ride hard; and to drive, chase, harry, as in the Gloucestershire usage: 'I skoused the mouse but could not catch it'.

regional cultural stereotypes – black pudding is to the industrial north what scouse is to Liverpool. Few groups, however, choose to name themselves after a particular (and humble) dish. The first recorded use of the term was in 1837 by the cost-conscious Chadwickian surgeon of the Liverpool workhouse who reported on the successful application of the 'evaporating process' to 'Meat Scouse', leaving 'a solid mass of nutritious food'.[19] Despite its continued association with pauperism,[20] scouse became a popular local dish, always eaten with red cabbage pickled in vinegar – the presence of meat depended on economic circumstance, being absent from 'Blind Scouse'. Trade was brisk late on Saturday nights at the 'scouseboat', a steaming cauldron of stew strategically located on the junction of Wellington Street and Scotland Road. 'Scouse Alley' ran underneath Paddy's Market in St Martin's Hall, offering scouse for 1d a plate and wet nellies, another local speciality, at a halfpenny each.[21] A sense of pride and identity with the dish seems to have developed: to the consternation of middle-class Fabian women who ran the socialist Cinderella club in Falkner Street in the 1890s, the local children rejected cocoa and cake and insisted on being treated to scouse;[22] on arrival in Wales, wartime evacuees from Liverpool schools were greeted with scouse.[23] However, scouse was not the culinary highpoint for humble Liverpudlians: for the true Scottie Road scouser, as a spate of recent autobiographies attest, the real joy of the past was salt fish on Sundays (known in the Park Lane area as bacalhao).[24]

As the brief etymology suggests, there are historical gaps to fill and important historiographical questions to ask. Given its provincial pre-eminence, why did nineteenth-century Liverpool not acquire a distinctive

19] See the report of B. Nightingall, 15 Sept 1837 in a volume of correspondence of the Poor Law Commissioners with the Poor Law Union of Liverpool, in Public Record Office, Kew, MH 12/5966. I would like to thank Adrian Allan, University Archivist, University of Liverpool, for drawing my attention to this reference which pre-dates by three years the first recorded use in the *Oxford English Dictionary*.
20] See, for example, *Porcupine* 6 Nov. 1875, 505, a reference kindly provided by Fritz Spiegl.
21] Terry Cooke, *Scotland Road: 'The Old Neighbourhood'* (Birkenhead, 1987), 36 and 52.
22] *The Clarion* 18 Dec. 1897. For details of the Falkner Street Cinderella Club, see Krista Cowman, 'Engendering Citizenship: The Political Involvement of Women on Merseyside 1890–1920', unpublished PhD thesis, University of York, 1995, 158–61.
23] Frances Clarke, *At the Heart of it All: an Autobiography* (London, 1993), 29.
24] See, for example, Cooke, *Scotland Road*, 35, and Robinson, *Teardrops on my Drum*, 102. Jim Dillon kindly drew my attention to the Park Lane variety.

linguistic identity? What are the historical foundations for the 'scouse-ology' which now enlivens contemporary representations of 'heritage' Liverpool? How does the 'vile catarrhal accent' (to use Frank Shaw's description)[25] relate to the current image and perception of Liverpool as working-class, distressed and different?

From the construction of its innovatory wet-docks system in the early eighteenth century, Liverpool, the 'western emporium of Albion', identified its prosperity with commerce, not with manufacture.[26] 'The History of a place which chiefly subsists by foreign Commerce, cannot be expected to furnish many materials on the head of Manufactures', William Enfield attested in 1774 in his pioneer *Essay towards the History of Liverpool*.[27] When 'surfeited with capital', John Gladstone, a member of the migrant Scottish mercantile community and father of the future prime minister, followed the Liverpool tradition, studiously avoiding any form of industrial investment.[28] Guidebooks duly welcomed the absence of industry, noting with relief that the curse of the factory system stopped short of Liverpool and its independent workers.[29] Having overhauled Bristol, Liverpool was proud of its commercial image and provincial pre-eminence. Acknowledged in Moss's *Guide* of 1796 as 'the first town in the kingdom in point of size and importance, the Metropolis excepted',[30] Liverpool sought to rival London in its commercial infrastructure, to establish itself as a 'self-dependent financial centre'.[31] Vaunting its status as 'second metropolis',[32] nineteenth-

25] Shaw, *My Liverpool*, 15.
26] *Liverpool Repository of Literature, Philosophy and Commerce*, Jan. 1826. See also M.J. Power, 'The Growth of Liverpool' in Belchem (ed.), *Popular Politics, Riot and Labour*, 21–37.
27] William Enfield, *An Essay towards the History of Liverpool* (London, 1774), 90.
28] A leading merchant in the West India interest (an efficient slave-owner though never a slave-trader), Gladstone possessed an outstanding business brain, but took no interest in the industrial revolution. See John Vincent's review of a number of books on the Gladstone family in *Victorian Studies*, Vol. 16 (1972), 101.
29] See, for example, *The Stranger in Liverpool: or, An Historical and Descriptive View of the Town of Liverpool and its Environs* (Liverpool, 1846), 108–9.
30] William Moss, *The Liverpool Guide* (Liverpool, 1796), 1.
31] *Chamber of Commerce. Report of the Select Committee appointed to consider what steps can be taken for the purpose of constituting Liverpool a self-dependent financial centre* (Liverpool, 1863). As early as 1698, Liverpool had appeared to Celia Fiennes as 'London in miniature', see Power, 'The Growth of Liverpool', 21.
32] Liverpool's pretensions were acknowledged by outsiders: see, for example, the entry on Liverpool in *Mitchell's Newspaper Press Directory* (London, 1847), 161: 'Situated near the mouth of the Mersey, this *second metropolis*, has rapidly advanced in opulence and importance ... The public buildings are in a style of

century Liverpool, the 'modern Tyre', aspired to combine commerce, culture and civilisation. A kind of city-state, it craved recognition as 'the Florence of the north', a fitting tribute to William Roscoe, self-made role model and icon for the mercantile elite.[33] Picton's civic improvement proposals encouraged its citizens to 'render the external appearance of their town worthy the exalted role she seems destined to fill in the commerce of the world'.[34] Subscription societies attended to the promotion of literature and the arts, supplemented by a number of voluntary associations specifically geared to the education and recreation of young clerks, 'Liverpool gentlemen' – not 'Manchester men' – in the making.[35] Through the hasty invention of tradition, Liverpool acquired a number of 'old families' to attest to the nobility of commerce.[36] The ethos was to endure, preventing a wider (and much-needed) industrial diversification.

A northern outpost of gentlemanly capitalism with a flourishing extra-European trade, Liverpool defined itself against industrial Manchester and in rivalry with commercial London. Thomas Baines' *History of the Commerce and Town of Liverpool* provided the requisite historical perspective to confirm the port's commercial pre-eminence:

... the commerce of Liverpool extends to every port of any importance in every quarter of the globe. In this respect it far surpasses the commerce of any city of which we have a record from past times, as Tyre, Venice, Genoa, Amsterdam, or Antwerp, and fully equals, if it does not surpass, that of London and New York, the one the avowed capital of the first commercial state in the world, the other the real capital of the second.[37]

---

liberal expense and tasteful decoration, superior to those of almost any provincial town in England; and several of its institutions are honourable testimonials of the enlightened spirit by which commercial prosperity has been accompanied'. For the extension of the 'second metropolis' motif into popular fiction, see *The Life, Adventures and Opinions of a Liverpool Policeman, and his Contemporaries* (Liverpool, 1841).

33] Arline Wilson, 'Culture and Commerce: Liverpool's Merchant Elite c.1790–1850', unpublished PhD thesis, University of Liverpool, 1997.

34] J.A. Picton, *Liverpool Improvements, and How to Accomplish Them* (Liverpool, 1853), 24.

35] For a useful survey of societies and institutes, see *Roscoe Magazine*, March 1849.

36] Tony Lane, *Liverpool: Gateway of Empire* (London, 1987) ch. 2.

37] Thomas Baines, *History of the Commerce and Town of Liverpool, and of the Rise of Manufacturing Industry in the Adjoining Counties* (London, 1852), 840.

For all its concern with image and identity, however, Victorian Liverpool failed to establish a distinctive voice of its own, a deficiency which Picton, the 'annalist' of the town, sought to redress.[38] Outside the dialect culture and 'old codgers' speech of the industrial north, Liverpool was unable to match the rhyming slang and pearlie dress of the late Victorian music-hall cockney.

An early form of commercial culture, mid-Victorian dialect literature built upon the ballad tradition and oral culture that preceded it. In a spirit of self-conscious promotion, dialect 'texts' were recited in the home and spoken or sung in the various venues of working-class associational culture throughout the industrial districts of Lancashire and the West Riding. Parallel to the process of economic change in these manufacturing districts, dialect literature developed through symbiotic interaction of the familiar and the progressive. Language, Patrick Joyce insists, was the 'central symbol' of the culture of the working people, the medium through which they handled change and created new identities. Although phrased in linguistic post-structuralism, Joyce's study of dialect and the making of social identity draws heavily on recent research in economic and social history, stressing continuity and adaptation in the industrial revolution: the phased movement to larger towns, the cellular growth of towns around earlier settlements, the similarity of environment between different urban-industrial situations, and the role of the family in mediating the transition to urban factory life.[39] However, these revisionist perspectives – which no longer equate industrialisation with the breakdown of previous patterns of community and family life – may not apply outside the emblematic (and much-studied) northern heartlands. A short distance away, economic and social change – and ultimately the pattern of speech – differed markedly. As the emergence of scouse confirmed, Liverpool was in the north of England, but not of it.[40]

Liverpool sits awkwardly outside the main narrative frameworks of economic history (just as it was excluded from the Victorian social novel).[41]

38] *Notes and Queries*, 7th series, Vol. 6 (1888), 210–11.
39] Joyce, *Visions*, chs 11–12.
40] Liverpool is 'in a number of ways linguistically as southern as it is northern' (Hughes and Trudgill, *English Accents and Dialects*, 20).
41] 'The Liverpudlian, by birth or adoption, confesses to a certain jealousy of Manchester and London and towards the hardened literary convention which sees the Victorian industrial novel as the product of one, and the Urban novel of the other. Now Liverpool is neither "urban" nor "industrial", neither Hogarthian/

Accounts of the industrial revolution, revisionist and otherwise, privilege the manufacturing north (the setting of the 'industrial' novel). Alternative studies of economic history, which recognise Victorian England more as the clearing-house than the workshop of the world, have a restricted vision that tends not to extend beyond London (the city which preoccupied the urban novelist).[42] Liverpool's commercial and mercantile significance is thus overlooked. As a great seaport and commercial centre, Liverpool underwent exponential growth, attracting long-distance migrants, primarily the Irish, but also significant numbers of Welsh and Scots, to its various labour markets. Beneath the skilled city trades and the booming commercial services sector, the casualism of the docks – 'the mecca of all British jetsam'[43] – facilitated ready ease of entry. Here, indeed, the swelling numbers of long-distance migrants (most pressing, of course, at the time of the Irish famine) may have exercised a 'crowding-out' effect, limiting the extent of in-migration by poor labourers in agricultural areas adjacent to Liverpool. Then there were the unsettled transient poor, caught in a 'curious middle place'. Disoriented by the lack of funds for further travel, they found themselves unexpectedly stuck in Liverpool, the human entrepôt for trans-continental emigration. In its pattern of growth and in-migration, Liverpool differed significantly from other northern conurbations (and, as a recent comparative study has emphasised, from other European 'grandes villes').[44]

Dickensian nor Mrs Gaskellish, nor certainly was it so tightly-knit and self-contained as to be "provincial".' Ian Sellers, *Nineteenth-Century Liverpool and the Novelists* (Warrington, 1979), 3.
42] Liverpool does not appear in the index of the latest two-volume study of 'gentlemanly capitalism', P.J. Cain and A.G. Hopkins, *British Imperialism: Innovation and Expansion 1688–1914* (London, 1993) and *British Imperialism: Crisis and Deconstruction 1914–1990* (London, 1993).
43] Pat O'Mara, *The Autobiography of a Liverpool Irish Slummy* (London, 1934), 17.
44] See below, ch. 8, 'Grandes villes: Liverpool, Lyon and Munich'. Wilfred Smith drew attention to the 'illuminating' contrast between Merseyside and Greater Manchester: 'While Merseyside is foreign to and has been superimposed on the rural landscape of South-west Lancashire and Wirral, Greater Manchester is autochthonous and has its roots deep in the roots of South-east Lancashire ... On Merseyside, the life of the place centres on the axial line of the river; in South-east Lancashire, human activity displays similar qualities at many points widely diffused over an extensive industrial terrain. The one represents the outgrowth from a single cell, the other registers the aggregation of a whole mass of similar cells', 'Merseyside and the Merseyside District' in *A Scientific Survey of Merseyside*, ed. W. Smith (Liverpool, 1953), 1–2.

Industrial conurbations usually grew out of conglomerations of small towns and villages, augmented by short-distance rural in-migration which tended to reinforce their culture, character and status as regional centres. The urban speech of Manchester-Salford and Leeds-Bradford differed from that of the surrounding countryside, but it remained speech of the same kind. Long-distance in-migration – the multi-ethnic, mainly celtic inflow – transformed Liverpool, setting it apart from its environs. When Liverpool eventually acquired its own voice – by general consent, John Kerrigan notes, 'a mixture of Welsh, Irish and catarrh'[45] – it contrasted sharply with the surrounding dialects of Lancashire and Cheshire.[46]

As it grew from the central waterfront, Liverpool expanded outwards in a cultural vacuum, as it were, urbanising an area largely without previous geographical and occupational identities. An isolated port, Liverpool was transformed into 'the supreme transportation node of the North West' by infrastructural development in the late eighteenth century, prompting an 'industrial efflorescence' which, Langton notes, was 'as brief as it was spectacular'. By 1800, Liverpool was 'set fair on the course which led to the status of entrepôt'. Dock development was accompanied by de-industrialisation: waterfront craft industry was driven far away, to be followed by heavy industry as Liverpool chose not to exploit its near monopoly hold of raw materials, particularly coal, from the 'inner ring' of its hinterland. Unable to challenge the dominance of the Atlantic shipping trades and commerce, industry re-located in specialist fashion well out in the hinterland itself, distinct and apart from Liverpool.[47] In the absence of surrounding (and/or single-industry) out-townships, Liverpool – an urban island superimposed on a landscape of good husbandry[48] – lacked the autochthonous cultural legacies and 'structural' foundations upon which

45] John Kerrigan, 'Introduction' in *Liverpool Accents: Seven Poets and a City*, ed. P. Robinson (Liverpool, 1996), 2.

46] Knowles, 'Scouse', ch. 2. Areas on the periphery of Merseyside, such as West Wirral, are especially suitable for study since it is possible to identify features as being distinctively 'Merseyside' or 'Cheshire' to a much greater extent than would be possible with the equivalent characteristics for most other urban areas, see Newbrook, *Sociolinguistic Reflexes*, 15 and passim.

47] J. Langton, 'Liverpool and its Hinterland in the Late Eighteenth-Century' in B.L. Anderson and P.M.L. Stoney, *Commerce, Industry and Transport: Studies in Economic Change on Merseyside* (Liverpool, 1983), 1–25.

48] Wilfred Smith, 'Merseyside', 2.

northern industrial dialect was readily constructed.[49] The obscure Dicky
Sam apart, there was no Liverpudlian equivalent of such long-established
identity figures and subsequent dialect heroes as Tim Bobbin, the Lancashire weaver, or Bob Cranky, the Geordie pitman.[50] Nor, as will be shown
later, was there anything to match the London cockney for whom
consumption and display, not occupation or craft skill, was the defining
motif.

Liverpool, one of the publications in 1907 commemorating the 700th
anniversary of the granting of its first charter observed, was 'a city without
ancestors':

> Its people are people who have been precipitately gathered together
> from north, from south, from overseas by a sudden impetuous call. Its
> houses are houses, not merely of recent birth, but pioneer houses,
> planted instantly upon what, so brief a while ago, was unflawed meadow-
> land and marsh.[51]

This remarkable pattern of in-migration, 'the precipitancy of her uprising',
also accounts for another distinctive feature: spatial segregation. As
historical geographers have shown, Victorian Liverpool emerged in
precocious manner as the prototype of the modern twentieth-century city
with distinct social areas. The 'collar gap' widened as clerical workers took
advantage of by-law housing and transport improvements to move out to
new suburbs. Within the working class, residential location was a similar
compromise between proximity to work and a suitable residential area in
terms of cost (often linked to position in the family life cycle), social status
and ethnic affiliation. The inner residential suburbs were favoured by
skilled workers and by Welsh and Scottish minority groups. A large proportion of the unskilled and semi-skilled working class clustered close to
casual labour markets of the city centre and the waterfront, areas

49] These cultural and structural factors also facilitated working-class collective
action, which perhaps accounts for Liverpool's backwardness in Chartism and
other movements. See John Belchem, 'Beyond *Chartist Studies*: class, community
and Party in Early-Victorian Populist Politics' in *Cities, Class and Communication:
Essays in Honour of Asa Briggs*, ed. Derek Fraser (London, 1990), 105–6, 120–21.
50] For an excellent analysis of the construction of Geordie through the interaction
of community and culture in the mining villages of the north east, see Rob Colls,
The Collier's Rant: Song and Culture in the Industrial Village (London, 1977).
51] Walter Dixon Scott, *Liverpool 1907* (1907: rpt, Neston, 1979), 6 and 24.

associated with the Irish.[52] These spatial variations, however, did not prevent the emergence of a common accent: only the trained local ear could appreciate micro-cultural nuance.

Little has been recorded of the development of scouse, but what seems to have happened, Gerry Knowles maintains, was an initial linguistic polar-isation, followed by a remarkable two-way flow across the boundaries of social segregation. On its emergence, some time after the famine influx, the Anglo-Irish vernacular of the central area became the non-prestige form, opposed by those who upheld traditional north-western English (as modified by other in-migrants) as the local standard. Throughout the next hundred years, Knowles suggests, prestige grammar, vocabulary and phonological structure percolated downwards to impose considerable uniformity on working-class speech, while the phonetic forms and tonetic features of Anglo-Irish – linguistically the defining characteristic of scouse – spread upwards and outwards.[53] Unfortunately, Knowles produces little evidence to substantiate his thesis. Viewing 'non-prestige' scouse as an Irish implant, he attributes its influence to a process not dissimilar to the 'contamination' observed by Dr Duncan, Liverpool's pioneer medical officer of health:

> ... the native inhabitants are exposed to the inroads of numerous hordes of uneducated Irish, spreading physical and moral contamination around them ... By their example and intercourse with others they are rapidly lowering the standard of comfort among their English neighbours, communicating their own vicious and apathetic habits, and fast extin-guishing all sense of moral dignity, independence and self-respect.[54]

In-migration undoubtedly accentuated Liverpool's notorious public health problems, but the linguistic impact of new arrivals is much more difficult to assess. The Irish contribution to the making of scouse may well have been more complex and protracted than Knowles implies. Comprising both transients and settlers, the famine Irish were by no means as discrete,

52] R. Lawton and C.G. Pooley, 'The Social Geography of Merseyside in the Nineteenth Century', Final report to the Social Science Research Council (Dept of Geography, University of Liverpool, 1976).
53] Knowles, 'Scouse', 23–24.
54] W.H. Duncan, 'On the Sanitary State of Liverpool' (1842) quoted in G. Kearns, P. Laxton and J. Campbell, 'Duncan and the Cholera Test: Public Health in Mid Nineteenth-Century Liverpool', *Transactions of the Historic Society of Lancashire and Cheshire*, Vol. 143 (1994), 98–99.

linguistically and otherwise, as other migrants, most notably the Liverpool Welsh. Being dispersed throughout the conurbation, the Welsh contributed little to the pattern of urban speech on Merseyside. They kept their own language for themselves: families travelled long distances to worship together in Welsh-speaking Calvinist chapels; Welsh newspapers circulated in the city; and the National Eisteddfod was held there on several occasions.[55] While the Irish lacked such cultural insulation – Irish gaelic was seldom heard in Liverpool – oral history casts doubt on the speed and extent of their 'contaminating' linguistic impact on others. Indeed, some oral historians attest that many working-class Liverpudlians failed to exhibit any 'scouse' characteristics (Irish or otherwise) in their speech until well into the twentieth century.[56]

At first, Irish migrants were curiosity figures whose dialect, demeanour and appearance caused much amusement, prompting the *Picturesque Hand-Book to Liverpool* to recommend a visit to the Clarence Dock when the Irish packets docked: 'At the stern will be seen, as usual, a freight of bipeds, old and young, holding converse in a jargon that it would be difficult to interpret; whilst the rest of the deck will be crowded with a medley of sheep, pigs, and oxen'.[57] Literary and journalistic sources continue to suggest a sense of vernacular apartness, as in Dickens' night out on the Liverpool waterfront – where Irish and 'negro' characters are distinguished by phonetic spelling[58] – and in Hugh Shimmin's delight in

55] Richard Dennis, *English Industrial Cities of the Nineteenth Century: a Social Geography* (Cambridge, 1984), 228–30. C.G. Pooley, 'The Residential Segregation of Migrant Communities in Mid-Victorian Liverpool', *Transactions of the Institute of British Geographers*, Vol. 2 (1977), 364–72. Hall Caine noted of William Edwardes Tirebuck, the most talented of the Liverpool-Welsh novelists, that he 'was only the foster child of the great city on the Mersey and much as he loved and intimately knew her, at the bottom of his nature he was a Welshman, body and soul', quoted in Sellers, *Nineteenth-Century Liverpool and the Novelists*, 52. Another Liverpool-Welsh novelist, Eleazar Roberts assured his readers that the Liverpool setting of his writings would not 'detract in the least from its faithfulness to its Cymric perspective', ibid., 59.
56] I thank Tony Lane and Jim Dillon for their critical comments and knowledge of oral history.
57] Quoted in R.J. Scally, *The End of Hidden Ireland* (New York, 1995), 189.
58] *The Uncommercial Traveller* (final edition, 1869), ch. 5. 'Negro' characters were also often identified by their flamboyant wardrobe, as in the case of 'the Bouncer', a notorious figure in the Scotland Road district who sold pills on street corners, frequented the races to play the 'purse trick', but had, alas, fallen on hard times (and into sartorial ordinariness) when spotted by the social explorers of *Squalid Liverpool, By a Special Commission* (Liverpool, 1883), 88.

encountering the 'rich smack of the true Milesian brogue'.[59] Dixon Scott's investigation into the slums, published in 1907, revealed a less attractive linguistic apartness:

... the majority here are either Irish or of Irish descent. It follows, therefore, that here alone in Liverpool do you get a specific dialect. They speak a bastard brogue: a shambling, degenerate speech of slip-shod vowels and muddied consonants – a cast-off clout of a tongue, more debased even than Whitechapel Cockney, because so much more sluggish, so much less positive and acute.[60]

Although problematic in its immediate post-Famine origins, Knowles' account of the subsequent diffusion of scouse accords well with Liverpool's distinctive socio-economic and topographical structure. Once established as the vernacular of the central areas, 'slummy' scouse flourished in a nodal position at the heart of the Merseyside communications network and the main labour market. While residential distance from the centre was increasingly possible and desirable, everyday working contact with scouse was unavoidable. Unlike London, there were no boundaries for flaneurs to transgress:[61] commerce, the waterfront and the 'secondary economy' of the slums were coterminous in central Liverpool. The central landing-stage, 'the half-mile raft, moored to the City's gates', encouraged social inter-mingling: 'Half of Liverpool uses it as a matter of business, the other half as a matter of health and pleasure, and it presents all day long the appearance of a democratic promenade'.[62]

Casualism too facilitated the diffusion of a distinctive vernacular. There was considerable mobility and cultural interaction throughout the dockside labour market despite the sectarian geography of a Catholic north and a Protestant south, and increasing job specialism according to type of cargo, dock, vessel or employer.[63] Whatever their ethnic origin or

59] J.K. Walton and A. Wilcox (eds), *Low Life and Moral Improvement in Mid-Victorian England: Liverpool through the journalism of Hugh Shimmin* (Leicester, 1991), 212.
60] Dixon Scott, *Liverpool 1907*, 144.
61] J.R. Walkowitz, *City of Dreadful Delight: Narratives of Sexual Danger in Late-Victorian London* (London, 1992), ch. 1.
62] Dixon Scott, *Liverpool 1907*, 38–39.
63] For the best analysis of waterfront casualism, see Eric Taplin, *Liverpool Dockers and Seamen 1870–1890* (Hull, 1974), and *The Dockers' Union* (Leicester, 1986).

sectarian affiliation, dockers cherished the variety and sociability of their itinerant work culture as they moved along the 'seven-mile sequence of granite-lipped lagoons',[64] relying on scouse, the vernacular of the central waterfront, as a lingua franca. In establishing credentials and comrade-ship along the waterfront, casual workers – prototype 'stage scousers' – accentuated the phonetics and the humour:

> We went wherever a ship was, all along the docks, meetin' 'undreds of different characters, both bosses an' men. Like der Music Halls, hundreds of different turns, all travellin' der country, usin' one act, an' bringin' down der 'ouse, but we only seen it once. Same on der docks; yer travelled all over, meetin' perhaps once every six weeks or maybe more. So yer see, yer'll soon get fed wid Wally tellin' 'is same stories, even though 'e's great when 'e tells 'em.[65]

This is to suggest that the pronounced adenoidal quality of scouse was a form of linguistic bonding, an assertion of group identity, rather than a symptom of the notorious problems of public health which made Victorian Liverpudlians prone to adenoids and respiratory disease. The wit and humour, it seems, soon spread from the waterfront to the commercial offices. Ron Garnett's autobiography revels in the author's 'junior clerical work-experience as a series of send-ups and shambles in true Liverpool tradition'.[66]

Once scouse emerged as a distinctive voice, Liverpudlians took exag-gerated delight in their divergence from the industrial north – 'strange places like Wigan and St Helens, never mind the dark interior called Manchester'[67] – and its dialect culture. *Scouse Wars*, one of the more humor-ous publications of the current nostalgia boom, revels in cultural stereo-types as it celebrates the 'ancient conflicts of Woollybacks and Wackers':

64] Dixon Scott, *Liverpool 1907*, 26.
65] L.T. Roche, *Down the Hatch* (Liverpool, 1985), 219.
66] Garnett, 3.
67] John Kerrigan in *Liverpool Accents*, 3. Noting the relative lack of overland travel eastward from Liverpool, Ron Garnett has some interesting observations on the micro-geographical distribution of the Liverpool dialect and the boundaries of 'Liverpool suzerainty': 'Wigan was disparaged by Merseysiders as a joke; Ormskirk, St Helens, Runcorn, Widnes, were on the frontier – beyond which the Lancashire accent held sway. The pattern of incursion of the "scouse" tongue was largely littoral – Southport, the Wirral, and Chester (despite its well-heeled residents and county town atmosphere) were all in scouse territory. Lancashire was alien and Liverpool did not consider itself to be within the confines of Lancashire'. Garnett, 13–14.

Woollybacks come from Woollydom, in the North of England. Woollydom is a land of cobbled streets, mills, pits and flat caps, where men are fed on pie and mushy peas, black-pudding and tripe; a land where men prize their pigeons, worship their whippets and fondle their ferrets; a land where men are bred not merely born. Wackers are the inhabitants of the city of Liverpool – famed for their humour, football, dockers and judies. Wackers eat scouse and wet nellies. Wackers and Woollybacks are tough yet warm breeds. Although both are Northerners, they are different in many ways; culture and traditions and even language divides them.[68]

The sub-text here hints at a common antipathy to London and the south. Forced by jealous rivalry of London into conditional alignment with the north, Liverpool brought a special angle to the north/south divide. Throughout the nineteenth century, London was much resented for its monopolistic privileges and practices, anachronistic obstacles in the path of Liverpool's rise to commercial pre-eminence:

Whilst Liverpool yields to London in the extent of its trade with the continent of Europe, it surpasses the capital in its trade with America, and already rivals it in the trade with the East, although it was not allowed to have any commerce with India previous to the renewal of the company's charter in 1813, nor with China previous to the subsequent arrangement of the Indian Government in 1833.[69]

To Liverpudlians, unfair commercial privileges and practices were personified in the character of the arrogant cockney. When James Morris, a director of the Bank of England, came up from London as Ewart's running mate in the 1835 parliamentary election, he was immediately stigmatised as a 'cockney' by local Tories envious of metropolitan monopoly and chartered commercial privilege. In a posting-bill advertising two hacks for sale, Ewart was offered as 'Lot 1: NONENTITY', while Morris was paraded as:

68] Anthony Griffiths, *Scouse Wars* (Liverpool, 1992), 6.
69] Baines, *History*, 769. The rivalry extended to philanthropic and missionary zeal, hence the alacrity with which Liverpool followed London in establishing a Merchant Seaman's Auxiliary Bible Society: 'A corresponding interest to that which the moral want and misery of seamen in London had originated was quickly communicated to Liverpool, and a desire was excited of imitating the judicious bounty of the metropolis, no less than of following hard in the captivating career of its maritime greatness; a holier rivalry was superadded to the energies of

Lot 2: COCKNEY: a South Country Horse, 11 1/2 hands high, sent here with a *false pedigree*; Sire stated to be *Free Trade*, but though *quite unknown* here, he is ascertained to have been got by *Monopoly*, trained in Threadneedle-street, where he has been used by an *Old Lady*, who has got a Patent, for making Rags into Money, and who prosecutes with the utmost rigour anyone else that attempts to follow the same trade. Though not vicious in other respects, 'COCKNEY' like all *London*-bred Horses, is very *jealous* of those bred in the *North*, particularly *Liverpool*.[70]

Commercial rivalry was compounded by matters of style and taste. While Liverpool aspired to 'second metropolis' status, it was adjudged provincial by cultured Londoners, by those who spurned the designation 'cockney'.[71]

In early nineteenth-century London, as Gareth Stedman Jones has shown, use of the term 'cockney' mediated between the aesthetic and the political, distinguishing the cant of the vulgar from the refined language of the educated. The distinction, Stedman Jones notes, 'referred to a difference not between middle and lower, yet alone working, class, but between the citizen and the courtier, the plebeian and the patrician, the vulgar and the genteel'.[72] With a metropolitan arrogance which offended the Liverpolitan mercantile elite, refined Londoners refused to extend these distinctions beyond the capital: provincial culture was assumed to be vulgar. John Walker epitomised the attitude in his *Critical Pronouncing Dictionary* of 1791:

> The grand difference between the metropolis and the provinces is that the people of education in London are free from all the vices of the vulgar; but the best educated people in the provinces, if constantly resident there, are sure to be tinctured with the dialect of the country in which they live.[73]

---

commercial speculation'. *Eighth Report of the Liverpool Auxiliary Bible Society* (Liverpool, 1819), 13.
70] Posting-bill in British Library, call-mark 10349f8.
71] One of the lesser Liverpool-Welsh novelists who wrote under the pseudonym Powys Oswin was scathing in his criticism of metropolitan pretensions of the Liverpool mercantile elite in *Liverpool Ho!* (1857): 'Proud, showy imitators of London absurdities ... Liverpool ladies poor players upon the second fiddle, weavers of old garbs, pickers up and misers of metropolitan cast-offs and farce-robes' (quoted in Sellers, *Nineteenth-Century Liverpool*, 30–31).
72] Jones, 'The "Cockney"', 280–84.
73] Quoted in ibid., 280.

On a visit to Allerton Hall in 1813, Maria Edgworth was impressed by Roscoe's learning but repelled by his 'strong provincial accent which at once destroys all idea of elegance'.[74] Others described the great renaissance scholar's accent as that of a 'barbarian',[75] while later in the century, as noted above, the residual provincial tones of another Liverpudlian scholar-politician, W.E. Gladstone, were cause for comment. What prompted the correspondence in *Notes and Queries* was the question of whether Gladstone had a 'provincial' accent.[76] It was not 'scouse' which betrayed Victorian Liverpudlians, but a basic provincialism.

While a distinctive 'scouse' accent had yet to be identified in the age of Gladstone, a new populist 'cockney' culture was celebrated nationwide. In the superdromes of late Victorian commercial music-hall, where polite, bohemian and popular culture intersected, 'cockney' underwent rapid social descent. The solid burgher was replaced first by the sham-genteel swell, hero of the 'Arry-stockracy' of office clerks, and then by the coster-monger pearlie, immortalised on stage by Albert Chevalier.[77] These new representations were to resonate with Liverpool audiences. From the time of the short-lived Roscoe Club, the pretensions of junior young office clerks featured prominently in local satirical publications.[78] Costermongers and hawkers – trades dominated by Irish women, or 'Mary Ellens' as they were known on Scotland Road – were a pervasive presence. Along with bookies, pawnbrokers, common lodging-house keepers and prostitutes, they serviced Liverpool's thriving 'secondary economy' of the streets. Constantly moved on from respectable areas, this boisterous arena catered for the needs of the city's poorest inhabitants and least wary visitors.[79] While responding to new representations of the cockney, Liverpudlians still lacked their own stage identity: scouse humour had yet to transfer from the docks and the streets to the boards of the national music hall circuit.

74] C. Colvin (ed.), *Maria Edgworth: letters from England 1813–44* (Oxford, 1971), 10.
75] *Creevey Papers*, Vol. ii, 256–57.
76] *Notes and Queries*, 7th series, Vol. 6 (1888), 124–25, 153, 178, 210. See also R.T. Shannon, *Gladstone* (London, 1982), Vol. i, 93.
77] Jones, 'The "Cockney"', 284–300.
78] See, for example the innumerable cartoons and articles satirising the club in *Liverpool Lion*, Vol. i (1847).
79] M. Brogden, *The Police: Autonomy and Consent* (London, 1982), 43–73.
80] Jones, 'The "Cockney"', 276. Tony Lane informs me that shop stewards on the Liverpool docks in the 1960s and 1970s still referred to their London counterparts (not least Jack Dash) as 'pearlie dockers'.

Having been adopted by the poor on the streets, Chevalier's cockney enjoyed considerable longevity. The speech patterns, dress, gestures and milieu offered a culture for populist celebration. By the end of the First World War, however, the cockney was an increasingly elusive figure on the streets. Until re-incarnated in air-raid shelters as the spirit of the nation, cockney pride was marginalised in Baldwin's middle England: 'safety first' policies drew upon the culture of the shires.

As the pearlie cockney ossified into a nostalgia figure – 'an inter-mittently renewed metaphor for the corrosive character of modernity'[80] – a succession of Liverpool-raised (and 'slightly touched') comedians (Arthur Askey, Tommy Handley, Derek Guyler, Ted Ray, Bill Danvers, Harry Angers, Billy Bennett, Robb Wilton, Billy Matchett, Beryl Orde, Norman Evans, and on to Ken Dodd, et al.) acquired national celebrity for their humour. Although at the time there was little emphasis on Liverpud-lianism, this comic efflorescence appears as a defining moment for scouse, an early instance of the Merseyside symbiosis of economic decline and cultural assertion. As a major export port, Liverpool was hit dispropor-tionately hard by worldwide depression as trade declined more rapidly than production. Throughout the 1930s, the local unemployment rate remained resolutely above 18 per cent, double the national average.[81] Even so, Merseyside was not designated as a depressed area in the legislation of 1934. Liverpool found itself disabled within interwar discourse of unemploy-ment and economic policy. Priority was accorded to the problems of the industrial north and other distressed manufacturing areas, while efforts to regain comparative advantage as the world's clearing house were exclu-sively centred on the city of London. Having to come to terms with its distinctive and accentuated structural problems, Liverpool of the depres-sion made itself heard through humour. When asked why Merseyside produced so many comedians, Arthur Askey replied: 'You've got to be a comic to live in Liverpool'.[82]

Radio was the medium which brought scouse comedians national recog-nition. In the transition from music-hall to radio comedy, Tommy Handley was probably the most innovative figure, pointing the way forward to the zaniness of the *Goons*. Where other Liverpool comics like Askey and Ray tried (not always successfully) to conceal their vernacular nasality by

81] S. Davies, P. Gill, L. Grant, M. Nightingale, R. Noon and A. Shallice, *Genuinely Seeking Work: Mass Unemployment on Merseyside in the 1930s* (Birkenhead, 1992).
82] Quoted in Shaw, *My Liverpool*, 25.

adopting north country or standard stage accents, Handley – ably assisted by Deryck Guyler's Frisby Dyke – was unashamedly scouse (although his repertoire was by no means exclusively Liverpudlian). Through Handley's contribution to the writing and performance of *Itma*, the Liverpool accent became synonymous with verbal wit, holding its own against Mona Lott, the cockney char.[83] During the war, the pronounced scouse humour of *Itma* offered an alternative to the 'carry-on spirit' cockney revival. For local inhabitants – who celebrated Handley as 'one of ours' – it served as some recompense for news broadcasts which failed to recognise Liverpool's special plight:

> On the radio, Liverpool was never specially mentioned for being bombed; you heard only of 'the north-west'. This was a propaganda exercise because Liverpool was a strategic target for enemy bombers, but it demoralized the people of the city because they felt – as they feel today for different reasons – that they were ignored and perceived to be of no consequence.[84]

By the end of the Second World War, humour was firmly established as Liverpool's response to its psychological, economic and structural problems. Verbal wit – a cultural form which, like football, seemingly extended across sectarian boundaries[85] – spread beyond the bonding rituals of workplace and local pub to become the defining characteristic of the scouser. Surreal word-play was highly prized, distinguishing scouse humour from the slow-building, anecdotal, character-based northern monologue and the fast patter of cockney dialogue.[86] Young men in particular prided themselves on their wit, mouthiness and verbal invention, attributes which set the real scouser apart from other lads or 'bucks':

83] Ibid., 160–64.
84] Clarke, *At the Heart of it All*, 26. For a major reassessment of Liverpool and the blitz, see Garnett, ch. 6.
85] Frank Boyce has reminded me that the early radio comedians tended to come from Protestant backgrounds. More recently, television comedy and soap opera have redressed the balance, delighting in Catholic stereotypes and in-jokes (such as the inability of Mrs Boswell, matriarch of *Bread*, to cross herself correctly). On the absence of sectarianism in football allegiance, see Tony Mason, 'The Blues and the Reds: a history of the Liverpool and Everton Football Clubs', *Transactions of the Historic Society of Lancashire and Cheshire*, Vol. 134 (1985), 107–28.
86] Jeffrey Richards, *Stars in our Eyes: Lancashire Stars of Stage, Screen and Radio* (Preston, 1994).

The difference between a buck and an everyday scouse is this: The buck is aggressive. He says, 'Warra yew luken at?' The scouse replies, 'I dunno, the labels fell off'. The buck threatens to hit you with a brick; the scouse says, 'Gowome, yermum's got cake!' A stranger on asking a buck a simple question like, 'Where's the urinal?' would be given a surly look and the words, 'Fuck off, wack!' The scouse would reply to the same question, 'How many funnels has she got?' Verbal badinage comes natural to the scouse but one gets only abuse from the buck.[87]

This is not to suggest the absence of violence in the scouse mentality. Besides humour, the macho world of the docks produced a proud boxing tradition and a shamefully high incidence of domestic violence directed against females.[88]

Just as Chevalier's cockney had been to the London poor, so the scouse comedian – as projected first on the radio and then in innumerable television soap-operas – has offered humble locals an attractive and attainable role model. 'Every Liverpudlian', Alan Bennett rued, 'seems a comedian, fitted out with smart answers, ready with the chat and anxious to do his little verbal dance.'[89] Aided by broadcasters like Billy Butler and Brian Jacques on local radio, nostalgia and the heritage industry have fortified the cultural inheritance: there are collections of children's rhymes[90] and multi-volume thesauri – or 'cacologies' of 'scouseology' – produced by Scouse Press, 'Liverpool's first publisher of local humour and local history'.[91]

87] Robinson, *Teardrops on my Drum*, 32.
88] Pat Ayers and Jan Lambertz, 'Marriage Relations, Money and Domestic Violence in Working-Class Liverpool, 1919–39', in *Labour and Love: Women's Experience of Home and Family 1850–1940*, ed. Jane Lewis (Oxford, 1986), 195–217. The emergence of Women of the Waterfront during the (1995–96) dock dispute points to an important cultural and political change. See 'Support on the Waterfront', *The Big Issue in the North*, 2–8 Jan. 1996, and Merseyside Port Shop Stewards Committee, *Never Cross a Picket Line* (Liverpool, 1996), 23–27. On the television, the fist-happy Liverpudlian is to the fore in Harry Enfield's Brookside parody, *The Scousers*.
89] Bennett, *Writing Home*, 143–44 and 289. In their introduction, Young and Bellew point out that their 'A-Z of Scouseology isn't just a massive list of facts. It's put together with the humour and the asides Scousers are noted for.'
90] Frank Shaw, *You Know Me Anty Nelly? Liverpool Children's Rhymes* (London, 1970).
91] Fritz Spiegl (ed.), *Lern Yerself Scouse, Vol. 1* (Liverpool, 1966, rpt. 1988); Linacre Lane, *Lern Yerself Scouse, Vol. 2: The ABZ of Scouse* (Liverpool, 1966); Brian Minard, *Lern Yerself Scouse, Vol. 3: Wersia Sensa Yuma?* (Liverpool, 1972); and Fritz Spiegl, *Lern Yerself Scouse, Vol. 4: Scally Scouse* (Liverpool, 1989). Scouse Press has

Somewhat belatedly, Liverpool has acquired its dialect literature, works of reference and reverence in which native wit is accentuated by such devices as circumlocution, an Irish-like preference for the long-winded picturesque and aphoristic phrase; 'diddymisation', a seemingly contradictory liking for short forms and pet names formed by adding a 'y' to the first syllable (much favoured in *Brookside*, the soap which relies on 'professional' scouse); and the comic malapropism, verbal 'near-misses' known locally as Malapudlianisms or Merseypropisms. It is an unfortunate irony that while lovingly preserving the wit and wisdom of yesteryear, 'heritage' publications have perpetuated some of the unflattering myths and misconceptions about contemporary Liverpool.

As with cockney, scouse has acquired metaphoric force in hostility to modernity. Prefaces to individual volumes of *The Great Scouse Tetralogy* splenetically chart the baleful and irresistible influence of television and drug-related inner-city crime, developments which have fractured the unity and decency of scouse culture. 'While the good, old-fashioned Scouse people have lost none of their charm, wit and friendliness, those disposed to evil-doing have, alas, got worse', Fritz Spiegl rues in his 'Serious Foreword' to *Scally Scouse*. Through the curse of television, adolescents (or rather, 'the aggressive, unthinking young') have become 'prey to every pressure: greed fed by television advertising, cops-and-robbers violence and the grubby life-styles of "soap" heroes'. In seeking a return to a golden age, Spiegl and other contributors to the Scouse Press look back beyond the early 1960s when the Beatles – four lads who shook the world – brought Liverpool global attention. In conservative nostalgia, there is no place for the 'amphetamine-boosted talents' of the Fab Four. As hero-worshipped drug-abusers, they stand condemned along with other exponents of the Mersey sound, and the accompanying (but soon southern-based) 'professional scousers', the novelists, poets and playwrights of the 1960s Mersey boom: 'The swinging, pop-crazed 60s led directly to the present drugs scourge, to narcotics-related crime and junkie-spread AIDS ... Liverpool could have

---

now been joined by several other heritage and local history publishers, including Countyvise, Liver Press, Bluecoat Press and the Harbour Publishing Company. Mention should also be made of the publications of the Docklands History Project, and of the O'Connor brothers' superb photographic reminders of Liverpool's past: *Liverpool: It All Came Tumbling Down* (Liverpool, 1986), 'testimony to our very own "scouse heritage"', Billy Butler writes in his foreword, and *Liverpool: Our City, Our Heritage* (Liverpool, 1990). Note the difference in tone and terminology from the earlier heritage publication of the Merseyside Civic Society, *Liverpolitana* (1971).

done without such heroes.'[92] Viewed through this jaundiced perspective, the cultural efflorescence of the 1960s – a remarkable accompaniment to adverse structural change as the port adjusted to the end of Empire, containerisation and eventual entry into the EEC – marked a sorry turning-point. Abandoning the standards of the past, Liverpool set itself on course to become the 'shock city' of post-industrial Britain. 'Suicidal' industrial militancy and 'toy town' political extremism were symptoms of cultural collapse as decent honest scouse was transmogrified into 'whinge-ing scouser': even the accent lost appeal, becoming associated 'more with militant shop-stewards on television than comedians as of old'.[93] Heritage 'scouse' has thus reinforced external perceptions of 'self-inflicted' decline in Liverpool, now the country's most working-class and deprived city.

In the early 1980s, the *Daily Mirror* advised Liverpudlians to build a fence around their city and charge admission: 'For sadly, it has become a "showcase" of everything that has gone wrong in Britain's major cities'.[94] In media and popular perception, Liverpool has paid the price for its cherished but self-defeating 'otherness', its refusal to comply with the economic 'realities' of enterprise Britain. Media images of the 'militant' 1980s have endured, undermining the prospect of rebirth as the nation's 'city of architecture':[95]

The long lens view of the heroic towers of the Liver Building, with the Pierhead in the foreground apparently swamped by mountains of rubbish left by striking municipal workers, but actually separated from it by the Mersey, still seems the personification of civic squalor. And

92] Spiegl, *Scally Scouse*, 5–10.
93] See Fritz Spiegl's 'Preface' to the 1984 reprinted edition of the first volume of *Lern Yerself Scouse*.
94] *Daily Mirror* 11 Oct. 1982 quoted in C.M. Czypull, 'Liverpool's Economic Decline since World War Two: an Approach Towards the Structural and Historical Problems of the Region', unpublished MA thesis, University of Hannover, 1992.
95] In the 1960s, there was a flourishing of pre-tourist 'heritage', focused on the rescue and retrieval not of the local dialect but of the city's commercial and public architecture, best exemplified in Quentin Hughes, *Seaport* (Liverpool, 1964), reprinted in 1993 with a 'Postscript' applauding the complementary efforts of the council's Heritage Bureau, the Merseyside Civic Society and the first regional branch of the Victorian Society. It has recently been supplemented by a sumptuous collection of coloured illustrations in Quentin Hughes, *Liverpool, city of architecture* (Liverpool, 1999), a fitting tribute to Liverpool's (alas) unsuccessful bid for the Arts Council's City of Architecture and Design Award. Glasgow, the other 'second city' gained the prize.

Giles Gilbert Scott's masterpiece, the Anglican cathedral, Britain's largest, marooned in an urban free-fire zone more like the South Bronx than anything in an English city, was witness to decay on a frightening scale.[96]

As shock city – Britain's Beirut[97] – Liverpool (and its inhabitants) have been accorded a crucial role in dominant political discourse. Where cockney had been evoked as the essential spirit of the nation, an emblematic figure of wartime and Butskellite consensus, the whingeing militant scouser has come to personify the 'other' against whom the respectable, responsible and 'realistic' define and align themselves. United in rejection of the Liverpool spectre of self-destructive working-class militancy, diverse social groups are brought together in a conventional wisdom of economic and political 'realism'.[98] Liverpool's recalcitrance, its undue reluctance to accept market realities, is given an ethno-cultural explanation which emphasises its class 'otherness'. Scouse militancy is not only irrational but also un-English, deriving its impetus from celtic truculence, from the city's Irish heritage.

The Liverpool-Irish (of whom Heathcliff, the great other/outsider of Victorian literature, brought starving and houseless from the streets of Liverpool, may well have been one)[99] have always suffered the prejudice and negative reputation which now blight the city itself. Condemned by Dr Duncan as a contaminating presence, they have yet to be rehabilitated. They have no place in the revisionist narrative of the Irish in Britain, a celebration of widespread distribution, successful integration and 'ethnic fade'. Labelled as 'the dregs' by Father Nugent (an Irish-Liverpudlian himself), those who remained in the port of entry have been dismissed as the *caput mortuum*, a kind of under-class, as it were, unable, unwilling or

96] 'The quality of Mersey is not strained', *The Guardian*, 6 Sept. 1994.
97] P. Scraton, A. Jemphrey and S. Coleman, *No Last Rights: The Denial of Justice and the Promotion of Myth in the Aftermath of the Hillsborough Disaster* (Liverpool, 1995), 226.
98] This is to suggest a later application of the process analysed by Ross McKibbin in 'Class and Conventional Wisdom: The Conservative Party and the "Public" in Inter-War Britain', in *The Ideologies of Class* (Oxford, 1990), 259–93. There is now some evidence of a turn-round in media attitudes. See, for example, 'Hall of Fame no.1: Liverpool', *Guardian* 24 Apr. 1999; and Linda Grant's essay in the 'Weekend' section of the *Guardian* 10 July 1999, headlined: 'From wags to scallies to scumbugs. Why has everyone got it in for Scousers?'
99] Terry Eagleton, *Heathcliff and the Great Hunger* (London, 1995), 1–26.

unsuited to take advantage of opportunities elsewhere in Britain or the new world.[100] An enduring cultural legacy of immobility, inadequacy and irresponsibility, this 'Irishness' has purportedly set Liverpool apart. Immune from the enterprise culture, their descendants have sunk further into economic depression and (ungrateful) welfare dependency, remaining working-class when all around have moved onwards and upwards. An anachronism elsewhere in Thatcherite Britain, the term 'working-class' retained a residual pejorative relevance – a form of linguistic devaluation – when applied to Liverpool and its 'celtic' lumpenproletariat.

Unfortunately, this crude but effective ahistorical ethno-cultural stereo-typing has not been challenged from within. In Liverpudlian popular history and working-class autobiography, the unadulterated image of the lowly Irish 'slummy', reckless and feckless, has been adopted as the foundation character, a symbolic figure of inverse snobbery and pride in the evolution of the true Scottie Road scouser.[101] Furthermore, the dialect-heritage industry has traced the perceived slovenliness of the local accent back to the assumed laziness and casualism of its Irish originators. The fugitives from the Potato Famine, Spiegl contends, 'gave the Liverpudlian

100] See the essays by David Fitzpatrick, Colin Pooley and Graham Davis in R. Swift and S. Gilley (eds), *The Irish in Britain 1815–1939* (London, 1989), and Graham Davis, *The Irish in Britain 1815–1914* (Dublin, 1991). For an alternative perspective on the Liverpool-Irish, see John Belchem, 'The Immigrant Alternative: Ethnic and Sectarian Mutuality among the Liverpool Irish during the Nineteenth Century' in *The Duty of Discontent: essays for Dorothy Thompson* ed. O. Ashton, R. Fyson and S. Roberts (London, 1995), 231–50.

101] The great north-end thoroughfare of nineteenth-century Irish-Liverpool, Scotland Road has established itself as the 'hallowed patch' of Liverpool's heritage and identity, aided by the presence of a local writers' workshop. According to Terry Cooke's blurb: 'There was nothing like it anywhere else in the world, and it was known world-wide thanks to the many Scotland Road men who went to sea and talked nostalgically about it. In spite of the many fine buildings that Liverpool possessed it epitomised Liverpool and that special Liverpool spirit that could survive any disaster and then recount the event with typical Scouse humour.' Besides the autobiographies already mentioned, J. Woods, *Growin' Up: One Scouser's Social History* (Preston, 1989) is also set in Scotland Road, 'one of the "rougher" districts of the city'. Written long before the heritage boom, Pat O'Mara's harrowing autobiography (which makes no reference to scouse) is set for the most part in the south-end slums. For some unexplained reason, the word 'Irish' has been deleted from the title of the recent (but undated) reprint by the Bluecoat Press. The 'demonisation' of the Scotland Road district can be traced back to the 1880s when its inhabitants were described as 'the lowest type of squalid life. They are more uncivilised, more dangerous, more ignorant, more drunken than any to be found elsewhere', *Squalid Liverpool*, 50.

(whose speech was formerly Lancastrian rustic) not only his accent but also his celtic belligerence'.[102]

While these images, myths, and stereotypes await historical deconstruction, linguistic studies have begun to point the way forward, undermining preconceptions and prejudice about the nature of scouse. Without denying the substantial Irish input, application of Labovian and other forms of sociolinguistic analysis has underlined the systemic nature of Merseyside vernacular speech. By no means unpatterned and slovenly, the vernacular discipline extends across local micro-cultural variations of scouse. Furthermore, aesthetic prejudice against the accent seems inconsistent: although more open to innovation than the dialect of many northern towns, it has kept closer to the standard of grammar, vocabulary and pronunciation. In phonological evolution, indeed, scouse has undergone sound changes similar to those which occurred in the ancestor of RP (received pronunciation) some centuries ago, developments then considered high-status and prestigious.[103]

While still stigmatised as slovenly and working-class, even by some native speakers, scouse is not considered as unattractive as the accents of the West Midlands in general and Birmingham in particular.[104] Scouse, indeed, has proved a cultural force of growth, extending both its geographical and social field of force.[105] In Knowles' study, middle-class informants in Aigburth studiously avoided the shibboleths of scouse, but even when using 'prestige' forms, they were still recognisably Liverpudlian.[106] As Carla Lane, Jim Hitchmough and other writers have appreciated, the external

102] Spiegl, 'Preface' to 1984 reprinted edition of *Lern Yerself Scouse*. See also his 'Foreword' to *The ABZ of Scouse* on how nineteenth-century Merseyside was a Mecca for 'would-be workers who lacked the ability to acquire skills or, being shiftless, lacked the ambition ... Let us face the awful fact: it is from the uneducated and in some respects uneducatable stratum of Merseyside life that Scouse has arisen and developed.'
103] Andrew Hamer, 'Scouse Boundaries', paper presented to Liverpool Studies Seminar, 15 Nov. 1995, and his paper, 'Non-Standard Accents and the Classroom'. See also, Knowles, 'Scouse', De Lyon, 'Sociolinguistic Study' and Newbrook, *Sociolinguistic Reflexes*.
104] Peter Trudgill, *On Dialect* (Oxford, 1983), 218–19.
105] Knowles, 'Scouse', 14–15, charts its progress north to Southport, north-east to Maghull, Lydiate and Ormskirk, east to St Helens (although Andrew Hamer has noted resistance here – the boundary of woollydom, perhaps?), and south-east beyond Halewood to Runcorn and Widnes. See also Newbrook, *Sociolinguistic Reflexes*, for its dominance in West Wirral.
106] Knowles, 'Scouse', ch. 8.

ear can readily distinguish between 'posh' and 'popular' in Liverpudlian vernacular, an essential juxtaposition for the comedy of manners. Through a process of historical inversion, snobbish pretension, the original hallmark of the Liverpool gentleman, is now the butt of humour in which 'dead' scousers, true working-class Liverpudlians, have all the best lines (suitably domesticated of course for a mass television audience).[107] Furthermore, the new climate of populism has brought a fashionable edge to certain non-standard accents in middle-class professional circles, accompanied by a new-generation nostalgia beyond the limits of conventional heritage. The Merseybeat of the 1960s has become retro-chic, celebrating a 'scouse style' linked with 'the birth of the original Britpop and the lairy humour of TV series like *The Liver Birds*'.[108] A fashionable accessory, scouse is now accentuated and cultivated, no longer concealed. In the very latest stylistic stakes, however, it seems to be losing ground to estuary English, the new watered-down (and much broadcast) form of cockney.[109]

The cultural spread of scouse stands in marked contrast to Liverpool's continuing economic and demographic decline, its spiralling descent into European 'Objective One' funding status. The media myth and political rhetoric of militant Merseyside aside, scouse 'otherness' has a wide appeal, prompting some to emulate (and thereby fragment) its accent. A series of writers and dramatists, including Alun Owen, Neville Smith and Jim Allen, brought Liverpool to national attention, enabling the next generation of playwrights (often ex-schoolteachers) – Willy Russell, Alan Bleasdale, Jimmy McGovern et al. – to probe more deeply into scouse surrealism (from wacker to wacky?) and Merseyside exceptionalism. Humour and black-market ingenuity – a natural extension of the traditional 'secondary economy' of the streets – are now privileged in cultural celebration of the 'scally' scouser. Incorporated into comedy series and soap operas, scallies are distinctly less laudable and heroic than war-time cockneys, but they evince their own form of 'carry on spirit'. Their dubious tricks, ploys and survival techniques[110] – what might be called a liminal form of British endurance – offer much amusement to nationwide television audiences. In true Liverpool fashion, scallies exemplify what Matt Simpson describes as 'a come-day-go-day attitude to life born out of the seafaring traditions of

107] 'Liverpudlians are paranoid about what they consider to be "posh"'; Matt Simpson, 'Voices, Accents, Histories', in *Liverpool Accents*, 167.
108] 'The Fab Fur', *The Observer* 26 Nov. 1995, Life Magazine, 58.
109] 'Fings ain't what they used to be, wack', *Guardian* 1 June 1999.
110] Spiegl, *Scally Scouse*, provides a useful introductory manual.

months at sea followed by a few days back home "blowing" pay as if it were an embarrassment'.[111] A counterbalance to the militant Merseysider, the scally scouser of popular cultural representation acts as a roguish saturnalian safety-valve, providing humour out of economic adversity.[112]

The 'scally' is the latest product of a scouse culture that is reactive to rather than causative of economic decline.[113] Admittedly, cultural factors may have hindered Liverpool's belated industrial diversification.[114] Workers in the new industrial plants of the Merseyside Development Area soon gained a reputation for antipathy to factory discipline and managerial prerogatives, prompting some observers to trace a cultural continuity back to the old traditions of waterside casualism and seafaring independence, the legacy of dockers who offered themselves for employment when they wished and of seamen who were able to pick and choose the ships.[115] Many of the plants were abruptly closed once development aid and other short-term advantages were exhausted, the alleged 'militancy' of the local workforce serving to justify a board-room decision taken far away from Liverpool. In the continuing tendency towards rationalisation, giant

111] Simpson, 'Voices, Accents, Histories', 167.
112] In its preview of *And the Beat Goes On*, the 'new Scouse extravaganza' on Channel 4, *The Guardian* notes how 'from the Liver Birds to Brookside, TV invariably portrays Liverpudlians as plucky underdogs ... a sort of run-down, put-upon natural fighter who's seen it all, done it all, and had it all done to them, but still faces life with a stoic sense of humour and an earthy honesty that's somehow difficult to find elsewhere' ('The Guide', 16 March 1996).
113] This is not to suggest, of course, that the militant scouser and the scally scouser are mutually exclusive. Jimmy Sexton's narrative of the great dock strike of 1889, the formative moment of Merseyside militancy, is punctuated by accounts of the practical jokes of some of its participants, most notably, one-eyed Blind Riley and the inebriate Christie Kenny. Sexton also appreciated the humour and culture of the old dockers' clubs and societies as they were gradually subsumed into trade unionism, such as the traditional grant of five shillings to coffin bearers at the funeral of a workmate: 'I recall one case where the bearers, anticipating the payment of five shillings, overspent it at the local pub before they had earned it, increased the deficit after they had discharged their melancholy duties, and eventually claimed another shilling piece, under trade union rules, on the ground that their job had been carrying dead meat, for which they were entitled to six shillings a day.' James Sexton, *Sir James Sexton, Agitator: the Life of the Dockers' M.P.* (London, 1935), 93–101 and 115.
114] For a full discussion, see John Belchem and Michael Power, 'Structural Change, Culture and Class in Early Industrial Liverpool' in Rainer Schulze (ed.), *Industrial Regions in Transformation* (Essen, 1993), 119–42.
115] R. Bean and P. Stoney, 'Strikes on Merseyside: a Regional Analysis', *Industrial Relations Journal*, Vol. 17 (1986), 9–23.

combines, as P.J. Waller has noted, seem always to single out the Liverpool limb for amputation.[116] Decline and disinvestment have reduced the local resource base, but 'scally' scouse resilience seems replenished.

Always vibrant in response to adverse structural change, scouse has periodically revitalised itself, taking a variety of cultural forms (such as the dramatic renaissance briefly noted above) since the radio comedy of the interwar depression.[117] Although he never visited the city, Jung captured its ambivalence in a famous dream, a 'pool of life' amid squalor and decay.[118] One new arrival in the economic blight of the early 1980s was immediately struck by the 'new Liverpool rock scene', the latest 'Scouse Phenomenon':

> Amidst all the well-documented problems that face Liverpudlians day in and day out, some things have never changed. The people remain confident, amusing and resourceful; the football teams beat everybody, and the music is as fresh, interesting and influential as ever. It's the music that grabbed me and made me stay![119]

Music offers perhaps the best insight into Liverpool's distinctiveness or 'otherness': significantly, tongue-in-cheek lyrics are the hallmark of the latest fashion, 'Scalpop'.[120] As with dialect, there is no indigenous 'folk' tradition in Liverpool – other than the sea-shanties of transient seamen. The Irish have contributed much to the local music scene, as the recent boom in Irish pub music attests, but they are only one voice within a wider mixture.[121] Although privileged in heritage and autobiographical accounts, the 'community' mentality of the slummy co-existed with a broader culture, a seafaring cosmopolitanism which made Liverpool particularly receptive to foreign ideas (syndicalism, for example) and to American popular music.

116] Merseyside Socialist Research Group, *Merseyside in Crisis* (1980). P.J. Waller, *Democracy and Sectarianism: a Political and Social History of Liverpool 1868–1939* (Liverpool, 1981), 351. For a critique of the pragmatic new realism of Merseyside workers since the recessionary 1980s, see Ralph Darlington, *The Dynamics of Workplace Unionism: Shop Stewards' Organization in Three Merseyside Plants* (London, 1994).

117] As Peter Robinson explains in the Preface, '*Liverpool Accents* is my attempt to demonstrate that in the field of poetry too, the city's hard years have been a goad to creative vitality and rebirth', p. iv.

118] *Liverpool Accents*, 67–68 and 90.

119] Con McConville's introduction to Klaus Schwartze, *The Scouse Phenomenon: the Scrapbook of the New Liverpool Rock Scene* (Birkenau, 1987).

120] 'Music Review', *The Big Issue in the North*, no. 116, 15–21 July 1996, 29.

121] Kevin McManus, *Céilís, Jigs and Ballads: Irish Music in Liverpool* (Liverpool, 1994).

Before the Beatles and the advent of the Merseysound, Liverpool had a reputation as the 'Nashville of the North', thanks to the cultural implant of the latest US albums which 'Cunard Yanks', sailors on the Atlantic run, brought back with them – back in the 1930s, indeed, Jimmie Rogers, 'The Yodelling Brakeman', had enjoyed considerable popularity.[122] Strengthened by cross-fertilisation with local country bands, Merseybeat arose in similar fashion: 'We used to get the soul records and the rock and roll records long before anyone else got them just because we were here and the sailors would bring them'.[123] The creative receptivity of scouse stands in marked contrast to cockney: rejuvenated by the 'Lambeth Walk', patriotic cockney offered hermetic protection against Americanisation or other alien cultural influence.

By no means restricted to music, cosmopolitanism accounts for other Liverpudlian cultural peculiarities, such as the distinctive 'expressionist' nature of working-class fiction in the inter-war years. While writers elsewhere reconstructed the enclosed world of the slum, the Liverpool school – George Garrett, James Hanley and Jim Phelan, all Liverpool-Irish *and* seamen – explored cultural multiplicity in water-front underworlds across the globe as they addressed issues of dislocation, rootlessness and alienation.[124] Beyond the 'inland' Irish Sea, Liverpool's private celtic empire, the city looked to the great oceans: as the aptly-named Irish-American historian Robert Scally has shrewdly observed, Liverpool at its height drew upon both an inner and outer world.[125] Unlike dialect culture, scouse thrived through interaction, a process encapsulated by L.T. Roche's account of the free-flowing wit (and drink) at the 'Winey' (Yates' Wine Lodge) after work on the docks:

> The Liverpool characteristic became obvious. A soft Irish humour, tempered by a Welsh wit. The ability to tell of travellers' tales, through personal contact, or from a close relative; brother, nephew, uncle, or in-law ... The vast merchant fleet, arriving and departing, without a regular

122] I owe this reference to Jim Dillon whose uncles worked on Harrison boats and regularly brought back records from Galveston and New Orleans.
123] Kenny Johnson quoted in Kevin McManus, *'Nashville of the North': Country Music in Liverpool* (Liverpool, 1994), 2.
124] K. Worpole, *Dockers and Detectives: Popular Reading: Popular Writing* (London, 1983), ch. 4.
125] Scally, *The End of Hidden Ireland*, ch. 5, 'Liverpool and the Celtic Sea' is a masterly reconstruction of mid-nineteenth-century Liverpool.

time-table, set the base at casual. The immigrants, transients in the main, swelled the complex of Liverpool. Songs and stories from lands afar widened and increased the normally narrow-based traditions. Mixed religions incensed, or infused, the inhabitants. Mixed marriages, in religion and colour, diffused the conglomeration.[126]

It would be wrong to conclude in uncritical celebration of scouse cosmopolitanism and otherness. A culture of decline, scouse is unlikely to rejuvenate the local economy, the post-industrial investment in tourism and heritage notwithstanding.[127] Ironically, the award of Objective One status, some economists fear, 'may remind some outside Merseyside of the area's relative poverty and record of decline: deterring them from coming into the area'.[128] As the publicity surrounding the Jamie Bulger case attested – the abduction and murder of a toddler by two young boys – there is some impatience with Liverpool's 'self-pitying' insistence on its difference and particular problems. In reporting local reaction to the Heysel and Hillsborough disasters and the Bulger case, the quality press have constructed an image of Liverpudlian self-indulgence, self-pity and mawkishness, an unwelcome complement to the revived tabloid assault, otherwise on the wane in the absence of industrial and political dispute, against scouse violence, militancy and arrogance.[129] In the city at the time of the Hillsborough disaster, Alan Bennett found himself thinking: 'It *would* be Liverpool, that sentimental, self-dramatizing place'. Bennett, indeed, came to dislike Liverpool:

126] Roche, *Down the Hatch*, 111. The tone here is altogether more positive and convivial than in Dickens's famous account of mid-Victorian Liverpool's notorious waterfront drinking-houses (and other clip-joint temptations) in *The Uncommercial Traveller* (final complete edition, 1869), ch. 5 where 'Poor Mercantile Jack' is entrapped along with Loafing Jack of the States, Maltese Jack, Jack of Sweden, Jack the Finn and other vulnerable sailors ashore. See also, Matt Simpson, 'Voices, Accents, Histories', in *Liverpool Accents*, p. 167: 'the lingo and character of Liverpool are the result of cosmopolitan mix. Among the ingredients that go to make up the peculiar Liverpool stew you find Lancashire amiability, Irish blarney, Welsh acerbity, as well as bits of Chinese, German, Scandinavian, to name only the obvious ones.'
127] In '50 Great Merseyside Facts' and other promotional literature to attract investment, the Mersey Partnership places emphasis on 'the renowned warmth and sense of humour of Merseysiders themselves'.
128] P. Minford and P. Stoney, 'Objective One must be growth', *Merseyside Economic and Business Prospect*, Vol. 8 (1993), No. ii, 4.
129] For an excellent analysis of the media and Hillsborough, see Scraton, Jemphrey and Coleman, *No Last Rights*, ch. 5.

Robert Ross said that Dorsetshire rustics, after Hardy, had the insolence of the artist's model, and so it is with Liverpudlians. They have figured in too many plays and have a cockiness that comes from being told too often that they and their city are special.[130]

While acknowledging Liverpool's 'unrivalled tradition in entertainment', its propensity to exploit the rise of popular art forms over the past thirty-odd years, cultural critics can still be scathing of its insular style: 'Liverpool resembles an island with arcane customs and rituals, loosely attached to the north-west coast'.[131]

While this insularity may be called into question by the city's cosmopolitan past, Liverpool lacks a political culture and a historiographical tradition to incorporate its non-celtic in-migrants, the long-established presence of West Indians, Africans and Chinese notwithstanding.[132] Having captured control of the moribund party machine, Militant chose to operate municipal politics in typical Liverpool 'Tammany' style – Chicago rather than Petrograd on the Mersey. The associational endeavours and representational needs of ethnic, gender, special interest and minority groups, different in composition from the old sectarian and Irish formations, were snubbed and ignored, causing particular offence in the black community.[133] At a time of remarkable ecumenism in the 'hurt city', recent

130] Bennett, *Writing Home*, 289.
131] Adam Sweeting, 'With a Little Help from our Friends', *The Guardian*, 10 May 1995. While the original Liverpool gentlemen aspired to make their city the Florence of the North, contemporary scouse culture resembles the *campanilismo* of Naples: 'Neapolitans, like Liverpudlians, have a way of mythologizing and sentimentalizing the city, their humour, their hospitality, and like the Liverpudlians with some justice; also their songs and their musical and popular culture have put them on the map'; Jamie McKendrick, 'One to Spare?', *Liverpool Accents*, 91.
132] Having enrolled as a Special Constable for the night, Dickens was taken to waterfront entertainment houses where the dancers were black males, 'dancing with a great show of teeth, and with a childish good-humoured enjoyment that was very prepossessing'. Among the audience in other venues, he encountered 'Dark Jack, and Dark Jack's delight, his *white* unlovely Nan... They generally kept together, these poor fellows, said Mr. Superintendent, because they were at a disadvantage singly, and liable to slights in the neighbouring streets. But, if I were Light Jack, I should be very slow to interfere oppressively with Dark Jack, for, whenever I have had to do with him I have found him a simple and gentle fellow'. *Uncommercial Traveller*, ch. 5.
133] Gideon Ben-Tovim, 'Race, politics and urban regeneration: lessons from Liverpool', in *Regenerating the Cities: The UK Crisis and the US Experience*, ed. M. Parkinson, B. Foley and D. Judd (Manchester, 1988) 141–55. John Davies, 'Class Practices and Political Culture in Liverpool' (Lancaster Regionalism Group

historical studies have attempted a positive reassessment of sectarianism ('Catslicks' and 'Prodidogs'), and of casualism and the continuing propensity to riot,[134] but the 'black struggle for historical recognition in Liverpool'[135] continues:

> ... the notion of 'scouseness' was, and still is, something Black Liverpudlians are excluded from since to be 'scouse' is to be white and working class. One has only to examine the crowds at Anfield. Such exclusion relates to the broader issue of the way Black people continue to be perceived and treated as if they are immigrants when in reality the majority are Black British. This continues to reflect a deep-rooted racism that is as much a part of Liverpool's character as it is of Britain as a whole.[136]

Although giving a voice to Liverpool and to the casual, non-manufacturing working class, the language of scouse is not without privilege, prejudice and exclusion.

Historical deconstruction of scouse provides a useful corrective to the restricted concerns of conventional labour history. In the reconstruction that lies ahead, however, there is a need to transcend the in-built inequalities of the local vernacular, to establish better communication and understanding between the disadvantaged, exploited and marginalised elements of the post-industrial city.[137] Applied in this way, the 'linguistic turn' might yet reconstitute the working class.

Working paper 37, 1988). D. Worlock and D. Sheppard, *Better Together: Christian Partnership in a Hurt City* (London, 1989), ch. 8.

134] As well as studies by Lane, Waller, and Belchem, see also Frank Neal, *Sectarian Violence: The Liverpool Experience 1819–1914* (Manchester, 1988); R.S.W. Davies, 'Differentiation in the Working Class, Class Consciousness and the Development of the Labour Party in Liverpool up to 1939', unpublished PhD thesis, Liverpool John Moores University, 1993; and Joan Smith's important comparative analysis: 'Labour Tradition in Glasgow and Liverpool', *History Workshop Journal*, Vol. 17 (1984), 32–56, and 'Class, Skill and Sectarianism in Glasgow and Liverpool, 1880–1914', in R.J. Morris (ed.), *British Nineteenth-Century Towns* (Leicester, 1986), 158–215.

135] Mark Christian, 'Black Struggle for Historical Recognition in Liverpool', *North West Labour History*, Vol. 20 (1995–96), 58–66.

136] Diane Frost, 'West Africans, Black Scousers and the Colour Problem in Inter-war Liverpool', *North West Labour History*, Vol. 20 (1995–96), 56.

137] Paul Gilroy, *'There Ain't No Black in the Union Jack'* (London, 1987), ch. 6.

Part Two
IRISH LIVERPOOL

3

Ribbonism, nationalism and the Irish pub*

I n the taxonomy of drinking saloons, Irish pubs tend to be classified (in accordance with their present-day vogue) as 'universals' rather than 'ethnocentric', catering for a mixed clientele in prime thoroughfare sites. Publicans in the Liverpool-Irish enclave of the early nineteenth century, however, often chose to accentuate their ethnicity, to concentrate their efforts (in a notoriously competitive market) on the rapidly growing migrant clientele. Their methods differed from the linguistic and dietary provision – the ethnic (and autarkic) catering – undertaken by their Scandinavian, Italian, Bohemian and Polish counterparts in immigrant urban America. Without such cultural boundary markers, Irishness was asserted through promotion of various imported (or improvised) forms of convivial and bibulous male-based collective mutuality.[1] The continuum extended from 'Hibernian' burial and friendly societies, legally approved

* This essay draws upon and extends two of my previously published papers: '"Freedom and Friendship to Ireland": Ribbonism in early nineteenth-century Liverpool', *International Review of Social History*, Vol. 39 (1994), 33–56; and 'Sectarianism, Ethnicity and Welfare. Collective Mutuality among the Liverpool Irish' in *Labour, Social Policy and the Welfare State*, ed. A. Knotter, B. Altena and D. Damsma (Amsterdam, 1997), 35–44.
1] Perry R. Duis, 'The Ethnic Saloon: A Public Melting Pot' in *Ethnic Chicago*, ed. M.G. Holli and P.d'A. Jones (4th edn, Grand Rapids, 1995), 503–28. For a lurid description of the many pubs between central Liverpool and the Clarence Dock, disembarkation point from Ireland – 'a succession of red and blue lights to attract the incautious traveller' – see 'The World as It Is', *Temperance Gazette*, 7 July 1848. According to one estimate in 1850, there were 1480 public houses and 700 beershops in Liverpool, one to every 40 adult males in the population, 'Labour and the Poor: Liverpool letter xvi', *Morning Chronicle*, 2 Sept. 1850. Despite their plenitude, Liverpool pubs lack a study to match that of K.C. Kearns, *Dublin Pub Life and Lore: An Oral History* (Niwot, 1998).

and sanctioned by the Catholic Church, to secret 'Ribbon' branches linked to networks across the Irish Sea. The centre for collective mutuality, the Liverpool-Irish pub offered services and benefits that extended further than either the saloon-based 'padrone' operations on which Italians and other migrants in the new world depended, or the craft-based labour organisations (increasingly located away from the pub in specialist premises) privileged in conventional British historiography. As this study of 'migrant' Ribbonism shows, the pub and the publican were important proactive forces in the construction of a national or ethnic awareness among Irish Catholic migrant workers, initiating the process by which ethno-sectarian formations came to dominate popular politics in Liverpool. Nationalism took a variety of forms and meanings in Liverpool, but in most inflexions the pub was the centre of operations, the prime (but not uncontested) location for (male-based) political activity, from Ribbonite insurrectionary planning to home rule electoral canvassing.

As this study will show, nationalism – a consciousness of being Irish – was implanted through Liverpool Ribbonism, a multi-functional move-ment attending to the manifold needs of migrants. Support for nationalism and the extent of alcoholic consumption – both higher in nineteenth-century Liverpool than in Ireland itself[2]– were not symptoms of disloca-tion and exile, but mechanisms of migrant adjustment, convivial means of mutual support. Beyond the male-based pub-centred frameworks studied here were informal female networks of mutual aid and migrant adjust-ment in which those who gave expected to become recipients themselves when the wheel of fortune – or the family cycle – took a turn for the worse. Newcomers were quickly welcomed and enlisted, as an interviewee reported to Hugh Shimmin:

> Why, before my wife had got her furniture put into any sort of order, she had been visited by half the women in the court – in a friendly way, of course. One and all wished her good luck; some wanted to borrow pans and mugs, some wished her to join them in a subscription to bury a child that was dead in the top house; others that had joined for a little sup of drink, wished her to taste with them; some wanted her to subscribe to a raffle for a fat pig, which had been fed in the cellar where

---

2] C.L. Scott, 'A Comparative Re-examination of Anglo-Irish Relations in Nineteenth-Century Manchester, Liverpool and Newcastle-upon-Tyne', unpublished PhD thesis, University of Durham, 1998, 50.

it now was, and that was right opposite to the house in which I lived.[3]

While primarily instrumental in balancing the family budget – no mean achievement in a predominantly casual labour market – such female networks were by no means devoid of bibulous conviviality, good cheer and personal indulgence, as evinced by the Monday 'tea party' following the obligatory weekly visit to the pawnshop to pledge the Sunday best:

> On these occasions there appeared to be no lack of meat or drink, and immediately after the arrival of each visitor a little girl would be sent off to the grog shop for spirits ... There was generally a great bustle to get all indications of the tea party cleared off before the time at which the husbands might be expected home – that is supposing them to be at work – and the women separated with very loud protestations of friendship for each other.[4]

The location of mutual support, the streets also provided income opportunities for Irish and other women in 'outcast' Liverpool.[5] Social 'explorers' were censorious of the role of alcohol in the survival strategies of chip-sellers, watercress-sellers and other 'basket girls' who, in the absence of large-scale female employment, sought to make ends meet on (and through) the street. Local priests were more understanding of their 'habit of spending spare coppers in drink': "'Except that", said the priest, "as a rule they are good girls. They are chiefly Irish, and Irish girls don't often go wrong."'[6]

* * * * *

3] Quoted in H. Shimmin, 'The Courts at Christmas Time', in *Low Life and Moral Improvement in Mid-Victorian England: Liverpool through the Journalism of Hugh Shimmin*, ed. J. Walton and A. Wilcox (Leicester, 1991), 156.

4] H. Shimmin, 'The Social Condition of the People' in *Low Life and Moral Improvement*, 111.

5] Martha Kanya-Forstner, 'The Politics of Survival: Irish Women in Outcast Liverpool, 1850–1890', unpublished PhD thesis, University of Liverpool, 1997, ch. 2.

6] *Squalid Liverpool: By a Special Commission* (Liverpool, 1883), 42. This investigation drew particular attention to the plight of widows with children, apparently beyond any supportive network: 'These women struggle and strive to keep themselves and their children alive. They have nothing to spare for sick clubs. They probably have no friends, for, crowded together as these people live, they seem to have no inclination or ability for the formation of friendships. When the fever strikes down one of these widows no one may hear of it for days, and when it is known the surrounding neighbours probably consider it a circumstance which does not demand particular attention. There the woman may lie suffering, delirious, and dying, with her children starving round her. This is no fancy picture. It is terribly real. It represents one of the most appalling aspects of squalid life in Liverpool', ibid., 31.

Returning to the men, it is necessary to begin with a brief analysis of the controversial role of Ribbonism in Ireland itself. Secret societies were endemic in 'pre-modern' Ireland, but not all were the preserve of 'primitive rebels'. Traditionalist agrarian redresser movements operated alongside urban-based networks which combined labour protection and collective mutuality with forward-looking political and/or nationalist goals.[7] There was considerable, often confusing, overlap and fluidity in aims and functions, hence the difficulty in classifying and categorising Ribbonism, a new type of secret society which emerged around 1811. Some historians, echoing the loose use of the label in the post-Famine years, insist on its economistic purpose and generic character: Whiteboyism by another name, Ribbonism was the term applied to traditional and defensive agrarian protest, in which intimidation and violence sought to uphold a customary code (or moral economy) within the existing tenurial system.[8] Other historians, following the lead of the best-informed observers of the pre-Famine period, see a political (even republican) thrust that distinguished and distanced Ribbonism from traditional agrarian redresser movements, although in adjusting to local circumstances, Ribbonism was often responsive to rural grievances.[9] Viewed in this way, the Ribbonmen, with their sectarian blend of religion-based nationalism, secrecy and communal solidarity, occupy a pivotal role in the evolution of Irish nationalist politics: located midway between the Defenders of the 1790s and the militant organisations of the late nineteenth century, they maintained an organisational commitment within the Catholic community to national independence through rebellion and violence. However, direct links forward have yet to be traced: indeed, evidence from the last outbreak of Ribbonism in 1869

7] 'Secret societies appear to have been more "normal" in Ireland than elsewhere', T. Desmond Williams (ed.), *Secret Societies in Ireland* (Dublin, 1973), ix. See also, S. Clark and J.S. Donnelly, Jr, *Irish Peasants: Violence and Political Unrest 1780–1914* (Manchester, 1983); and more generally, E.J. Hobsbawm, *Primitive Rebels* (Manchester, 1959).

8] Joseph Lee, 'The Ribbonmen' in *Secret Societies*, Williams, 26–35.

9] Tom Garvin, *The Evolution of Irish Nationalist Politics* (Dublin, 1981), 34–43, and 'Defenders, Ribbonmen and Others: Underground Political Networks in Pre-Famine Ireland', *Past and Present*, Vol. 96 (1982), 133–55; M.R. Beames, 'The Ribbon Societies: Lower-Class Nationalism in Pre-Famine Ireland', *Past and Present*, Vol. 97 (1982), 128–43; and S.J. Connolly, 'Aftermath and Adjustment' in *A New History of Ireland, V: Ireland under the Union*, ed. W.E. Vaughan (Oxford, 1989), 19–20. See also, George Cornewall Lewis, *On Local Disturbances in Ireland* (London, 1836), 155–61 and 326.

suggests an economistic explanation for events in the notorious 'Ribbon-land' of Co. Westmeath.[10] Ribbonism, Donal McCartney judiciously con-cludes, 'occupied a limbo between the formidable United Irishmen and the Fenians without providing anything like a clear link between the two'.[11]

While a controversial presence in nationalist history, Ribbonism features prominently in early Irish labour history, reflecting its excep-tional success in urban areas, especially in Dublin. In Leinster, Ribbon lodges functioned as labour leagues, offering benefit and protection not only to artisans (as a supplement to unions and guilds) but also to unskilled workers in transport and carrying trades, such as the Dublin coal porters, the 'Billy Welters'.[12] Ribbonism, however, was not a class-based exercise in general unionism. As in the peasant societies, sectarianism provided the structural foundation for collective action. Leadership, as Tom Garvin notes, was often provided by the Catholic trading classes, shopkeepers, traders and publicans, who sought to deflect the forces of socio-economic conflict and unrest into nationalist channels.[13] Some contemporary observers were more cynical. In presenting evidence to the 1839 Select Committee of the House of Lords, Thomas Drummond, Under-Secretary at Dublin Castle, insisted that Ribbonism was no more than a confidence swindle operated by publicans, who pocketed the quarterly subscriptions as well as gaining custom, protection and prestige by serving as Ribbon masters.[14] Quasi-criminal elements were doubtless involved, seeking to transform Ribbonism from a protective association of collective mutuality into a protection racket – indeed, this was the charge brought by the breakaway Dublin-based lodges of the Irish Sons of Freedom against 'Captain' Rice, the powerful leading figure in the Northern Union, the senior Ribbon network. However, Ribbonism marked the beginning of the process by which sectarian collective mutuality moved away from the under-ground (and underworld) towards the integrative associational culture of

---

10] A.C. Murray, 'Agrarian Violence and Nationalism in Nineteenth-Century Ireland: the Myth of Ribbonism', *Irish Economic and Social History*, Vol. 13 (1986), 56–73.
11] Donal McCartney, *The Dawning of Democracy: Ireland 1800–1870* (Dublin, 1987), 82–89. See also the discussion of Ribbonism in Galen Broeker, *Rural Disorder and Police Reform in Ireland, 1812–36* (London, 1970), 6–13.
12] Emmet O'Connor, *A Labour History of Ireland 1824–1960* (Dublin, 1992),13–14.
13] Garvin, *Evolution of Irish Nationalist Politics*, 41–42.
14] Report from the Select Committee of the House of Lords appointed to enquire into the state of Ireland in respect of crime, Parliamentary Papers, 1839 (486), xii, 13, 317.

the Ancient Order of Hibernians. Significantly, the transformation was completed first in Irish migrant communities. [15]

As the main port of entry, Liverpool was the pivotal point for both Ribbon networks as they extended their operations among the large numbers of migrant workers who arrived in the decades before the Famine influx – the 1841 census recorded 49 639 Irish-born in Liverpool, some 17.3 per cent of the population. Ribbonism provided an important complement to the normal mechanisms of chain migration, serving as reception and assistance centre for migrant Irish Catholic workers. In sociological classification, chain migration replaced local and circular forms to become the dominant migration system in nineteenth-century Europe, facilitating long-distance movement from densely populated peripheral areas – particularly Ireland, Italy and the Polish provinces – to core industrial and commercial regions. Working through family networks, social connections and regional solid-arities, chain migration involved social arrangements with people already at destination, who characteristically helped newcomers to find jobs and housing, thereby protecting them from disorientation, dislocation and anomic behaviour. This functional analysis, however, should not be pushed too far. Information was shared by kin, friends and acquaintances, but there was considerable discrepancy in the knowledge and assistance – the 'personal information field' – available to individual migrants.[16] As the pace of Irish emigration increased dramatically from the 1820s, Ribbon-ism, with its extensive secret organisational structure, served both to fill the gaps in these informal networks and to provide cheap, flexible and mobile benefits for those unable to gain employment at the chosen destin-ation. The secret network that provided 'political' sanctuary for members in flight from the Irish authorities also offered 'tramping' benefits to itinerant migrant workers. In the process, it engendered a sense of identity wider than the familial and regional affiliations through which chain

15] There are brief references to Ribbonism among Irish migrants in L.H. Lees, *Exiles of Erin: Irish Emigrants in Victorian London* (Manchester, 1979), 223; Rachel O'Higgins, 'The Irish Influence in the Chartist Movement', *Past and Present*, Vol. 20 (1961), 85; J.H. Treble, 'The Attitude of the Roman Catholic Church towards Trade Unionism in the North of England, 1833–1842', *Northern History*, Vol. 5 (1970), 93–113; and G. P. Connolly, 'The Catholic Church and the First Manchester and Salford Trade Unions in the Age of the Industrial Revolution', *Transactions of the Lancashire and Cheshire Antiquarian Society*, Vol. 135 (1985), 125–39.
16] For a useful comparative and 'systemic' perspective on migration, see Leslie Page Moch, *Moving Europeans: Migration in Western Europe since 1650* (Bloom-ington, 1992), in particular, 16–18, and 103–60.

migration typically operated for 'moving Europeans'. Among Irish Catholics in Liverpool and Britain, Ribbonism helped to construct a national or ethnic awareness, a sense of Irishness.

*   *   *   *   *

Ribbonism, then, was multi-functional and morally ambiguous: its secrecy and ritual served *inter alia* to promote republican revolution, organised crime, sectarian protection and collective mutuality. Much of this complexity was implanted in Irish-Liverpool. On the waterfront, Ribbonism functioned as a form of primitive trade unionism, as Irish dock-labourers sought to corner a niche of the labour market by threats and violence against outsiders. Newly-arrived migrants unaware of the 'goods', the latest secret Ribbon grips and passwords, often found themselves at painful disadvantage within dock labour gangs.[17] Here, too, were a number of lucrative business opportunities for members of the 'friendship'. Ribbonmen, it was reported in 1840, were 'straining at a monopoly in the shipment of Irish emigrants. One man, from nothing, has realised a large fortune and has several Delegates on both sides in his employ as agents.'[18] Others sought financial gain at the movement's expense, selling their services within the shady intelligence network. Having failed in trade, E. Rorke moved in with his Liverpool mistress to exploit his old mercantile contacts with Irish connections, eliciting information which he then sold to the authorities. His main informant, P.H. McGloin, a respectable young businessman, employed by wool merchants on a salary of £100 per annum, later claimed that until approached by Rorke, he had 'taken very little part in the thing, because being in a respectable situation and having business to attend to, it was against his interest to spend his nights in attending meetings and "*boozing*", which the Officers of the Society must do'. In the aftermath of the major round-up of Ribbon leaders in Ireland in 1839, McGloin learnt of Rorke's disreputable morals and excessive middleman's commission. Having gained assurance that he would not be called as a witness himself, McGloin negotiated a direct deal with the authorities in Dublin Castle: 'He was formerly a Delegate, and might now take an office which would put him in possession of all their secrets. When he comes to

17] John Denvir, *The Irish in Britain* (London, 1892), 127–31. See also, *The Liverpool Irishman, or Annals of the Irish Colony in Liverpool* (n.p., 1909), 4.
18] Public Record Office, Kew: Colonial Office Papers (hereafter CO) 904/8 ff. 82–89.

Dublin he has to transact business (in trade) with a Delegate and would have many facilities of gaining extensive information.'[19]

McGloin's reports provide a useful insight into the operation of the Northern Union in Liverpool in the late 1830s. They should be read in conjunction with the vast amount of Liverpool material in the papers (191 items, all in shorthand) seized at the house of Richard Jones, national secretary of the rival Irish Sons of Freedom, following his arrest in the round-up of October 1839.[20] Liverpool, indeed, features prominently in the information gathered for the major Ribbon trials of 1840. Unfortunately, the same does not apply to the earlier round of arrests and trials in 1822, the first instance in which the authorities penetrated the upper echelons of the movement.

In the absence of local source material, evidence for the early 1820s is restricted to transcripts of the trials and confusing reports from informers summarised by Major Sirr, the Dublin police magistrate. However, it would seem that this was a period of major reorganisation, as the Dublin leaders, having abandoned plans for simultaneous insurrection with the English radicals – a scheme premised on a revolutionary outcome of the Queen Caroline Affair – sought to consolidate links not only with Ulster but with their compatriots in Britain. In June 1821, at a meeting chaired by Michael Keenan, a coal-porter with a reputation for toughness, a certain Fullinsby was appointed as special envoy to England: 'Keenan gave Fullinsby six tests and desired him to bring over the people of Liverpool and Manchester into Union with Dublin'.[21] An unhappy chapter of events ensued, typical of the confusion, suspicion and treachery which tended to prevail when secret societies extended from their base. Fullinsby was received in Liverpool by Campbell and Doogan. The former, a publican in Dickens Street, had close links with Ribbon activity in Ulster, travelling to Armagh every quarter,

19] Matheson's report to Drummond on his interview with McGloin in Dublin, CO 904/7 ff. 465–70.
20] The transcription of these papers proved difficult and contentious, see CO 904/7 ff. 313–28; hence only a small selection was produced at the trial. See M.J. Martyn, *An Authentic Report of the Trial of Richard Jones ... with an Appendix, Containing the Letters and Correspondence of the Secret Society Read in Evidence at Trial* (Dublin, 1840). However, transcriptions of all items can be found in the papers of Messrs Kemmis, Crown Solicitors, in National Archives, Dublin: Frazer Mss 43, transcript of the books written in short-hand found on the person of Richard Jones on 1 Oct. 1839 (hereafter Jones transcript). A near complete copy is available at the Public Record Office, Kew: Home Office Papers (hereafter HO) 100/263.
21] Trinity College, Dublin: Sirr Diaries, Mss N4/6 f. 88.

presumably to receive the 'goods'; the latter, a Dublin-born boot and shoe maker, was master of the Ribbon lodge which met in Campbell's pub, and apparently an expert in disguise. Having infiltrated a local Orange Order meeting, Doogan spotted one of the spies who had tailed Fullinsby across the Irish Sea. Suspicions soon fell on Fullinsby himself – there were rumours that he was a Protestant, his attendance at Mass notwithstanding, and that he wished to tell the Liverpool authorities 'the whole secret'. Campbell made a special trip to Dublin to express his concern, but what happened thereafter is impossible to disentangle. Reorganisation, however, was finally effected in February 1822 with the establishment of a national board, for which purpose Liverpool was considered an integral part of Ireland itself: listed as one of the nine committees 'in the North', it was entitled to send two delegates.[22] Shortly afterwards, Keenan and the other Dublin leaders were convicted for administering an unlawful oath, mainly on the evidence of the police informer Coffey.[23]

The trials brought an end to the first peak of Ribbon activity and to the hope of organisational unity. Henceforward, Ribbonism was split into separate Leinster- and Ulster-based societies, both of which contested for the allegiance of the Liverpool Irish. Both networks were hindered by the Catholic church, which strengthened its stand against oath-bound secret societies, after the trials (and Daniel O'Connell's subsequent evidence to the parliamentary select committee) had contrasted Ribbonite political conspiracy with Rockite agricultural disturbances in the south.[24] The Northern Union, or Sons of the Shamrock, duly concealed its operations behind the façade of clerically-approved benefit societies such as the Knights of St Patrick, and the St Patrick's Fraternal Society, an exclusively Catholic body 'to promote Friendship, Unity and True Christian Charity, by raising and supporting a stock or Fund of money for aiding and assisting its members when out of employment, and for no other purpose

---

22] Ibid., ff. 118 and 126; and N4/7 ff. 36 and 106.
23] *A Report of the Trial of Michael Keenan for Administering an Unlawful Oath* (Dublin, 1822); *A Report of the Trial of Edward Browne and others for Administering and of Laurence Woods for Taking an Unlawful Oath* (Dublin, 1822). They were described by the Attorney General as 'carmen, low artisans and others who, though not perhaps the dregs of society, are far below the order of persons competent to take a share in regulating the affairs of state'. See also, R.B. McDowell, *Public Opinion and Government Policy, 1801–1846* (London, 1952), 63–65.
24] Select Committee on the state of Ireland, Parliamentary Papers, 1825 (129), 71–72.

whatsoever'.[25] The various Hibernian benefit societies, which also offered sickness and death benefit, were originally the Liverpudlian extension of this dual-level practice, as here too the Catholic clergy – in accordance with a solemn Interdict of February 1831 – refused the sacraments to any known member of an organisation bound by secret oath.[26] By contrast, the Irish Sons of Freedom eschewed such deception, operating in secret without any façade. However, many of its members were attracted to other forms of associational culture, most notably the collective mutuality of affiliated friendly societies like the Oddfellows.

Founded in 1834, the Liverpool Hibernian Benevolent Burial Society provided the model for the expansion of Catholic collective mutuality throughout the Irish diaspora. Official histories of the Ancient Order of Hibernians acknowledge its pioneer status, praising its 'divine precepts' of charity and devotion, together with its public declaration of allegiance to the monarch, constitution and Catholic church.[27] As new societies were formed, the Hibernians underlined their clerical and constitutional loyalty by public disavowal of any connection with 'any illegal or excommunicated society in Ireland': 'The sole object of the Hibernian Society in England is to assist its Members in sickness and distress, and bury them when dead … no society in Ireland or elsewhere, has or shall have so long as such society shall be proscribed by the pastors of the church, any voice or influence in the government of our society, or the management of its finances'.[28] Such public proclamations notwithstanding, Hibernian societies acted as convenient cover, preserving the link, McGloin revealed, between English lodges and the Northern Union:

> A form of declaration has been adopted for the members at Liverpool, which begins by disclaiming all connexion with any societies in Ireland using secret signs and passwords; but this, like the article in the old declaration or oath of the Societies here, promising allegiance to the King or Queen, is only intended as a *blind*. The promise of allegiance

25] James J. Bergin, *History of the Ancient Order of Hibernians* (Dublin, 1910), 29–31.
26] For details of the Bishop's Interdict in the Northern District of England, see Connolly, 'Catholic Church', 132–33.
27] T.F. McGrath, *History of the Ancient Order of Hibernians* (Cleveland, Ohio, 1898), 51–55; Wayne G. Broehl, Jr, *The Molly Maguires* (Cambridge, Mass., 1964), 32–33. Papers produced by the society were found on a man arrested at a fair in Co. Louth, see Select Committee of the House of Lords … 1839 (486), xi, 4610–13.
28] Handbill, St Patrick's Hibernian Benevolent Society, CO 904/7 f. 149.

was always 'turned down' and not read, when a member was admitted – and the present disclaimer is to be treated in the same way.[29]

This subterfuge, however, was but the first step to full admission to the secret lodges, each consisting of a 'parish' master, two committee men, a treasurer and 36 members:

> Much precaution is used in the introduction of members, none but Roman Catholics being admissible; and a *report list*, with the name, age and residence, the parish and county where each candidate comes from, must be read out in each *body*, and afterwards in the General Committee of the Town ... each must be passed in two or more bodies and afterwards approved by the General Committee.[30]

There were at least thirty active branches (some well in excess of 36 strong) by the mid-1830s, despite persistent efforts by the clergy, mainly through rigorous interrogation of confessionists, to eradicate oath-bound societies. 'The clergy here this several years past', the Liverpool president of the rival Irish Sons of Freedom later reported to Dublin, 'were violently opposed against Irishmen on this side of the Channel holding a communication with Ireland. These Hibernians or Widgeons had recourse to every open artifice to deceive the clergy but God help them they were deceiving themselves when they would go to confession.' Under threat of denial of the sacraments, some Northern Unionists withdrew altogether; others alternated in attendance, according to conscience and need, between church and lodge; and certain sections of the leadership contemplated a range of exculpatory options, even severance of the offending link with Ireland. There was much internal dissension (and increased friction between the rival networks) when the Hibernians gave serious consideration to 'dropping Ireland ... of complying with the Bishops declaration and setting up shop for themselves confining their system, *as they say*, to England alone'.[31]

29] CO 904/7 ff. 465–70.
30] Extracts from communications from the informant AB, CO 904/8 ff. 309–10.
31] Jones transcript, no. 42: Wilson, Liverpool, 4 May 1838. Ribbonism was the main target, but clerical proscription applied to all forms of oath-bound societies: 'I should not feel myself justified in admitting to the sacraments any member of the trades' union, or of any society administering secret oaths' (evidence of Rev. Thomas Fisher, Liverpool, Royal Commission on the Condition of the Poorer Classes in Ireland: Appendix G, The State of the Irish Poor in Great Britain, Parliamentary Papers, 1836 (40), xxxiv, 23).

Clerical pressure notwithstanding, there was no unilateral restriction of operations to the Irish in Britain. The Northern Union retained its essential economic and political links with Ireland, the centre of operations, functioning as a form of affiliated friendly society for migrant workers, supplementing the informal mechanisms of chain migration by a tramping network of relief and assistance, irrespective of skill or trade. Basic cover was provided at modest cost, normally 1s for admission and a quarterly payment of either 3d or 6d. Sickness and death benefits were left to the discretion of the local branch or lodge: tramp relief, however, was distributed out of the 'box' (held at local headquarters – in Liverpool, the Grapes Inn, Grayson Street) through the highest local officer, the 'county delegate', and charged quarterly upon each branch. Elected by the branch officers at the quarterly meeting of the general committee, the 'delegate' was entrusted to attend the quarterly General Board of Erin or 'market' in Ireland to receive the 'goods', the latest signs and passwords, the correct version of which had to appear on the card or certificate presented by tramps seeking relief. The delegate's expenses in attending the General Board had the first call on funds, followed by relief and assistance for arrested or fugitive members in Ireland, leaving the remainder for benefit payments. On occasion, there was misunderstanding of this order of priority, although such matters were generally dealt with internally by the 'select', a gathering of the parish masters, sitting above the general committee to assist and advise the county delegate and act, if required, as arbitration tribunal.[32] There was considerable embarrassment in 1842 when Patrick O'Neill brought an action before the Liverpool magistrates against John McArdle, president of the Second Hibernians. Having joined the Provident Friendly Society, a society accorded legal recognition and approval by Tidd Pratt, the Registrar of Friendly Societies, O'Neill had fallen ill – and apparently into arrears – when the society was subsumed into the Second Hibernians, which then denied him sickness benefit. Under cross-examination, Patrick Doyle, president of the Provident Friendly Society, admitted that he had spent £6 of the funds of the society on a trip to Ireland to help raise bail for someone charged with Ribbonism.[33]

By operating in secret without such cover, the Irish Sons of Freedom avoided, or so its leaders believed, the duplicity, deception and financial

32] Extracts from communications of the informant AB, CO 904/8 ff. 309–17. Statement of John O'Brien, 3 Nov. 1841, HO 45/184.
33] *Liverpool Mercury* 29 Apr. 1842.

corruption inherent in the dual-layer Northern Union. Smaller in scale, the Liverpool branch of the Irish Sons of Freedom operated from head-quarters in George Carrick's Hibernian Tavern in Newton Hill Street, where much of the administration was left to the local 'president', equivalent in rank and role to the county delegate, but elected by all members. Within a few months of his election in 1838, William Wilson, a painter and decorator, complained of the disproportionate burdens of office, for which he received no expenses. On top of his onerous responsibilities for tramp relief, he had to 'attend the general meeting, take reports, read letters, in effect do the whole work of the society ... Every Sunday night either 3 or 4 of our bodies meet, they require my attendance every Monday night. I have to attend at Mr Carrick see the money forthcoming, receipt the Stewards books, see the sick money paid.'[34] Wilson's complaints were given a sym-pathetic hearing in Dublin where the central lodge, administered by Andrew Dardis, national president, and Richard Jones, national secretary, was nearly £20 in debt.[35] However, the Leinster network prided itself on its financial probity. Members paid 6d quarterly into the county fund, used to send the president to the quarterly board, to relieve tramps, to fee counsel for members of the friendship in jail, and to assist friends 'injured by opponents'. 'We or any other party', Jones wrote from Dublin, 'have no call on the money so collected ... no person out of your own County has any call on it.'[36]

Wilson's brief tenure of office, chronicled in detail in Jones's shorthand books, was full of controversy, complicated by personalities and a complex struggle for power which began earlier when Thomas Jones, a recent arrival from Co. Kildare, was ousted from the Liverpool presidency in 1837 on discovery that he had joined the Oddfellows.[37] His replacement, Kennedy, ruled against such dual membership, but was voted out of office soon afterwards for reasons which remain unclear. Kennedy, however, retained the confidence and ear of the Dublin leadership to whom he con-tinually traduced Wilson, his duly-elected successor. Ratification of Wilson's position, indeed, was delayed until thorough investigation of his back-ground – including detailed questioning of his old Dublin landlady about

34] Jones transcript, no. 80, Wilson, 22 Aug. 1838.
35] Jones transcript, no. 49: Dardis and Jones, 28 May 1838. Dardis was a publican, Jones a haymaker's clerk in Smithfield market, Dublin.
36] Jones transcript, no. 96: Jones, 19 Oct. 1838.
37] Jones transcript, no. 12: Thomas Jones, 24 Mar. 1838.

his attendance record at Mass – and a special 'mission' to Liverpool by Dardis and Jones in which they attempted to run an alternative candidate.[38] Thereafter, they established a relationship of mutual respect, symbolised by signing their correspondence with the current password, 'Freedom and Friendship to Ireland'. In this new spirit, Wilson offered financial assistance towards central printing and travel costs, notably the delegation sent to Belfast to initiate merger discussions with the Northern Union.[39] Wilson, however, lost local support as members queried the cost of his ambitious plans to institute a united framework of Ribbonite self-sufficiency, free from clerical interference or friendly society competition.

During the course of discussion with Patrick Cunningham and other members of the rival Northern Union, representatives of the Catholic clergy from Liverpool and industrial Lancashire displayed a willingness to relax the 1831 blanket proscription on secret societies by extending a measure of tolerance, not approval, to friendly societies such as the Oddfellows.[40] The Irish Sons of Freedom were encouraged further in this direction when they were invited to talks by a local Liverpool priest, the Rev. Wilcocks, as a gesture of gratitude for the society's £5 St Patrick's day donation to the parish school building fund. Wilson fell from favour when he refused to participate in these discussions, during which Wilcocks raised no objection to membership of the non-denominational Oddfellows. At the next election, Wilson was unseated by Michael Hanlon, an enthusiastic advocate of dual membership. On taking office, Hanlon wrote to Dublin, advising Jones to abandon discussions with the Northern Union and to give immediate approval to a dual membership policy in Liverpool, where the Oddfellows had acquired virtual control of the labour market in local yards and foundries.[41] His behaviour antagonised the local leaders of the Northern Union within whose sectarian perspective the non-denominational, apolitical Oddfellows were 'no better than Orangemen'. 'The other, the Leinster faction', McGloin reported at the time of Jones's trial, 'have applied to form themselves into a branch of the Independent

38] Jones transcript, nos 1–6, 14, 20 and 38.
39] Jones transcript, nos 48, Wilson, 25 May, and 49, Dardis and Jones, 28 May 1838. Tramps had to produce printed cards or certificates bearing the initial letters of the password. Others used after FAFTI include GUAI (General Union among Irishmen) and FNDO (Fear Not Danger Over), adopted by a cruel irony on 30 Sept. 1838, the day before Jones's arrest.
40] Connolly, 'Catholic Church', 134–36.
41] Jones transcript, nos 140–42, 144–45, 157, 173 and 186.

Order of Oddfellows which as a society with passwords and signs, neither sanctioned nor meddled with by the Law Authorities, they hope under its cloak to continue and meet as usual on their old affairs. Hence has arisen another feud between the two factions.'[42]

Liverpool, as noted above, was the pivotal point for both networks as they extended their cover among migrant workers. The local president of the Irish Sons of Freedom held 'the Prerogative of England', responsible not only for passing 'the goods' across the Irish Sea but for the adjudication of disputes over eligibility, subscriptions, arrears and benefits within English lodges.[43] Similarly in the Northern Union, the Liverpool county delegate served as national delegate for England at the Board of Erin, responsible for delivering the goods to lodges – 'on receipt of their proportions of the usual expenses' – throughout Lancashire, Cheshire, Yorkshire and the Potteries, 'in all places towards the North of England where any number of the lower class of Irish are found'.[44] Radiating from Liverpool, the two networks provided cover and benefits for migrant workers in 'unskilled' and mobile sectors of the labour market, often excluded from organised forms of working-class collective mutuality. In artisan networks, tramping was a means of control in the interests of local closed shops: in Ribbon networks, tramping facilitated mobility in pursuit of whatever work was available, while offering 'political' sanctuary for members in flight from the Irish authorities.[45] Railway navvies appreciated the advantages of membership, and were increasingly prominent in both networks. Hanlon passed the Leinster 'goods' to Preston, Manchester, Stalybridge, Rotherham and Cheshire, where 'there are many of our friends in the Cheshire railroad that is now making, and they are adding daily to our

42] Special Committee meeting, 30 June 1840, CO 904/8 ff. 225–28.
43] Jones transcript, no. 20: Dardis and Jones to Wilson, 31 Mar. 1838. Wilson spent much time on problems at Manchester, concerning Nowlan, a penitent defaulter, and on the eligibility of army pensioners.
44] Extracts from communications of the informant AB, CO 904/8 ff. 309–17. The Newcastle lodge, however, received quarterly instructions through the Glasgow-based national delegate for Scotland.
45] E.J. Hobsbawm, 'The Tramping Artisan', in his *Labouring Men* (London, 1968), 38. I have found no evidence of Ribbon benefits covering migrant Irish women. However, some oaths included a form of 'exclusive dealing': 'I also declare and promise, that in towns and counties I will give preference of my dealings to my Catholic bretheren'; see Lieut-Gen. Blacker, Third Report of the Select Committee on Orange Lodges, Parliamentary Papers, 1835 (476), xvi, 9111–134.

number'.[46] 'The persons employed on the different lines of Railway are principally Irish and are to a great extent Members of the Ribbon Society', Terence Dogherty, the Wigan-based informer and lifelong member of the Northern Union reported in 1848, 'and in case of any outbreak in Ireland would have to join their brethren there or break their declarations.'[47] Building labourers were another group in similar need of cheap, flexible and mobile benefits. Of the fourteen main figures in the Preston 'Hibernicans', the cover for the local lodge of the Northern Union, eleven were labourers in the building industry, including James Woods, the chair and secretary, and his two deputies, Pat Clancy and Pat Gill, a cellar-dweller at Canal Bridge. There was a distinct Ulster complexion: of the six labourers whose origins are recorded, three came from Co. Fermanagh, two from Co. Cavan and one from Co. Leitrim in neighbouring Connacht. The remaining main figures were John Daly, a sailor and shopkeeper of Friar-gate; Anthony Heany, a chair-bottomer, one of three Preston Ribbonmen who went on tramp to Sheffield where each received two shillings on production of their cards; and John Kelly, a stone-mason, who was accorded expenses to travel to Liverpool to receive the 'renewals'.[48] Unfortunately, detailed information of this order is not available on the social composition of Liverpool Ribbonism other than at delegate level. However, it was Irish labourers, apparently trained in the secret ways and means of Ribbonism, who came to the fore in the major building strike of 1833:

> The late turn-out of mechanics and labourers has been almost entirely organized by Irish: they are all bound together by secret oaths, which were probably suggested by the Irish; and, although the Irish were the poorest mechanics, they took the lead in this turn-out. The English submitted in the most singular manner to be led by the nose.[49]

46] Jones transcript, no. 157: Hanlon, 17 July 1839. J.H. Treble, 'Irish Navvies in the North of England, 1830–1850', *Transport History*, Vol. 6 (1973), 243 mistakenly refers to Ribbonism as 'essentially an agrarian secret society ... with little or no relevance to the English social scene'.

47] Information of Terence Dogherty, 14 June 1848, HO 45/2416. Fearful of the navvies' reputation, the authorities decided not to raid the local Ribbon pub on the following Saturday, the next scheduled meeting of the lodge, since it was races-day and pay-day for railway labourers.

48] Examinations as to Ribbonism at Preston in Lancashire, HO 100/263 ff. 340–56.

49] State of the Irish Poor in Great Britain ... 1836 (40), xxxiv, 28, evidence of S. Holme; see also 23, evidence of Rev. Robinson.

As the pivot of both networks, Liverpool bore a disproportionate financial as well as administrative burden, to the point where tramp relief payments had briefly to be suspended in actuarial crisis in the late 1830s. The main port of entry, Liverpool was the first place of refuge for Irishmen on the run, including bankrupts, criminals and disreputable members of the 'friendship' such as Robert McDonnell.[50] After being discovered selling the 'goods' for his own profit, McDonnell, a brogue maker, had turned to embezzlement and other crime before fleeing to Liverpool in the early 1820s, where he tried to defraud a local tontine by faking his death. Counterfeiting and other crimes followed (including 'dilapidating and gutting the house he occupied in Liverpool') until he discovered his true vocation as a Protestant preacher in Sheffield.[51] While criminals were left to their own resources, bona fide members in flight from the authorities had the first call on funds. Admittedly, such cases were generally recognised as a national charge: there were regular collections in England, Terence Dogherty reported, 'to aid persons in Ireland to get them out of the Country or to employ Counsel in case they may require such assistance at their trials'.[52] Once their credentials had been checked and approved in Liverpool, some fugitives went on tramp. 'The different Lodges in England', Dublin Castle reported, 'are so many safe harbours for culprits who have committed murder or other serious crimes in this country, where they are not only protected, but are certain of obtaining employment in the neighbourhoods of such Lodges.'[53] As the authorities became more vigilant, escape routes were changed to avoid the main ports. James Quinn, a lodging house keeper in Ilkeston, offered funds to Pat Hayes to help his father escape, guaranteeing his safety provided he used small coastal ports in Wicklow and Wales and kept away from Liverpool: on arrival in Derbyshire, he would find well-paid employment, the company of many fellow countrymen and immunity from detection, as individual identity was concealed beneath furnace and coal slack dust.[54]

50] A freelance informer kept a close watch for fugitive criminals and bankrupts, see National Archives, Dublin: Outrage Papers, Co. Cavan, 1839, 23994C, enclosing a letter from 'A Friend', Gt Homer Street, Liverpool.
51] Statement of John Kelly, CO 904/7 ff. 77–92.
52] Information of Terence Dogherty, 14 June 1848, HO 45/2416.
53] Inspector-General Brownrigg's report, enclosed in Larcom, 19 Mar. 1863, HO 45/7522.
54] Appendix A, HO 45/7522.

While the cost of relieving fugitives may have been spread throughout the movement, Liverpool bore the expense of aiding distressed members – economic migrants rather than political refugees – passing through the port. As numbers increased inexorably, there were rumours within the Irish Sons of Freedom that 'the Men of Liverpool were on the point of charging the Country a certain sum for the *Renewals* and that they did not assist *tramps*'.[55] The Northern Union experienced similar difficulties, compounded by the withdrawal of 'respectable tradesmen' and funds in the wake of arrests in Ireland in 1839. The number of branches, McGloin reported, fell from 30 to 20; funeral processions became less lavish; and the relief fund, previously assessed on the branches quarterly, 'got into disuse in toto', ending the standard arrangement by which tramps holding 'regular certificates' were given a bed for the night and a payment of 1s 6d. As 'respectable tradesmen' quit the general committee, the Liverpool lodges of the Northern Union were left in the hands of 'labourers, warehousemen, and lumbers and varied only by an occasional publican', without the necessary funds to serve as reception and assistance centre for migrant members.[56]

In the Leinster network, Wilson did what he could for tramps out of his own meagre pocket: 'I have nothing to depend upon but my hand. I have to support a helpless and motherless family and when a distressed friend comes my heart relents.' One of his main initiatives during his term as president, an attempt to introduce a properly-funded and administered system of tramp relief, left him so disillusioned that he decided to tender his resignation:

> Any good rules I propose I cannot get them carried into effect to meet the wants of distressed tramps. I proposed that each member should pay 1d per month that it be lodged in the hands of Mr Carrick and according as any distressed friend would come and apply to me for assistance for me to give a note to Carrick for the price of his bed and supper. Carrick to keep all these dockets and get credit for nothing at the quarterly settlement but what he could provide a docket for ... all we could get to pay was 22 men ... all my labour was in vain in introducing good discipline among them, they are all generals and no privates.[57]

55] Jones transcript, no. 49: Dardis and Jones to Wilson, 28 May 1838.
56] CO 904/8 ff. 82–89.
57] Jones transcript, no. 80: Wilson, 22 Aug. 1838. His wife died soon after he was elected president; see no. 38: Wilson, 2 May 1838.

Except at such times of actuarial crisis, however, the payment of relief at Liverpool seems to have been a matter of routine for members with regular certificates or 'cards', facilitating much two-way movement across the Irish Sea. Assessment of the socio-economic status of these pre-Famine migrants is particularly problematic. Considerable numbers of artisans and textile workers, victims of the delayed economic consequences of the Act of Union and the de-industrialisation of peripheral areas, came to Britain in search of similar employment, but were obliged to take whatever work was available. Denis Gilgun, an important witness at the trials in Ireland, moved back and forth between Co. Cavan and Preston in the late 1830s, aided by relief obtained from Brady's pub in Chistenhall Street, Liverpool. However, he was unable to continue in his trade as shoemaker in Preston, taking work as a builders' labourer. On his final return journey, Gilgun surrendered his 'card', issued by fellow labourer James Woods, 'headsman and Secretary' of the Preston Hibernicans, in return for relief and a new card signed in his presence by Brady, 'which I gave on my return to Ireland to my County Master McDonald, and continued a Ribbonman as before'.[58] Terence Dogherty appears more fortunate: having left Co. Cavan for Lancashire in the early 1820s, he was able to continue his trade as weaver, and his membership of the Northern Union, first in Manchester, then at Bolton, and finally in Wigan. When he eventually left Wigan in the trade depression of 1848 to return to Co. Cavan, however, he forgot to obtain a certificate from Terence McGlynn, the local delegate, and was thus refused admission to the lodge at Killeshandra. He travelled back to Wigan for the necessary documentation, for which he was charged an excessive re-admission fee of three shillings (one reason, perhaps, why he suddenly turned informer?), stopping off on return at John Carroll's pub in Crosbie Street, Liverpool to obtain one shilling in relief, on production of the valued certificate, from James Mullen, the Lancashire county delegate.[59]

Given its nodal location, Liverpool figured prominently in the unity discussions of 1838, providing a 'neutral' venue away from regional rivalry, and offering a ready-made communications network: 'as all persons going on tramp to England would have to call in Liverpool, they would be able to send word to all parts of Ireland'.[60] After the preliminary discussions in

58] Statement of Denis Gilgun, 15 Dec. 1840, HO 100/263 ff. 346–50. Gilgun had once run a Ribbon pub in Enniskillen.
59] Statement of Terence Dogherty, 6 July 1848, HO 45/2416.
60] Jones transcript, no. 75: Jones, 6 Aug. 1838.

Belfast in April, Wilson was instructed to report on 'the determination of the friends belonging to the Hibernians in Liverpool':

> If they act for the welfare of their native land they will join with these persons whose wish it is to see their native land free. The motto of every honest Irishman should be unite and free your native land.[61]

Wilson was an enthusiastic supporter of any arrangement that would 'cement all Roman Catholics in one bond of Brotherly love. Nothing would be more gratifying to me as to be in unity with men who address the same God, believe in the same Creed, kneel at the same Altar, and their Cause our Cause.' However, his efforts to institute the alliance in Liverpool were hindered by misinformation – he discovered that Patrick Cunningham, named at Belfast as the delegate of the Hibernians, had in fact withdrawn from office and 'felt more easy in his mind than when he communicated with Ireland, that he was now within the bounds of his Church and would continue so'[62] – and by the hostility of some of the current officers who remained loyal to 'Captain' Rice, President of the Board of Erin for the three kingdoms, specifically excluded from the Belfast unity discussions (along with his close associate, 'Captain' McGomley) on allegations of financial misdealing and peculation.

Wilson was one of four Liverpool representatives at the joint general board in Dublin on 1 July – attended by delegates from Antrim, Armagh, Down, Monaghan, Longford, Louth, Roscommon, Wicklow, Meath, Kildare and Dublin – which formally instituted the merger as the United Irish Sons of Freedom and Sons of the Shamrock and adopted 'a new form of Certificate to prevent persons that are opposed to us from being pawned upon us'.[63] The others were Thomas McConvill(e), local president of the Hibernians, described as 'the most violent advocate for the continuance of secret correspondence with Ireland'; Patrick Cavanagh (or Kavanagh), secretary of the Liverpool Hibernian Benevolent Burial Society, and general secretary of the Northern Union in Liverpool; and Thomas Burns, a pig jobber at the slaughter yard in Batchelor Street, president of the First Hibernian Friendly Society.[64] 'You may rest satisfied that England is with us to a man', Richard Jones reported in an optimistic circular letter, calling

61] Jones transcript, no. 33: Jones, 24 Apr. 1838.
62] Jones transcript, no. 38: Wilson, 2 May 1838.
63] Jones transcript, no. 66: Jones, 2 July, 1838.
64] Delegates in Liverpool since 1830, CO 904/8 ff. 79–80.

upon every delegate 'to convince the persons in your part of the Country of the folly of any longer adhering to Rice and his bloody faction'. To seal the union, the next joint board was to be held in Liverpool on 30 September: 'The Chief reason for having the meeting at Liverpool was that it would strike at the Root of the evil and as the persons there were from the different Counties in Ireland that they would be able to send Information from it to their friends of the folly of any longer being kept separated by any man or men'.[65]

Wilson returned from Dublin determined to ensure the success of the Liverpool board. Within a week, he obtained agreement for a unified structure within Liverpool itself, including a system of fines to curb those who placed regional loyalties and rivalries above national interest:

> Third, that any Officer or members belonging to either parties casting disrespectful allusions to on each others County or province or opposing each other will be tried by a mixed Committee – will be vested with power to levy the following fines for disrespectful allusions 5s, striking 5s, 10s if done unfairly.[66]

Wilson's efforts, and those of Jones in Dublin, were severely hampered in August, however, when Rice's supporters arranged a separate board at Dundalk. Among the three delegates from England was George Hamill, publican of the Grapes Inn, Liverpool headquarters of the Northern Union, and allegedly a former 'Servant man to Rice'.[67] Angered by the double-dealing of Reilly and the pro-Rice faction in Ireland – there were rumours that Rice had supplied the police with information about the Dublin 1 July board – Jones wrote to Wilson, insisting that matters be set straight in Liverpool:

> Dear Friend, you will please shew this to our friends Messrs Gonville [sic] and Kavenagh [sic] and send us word what the men of England are determined to do, we send them our advice which is as follows – that if they do not join with those persons who have the welfare of their Country at heart, that they in Justice to the land that gave them birth should withdraw from the society for ever, and why? Because they have sent their President and Secretary to make a union and empowered them with authority to do so.[68]

65] Jones transcript, no. 67: Jones, 3 July 1838.
66] Jones transcript, no. 73: Wilson, 31 July 1838.
67] Jones transcript, nos 191: Wilson, 15 Aug., and 78: Wilson, 20 Aug. 1838.
68] Jones transcript, no. 77: Jones, 19 Aug. 1838.

Although Cavanagh still appeared to favour the union, Hamill proved unrepentant and obstructive on return from Dundalk.[69] When the joint board finally assembled at Carrick's pub in Liverpool, Wilson, it seems, was the only local representative present.

One or two Irish delegates were unable to attend on account of the harvest ('it being the hurry time of business'),[70] but there were representatives from 'every County in the North', including two notable former opponents, James Brady of Co. Cavan and Michael O'Neal of Ballinamuck, Co. Longford. Besides Wilson, there was one other English delegate, Peter Fitzsimmons of Newcastle, another who had recently changed allegiance. Jones issued an upbeat circular report: 'We had representatives from every county in Ulster at our last meeting and our cause is progressing in the other Counties in England ... all the north of England is with us. The opponents to Freedom are on their last legs.' In a stock-taking exercise, he reported that tramp relief, henceforth to be restricted to the young, would be administered by three presidents in England: Wilson at Liverpool, Fitzsimmons at Newcastle, and Thomas Donoghue in Manchester. In Ireland, the united network covered every county in the north and midlands, but had yet to extend to Clare, Kerry, Limerick, Cork, Waterford, Kilkenny, Wexford, Galway, Sligo and Mayo.[71]

Further progress was halted by a number of factors: the duplicitous behaviour of the 'wretches' Cavanagh and McConvill(e), who sought to involve the clergy;[72] Wilson's unexpected dismissal from office, his earlier offer of resignation having been refused;[73] and the staunch anti-merger stance of his successor, Hanlon, who advised Jones to terminate talks with the deceitful 'Northerns': 'They will never adhere to any argument ... they want to outgeneral you'.[74] The presence of informers, despatched from Ireland, added to mutual hostility and suspicion.[75] Then came news of Jones's arrest and the seizure of his papers, describing 'the history of the Ribbon Society for the last two years'.[76] 'All the usual proceedings are now

69] Jones transcript, no. 84: Wilson, 18 Sept. 1838.
70] Jones transcript, nos 88 and 89: letters of apology from Lennon and Roche.
71] Jones transcript, nos 91, 96 and 97: Jones 7 and 19 Oct. 1838.
72] Jones transcript, no. 100: Jones, 26 Oct. 1838.
73] Jones transcript, nos 84 and 141: Wilson, 18 Sept. 1838 and 26 June 1839.
74] Jones transcript, no. 173: Hanlon, 2 Aug. 1839.
75] Jones transcript, no. 182: Jones, 9 Sept. 1839.
76] Jones was the first to be tried under new legislation in Ireland, 2 and 3 Victoria cap. 74, declaring illegal associations which communicated by secret signs and passwords.

suspended', McGloin reported, 'and intended to be so until after the Spring Assizes. No new members are admitted – no passwords circulated (as I understand), and no meetings held, except of the leaders whose proceedings are kept secret from the members at large.'[77]

'Tho' Ribbonism has received a great blow', McGloin concluded a few months later, 'it would be absurd to imagine it is extinguished.' During two days of 'drinking and squabbling' at the English national board at the Sefton Arms in St Helens in July 1840, all thirteen delegates, representing Bolton, Sheffield, Newcastle, Chester and other northern towns, reported a substantial decline in numbers. In Liverpool, regular members of the Northern Union were down to 320 from a total of 1350 three years previously. Thomas Burns was appointed national delegate, but this caused displeasure among those who now wished to by-pass Liverpool: 'Another division then occurred caused by a letter recd. from Michael Magrath, Delegate at Whitehaven, on the part of delegates in Cumberland, Durham, etc denying that they were under the jurisdiction of the Liverpool district and would form another board for themselves to communicate with Ireland'.[78]

* * * * *

'General Union among Irishmen', one of the quarterly passwords, proved impossible to effect, but Ribbonism contributed much to the construction of a sectarian *national* identity among the Liverpool Irish. Irish migrants were notorious for their intense regional and local loyalties, for importing their factional feuds, but such 'private battles' soon gave way to 'sectarian violence' in Liverpool, registering a wider sense of national identity.[79] Ribbonism was the proactive force in this sectarian implantation, able to extend its constituency among other Catholic migrants, while Orangeism, yet to be appropriated by the local Tory establishment, lacked resonance

77] Report of interview of McGloin, 27 Dec. 1839, CO 904/7 ff. 465–70. McGloin referred to the presence of a third network in Liverpool, which was 'seated in Connaught and has its head in Sligo', but I have found no other mention of it. At this stage a member of the Irish Constabulary Force was sent to Liverpool; see HO 43/58 f. 393.
78] Reports dated 26 July and 2 and 30 Sept. 1839, CO 904/8 ff. 225–28.
79] See the useful distinctions drawn by Anne Bryson in her study of 'Riotous Liverpool, 1815–1860', in *Popular Politics, Riot and Labour: Essays in Liverpool History 1790–1940*, ed. John Belchem (Liverpool, 1992), 98–134.

beyond the limited ranks of immigrant Ulster Protestants.[80] In organisational terms, Ribbonism remained a minority movement, strongest among
migrants from Ulster and adjoining counties, but its sectarian mentality
helped to construct a wider sense of national identity and affiliation in
which Catholic and Irish became synonymous. Having imported their
fierce sectarian loyalty – 'these silly people retaining here', Head Constable
Whitty reported, 'the absurd enmities which disgraced and degraded them
at home'[81] – the Ribbonmen from the north were to rally their fellow
countrymen and co-religionists against the hereditary enemy, the Orangemen. 'The Catholic labourers from the South of Ireland', Whitty later
observed, 'seldom belong to Ribbon Lodges, but they share freely in the
Catholic hatred of Orangeism, and as they are the more numerous, and not
the least reckless body, they are here, in times of disturbance the most
difficult to manage.'[82] Throughout the 1820s and 1830s, the Irish Catholics,
by force of numbers and/or reputation, were able to prevent the Orange
Order taking to the streets on 12 July.[83]

This sectarian national awareness was fostered first in the pub, later (as
the next essay shows) by the parish. Dublin Castle asked the Liverpool
police to keep a close watch on Jack Langan, a former Irish champion boxer,
who ran the most famous 'Irish' pub, strategically positioned opposite
Clarence Dock, the disembarkation point for Irish passenger traffic – it
was immediately recognisable by the effigy of St Patrick, shamrock in
hand, high on its walls. Langan enjoyed considerable fame and fortune in
Liverpool – his estate was valued at over £20 000 on his death in 1846 –
appearing on the platform when his hero, Daniel O'Connell, visited the
town. After close surveillance, the police concluded that the former pugilist
was 'too wealthy and too prudent' to engage in secret Ribbon activity.[84]

80] On the origins of Orangeism in Liverpool, see Frank Neal, *Sectarian Violence:
The Liverpool Experience 1819–1914* (Manchester, 1988), 17–32.
81] State of the Irish Poor in Great Britain … 1836 (40), xxxiv, 21.
82] Whitty's report, enclosed in Rushton, 2 Apr. 1842, CO 904/9.
83] The worst violence occurred in 1835, as detailed in P. M'Connell's evidence in
Third Report of the Select Committee on Orange Lodges, Parliamentary Papers,
1835 (476), xvi, 6620–22: 'a very determined outrage committed by the Roman
Catholics at Liverpool, crying out, "Ten pounds the head of an Orangeman";
disturbing the peace of the whole town; knocked down the authorities, injuring
several of the police, and displaying a degree of barbarous ferocity hardly ever
equalled in this country'.
84] Liverpool Police Office, 27 May 1839, CO 904/7 f. 192. *Liverpool Mercury*, 19
June 1846. John Denvir, *The Life Story of an Old Rebel* (Dublin, 1910), 3–4 and 52.

Lacking such celebrity, other Irish publicans undertook Ribbonite office, concealing the secret operations behind their promotion of legally-approved convivial and bibulous forms of associational culture. Hugh McAnulty, a Grayson Street publican and one of the founders of the Hibernian Benevolent Society, was 'by far the best-known man in Ireland', regularly representing Liverpool at the Board of Erin until his death in the mid-1830s. His various responsibilities were assumed by George Hamill, who married his widow, took over the pub, and attended the Board three or four times (including the pro-Rice assembly at Dundalk) before his own death a couple of years later. Undaunted, the twice-widowed Mrs Hamill proved a jealous guardian of the Ribbon tradition, one of several female licensees who provided important services for a male-based, pub-centred culture of secrecy.[85] Under cover of the legally-approved Provident Friendly Society, the Grapes Inn remained the most important Ribbonite venue in Liverpool – 'the general Box is kept at the Widow Hamills, Grayson Street which is therefore Head Quarters'. Some publicans, however, proved reluctant to commit themselves beyond the provision of premises. John McArdle, an Ulster Catholic by birth, hosted a number of societies at his Crosbie Street pub, famous for its Sunday night readings from *The Nation* – including the Second Hibernian Friendly Society, the Third Hibernian Mechanical Society, and one of the earliest lodges of the Ancient Order of Hibernians – some of which, as the action brought against him in 1842 revealed, were undoubtedly a cover for Ribbon activities. According to informers, however, McArdle was 'a decent and honourable man who always opposed the continuation of Secret Communication with Ireland'. Having the misfortune to be appointed Liverpool delegate at the time of the arrests and trials of 1840, he chose not to fulfil his duties. An accomplished ethnic entrepreneur, McArdle briefly diversified into the grocery and provision trade to cater for the temperance fad in the Irish community following a visit by Father Mathew.[86] In 1842, by which time the movement was past its peak, Whitty calculated that there were still thirteen Ribbon pubs in Liverpool, although most were 'used only as houses of resort, for ordinary

---

85] Widow McNamara provided similar services at her jerry shop in Union Street, Preston; see Gilgun's statement, 5 Dec. 1840, HO 100/263 ff. 346–50. Women also provided the premises for clerically-approved societies, such as the St Anthony's Society at Ellen Wood's, Cockspur Street, and the Roman Catholic Teetotal Association at Mrs Mountain's, Flood Street, Liverpool.
86] Delegates in Liverpool since 1830, CO 904/8 ff. 79–80. Denvir, *Life Story*, 15–16.

rather than special communication'.[87] At some Irish pubs, however, the old faction-fighting culture still prevailed, as at the alehouse in Sawney Pope Street, venue of the Molly Maguires. In this Liverpudlian manifestation, the Mollies were sworn to give mutual help, an insult to one 'being taken as an insult to all, for which is sought satisfaction'.[88]

Pubs and publicans were essential to the operation of Liverpool Ribbonism, but there was a teetotal nationalist alternative. While passing through Liverpool to advocate total abstinence, James McKenna admitted that 'the repeal of the Union is the grand object of his mission'. A schoolmaster and founder of several Ribbon lodges in Ireland, McKenna insisted that if the people 'kept themselves sober, we would not be now under the British yoke ... there is no way of freeing ourselves from that odious Impost but by uniting the Catholic Population of the two countrys [sic] together as one body, to do away with Drunkenness'.[89] The secretary of the Roman Catholic Total Abstinence Association was John Doyle, but it is not clear whether this was the same person as the stout and pugnacious tailor, Johnny Doyle of Lumber Street, a committee member of the Liverpool Hibernian Benevolent Burial Society, and Cunningham's replacement as Liverpool delegate to the General Board – a number of other Doyles (Peter, Patrick, Terry and Kenny) were prominent office-holders in the Northern Union.[90] In 1848, delegates from the Irish Confederation, the militant wing of 'Young Ireland', were received at James Lennon's Temperance Hotel in Houghton Street, regarded by J.D. Balfe, a high-placed informer, as the centre of insurrectionary planning. The extension of Confederate Clubs throughout Liverpool was coordinated by another tailor, James

87] Whitty's report, 2 Apr. 1842, C.O. 904/9 ff. 210–15.
88] *Liverpool Journal*, 17 Apr. 1858, quoted in Anne Bryson, 'Riot and its Control in Liverpool, 1815–1860', unpublished MPhil thesis, Open University, 1989. The Molly Maguires are best known for their violent and intimidatory industrial tactics in the anthracite coal region of northern Pennsylvania.
89] Kemmis and Carmichael, 29 Sept. 1838, CO 904/7 f. 100. For the remarkable impact of Father Mathew's visit to Liverpool in 1843 (during which the young Denvir took the pledge three times), see Denvir, *Life Story*, 12–17, and Thomas Burke, *Catholic History of Liverpool* (Liverpool, 1910), 73–74.
90] See the printed rules and regulations of the association in CO 904/7 ff. 160–62. On the Doyles, see CO 904/8 ff. 79–80. Another tailor, Mark Brannon, served as Liverpool delegate until his expulsion in 1832. A sample of the 1851 census has shown that 57.5 per cent of workers in this sweated trade were Irish; see I.C. Taylor, '"Black Spot on the Mersey": a Study of Environment and Society in 18th and 19th Century Liverpool', unpublished PhD thesis, University of Liverpool, 1976, 7.

2. J.A. Picton, architect, local historian and 'annalist' of Liverpool, from the *Liverpool Leader Album*, 1874.

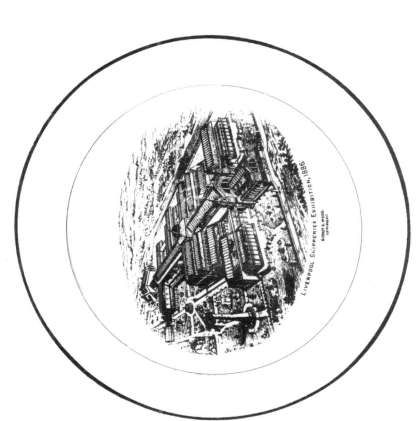

1. Liverpool Shipperies Exhibition plate, 1886, from the International Exhibition of Navigation, Commerce and Industry held at Wavertree.

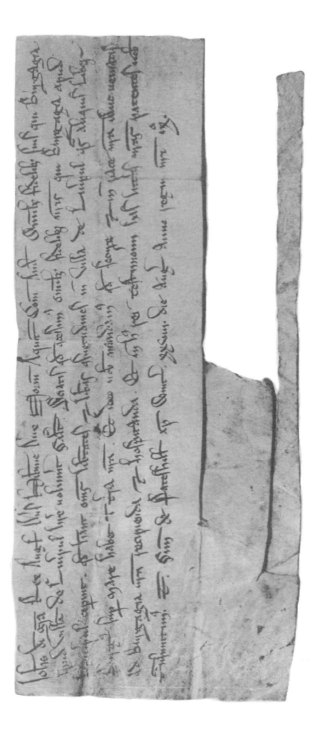

3. Letters Patent of King John, founding the Town of Liverpool, 28 August, 1207. *Free translation* 'John, by the grace of God, King of England, Lord of Ireland, Duke of Normandy and Aquitaine, Count of Anjou, to all his faithful subjects who wish to have burgage-holdings in the township of Liverpul, greeting. Know ye that we have granted to all our faithful subjects who take burgage-holdings in Liverpul that they shall enjoy within the township of Liverpul all the liberties and free customs which any free borough upon the sea hath within our land. Wherefore we command that ye come hither unmolested and under our protection to receive and dwell in our burgage-holdings. In witness whereof we send unto you these our letters patent. Witness, Simon de Pateshill. At Winchester, the twenty-eighth day of August, in the ninth year of our reign.'

PROGRAMME: PART ONE

A Selection of Liverpool Music chosen from the following items and sung by A. L. Lloyd and Ewan MacColl (Folksingers), with Alf Edwards (Concertina): The Ballad of Johnny Todd; Paddy West; Blow the Man Down; The Black Ball Line; Van Diemens Land; The Liverpool Girls; Maggie May; The Liverpool Landlady; The Birkenhead Ferryboat Shanty, etc., introduced by Fritz Spiegl, with readings by Bernard Miles.

INTERVAL OF FIFTEEN MINUTES

PART TWO

EMILIA DI LIVERPOOL

Melodrama Semi-serio

Poesia del Signor Giuseppe Checcherini : Musica del Maestro Signor Gaetano Donizetti

Emilia (*Soprano*) : Doreen Murray

Candida (*Emilia's Companion*) : Barbara Delano Laing

Bettina (*Soprano*) : Barbara Delano Laing

Colonello Villars, alias Tompson (*Tenor*) : Alexander Young

Claudio di Liverpool (*Baritone*) : Norman Platt

Conte Asdrubale (*Baritone*) : William Coombes

Narrator : Bernard Miles

(First performance in England and first modern performance)

6

Donizetti seems to have had a peculiar liking for operatic libretti on English subjects. Apart from *Emilia di Liverpool* he also wrote *Il Castello di Kenilworth* (1829), *Anna Bolena* (1830), *Rosmonda di Inghilterra* (1834), *Lucia di Lammermoor* (1835) and *Roberto d'Essex, Conte d'Essex* (1837), and one would be tempted to attribute this predilection to his supposed descent from a Scotsman of the name of Don(ald) Izett, had not this theory been recently discounted. *Emilia di Liverpool* dates from 1824 and although a comparatively early work it is the seventeenth of the composer's seventy-odd operas. The libretto by Giuseppe Checcherini is entitled *L'Eremitaggio di Liverpool* (sic) and was published in 1888; Schonenberger of Paris brought out a vocal

4. [*left*] Postcard celebrating the 700th anniversary of the granting of letters patent to Liverpool, 1907.

5. [*above*] From the programme of the concert to celebrate the 750th anniversary of the granting of letters patent to Liverpool, 1957.

6. [*left*] Liverpool and Africa exhibition at Liverpool Library, 1957. Dr Chandler, Councillor Edwards and Father Huddlestone examine an exhibit.

7. [*above*] Multi-racial Community exhibition, Toxteth Library, 1979.

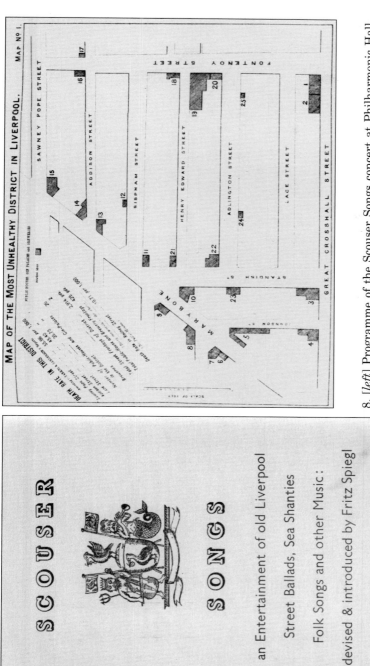

8. [*left*] Programme of the Scouser Songs concert at Philharmonic Hall, Liverpool, 3 March 1962.

9. [*above*] Map of the most unhealthy district in Liverpool, by Nathaniel Smyth, c. 1875. As the numbers indicate, there was a public house on virtually every corner.

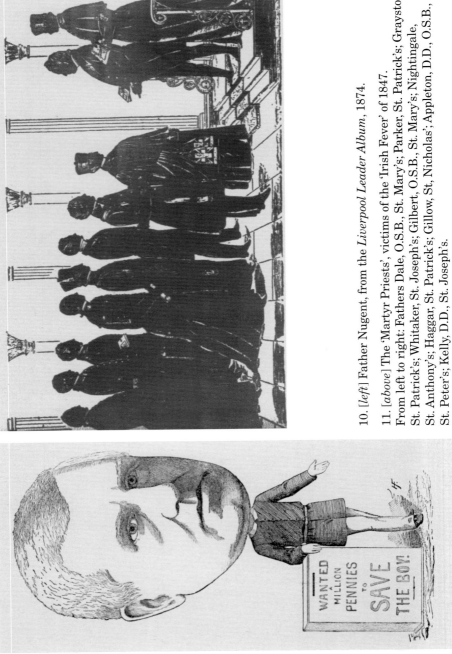

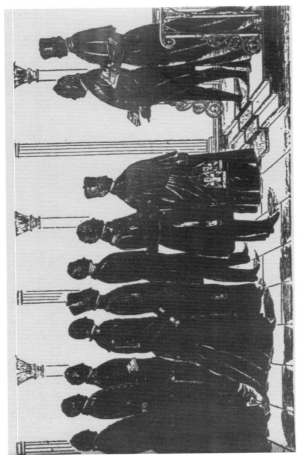

10. [*left*] Father Nugent, from the *Liverpool Leader Album*, 1874.

11. [*above*] The 'Martyr Priests', victims of the 'Irish Fever' of 1847. From left to right: Fathers Dale, O.S.B., St. Mary's; Parker, St. Patrick's; Grayston, St. Patrick's; Whitaker, St. Joseph's; Gilbert, O.S.B., St. Mary's; Nightingale, St. Anthony's; Haggar, St. Patrick's; Gillow, St, Nicholas'; Appleton, D.D., O.S.B., St. Peter's; Kelly, D.D., St. Joseph's.

13. Samuel Holme, Mayor of Liverpool 1852-3, by E. Patten.

12. Photograph by T. Burke of the 'Dandy' Patrick Byrne memorial drinking fountain, Scotland Road, late nineteenth century.

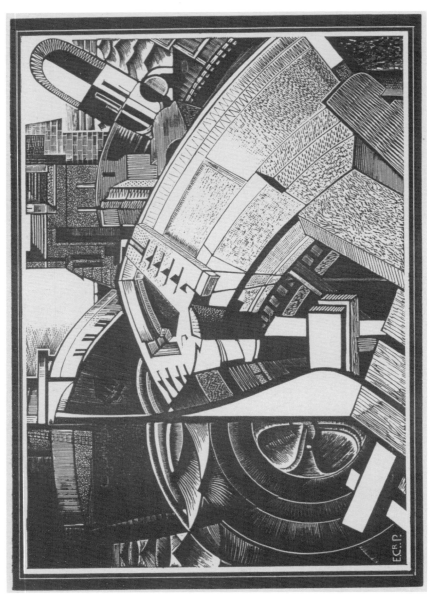

14. Wood engraving by Edward Carter-Preston, one of a series on Liverpool Cathedral themes produced in the nineteen thirties.

Laffin, using James Ord's temperance coffee-house, venue of the Roman Catholic Total Abstinence Benevolent Society, as his operational base.[91]

Liverpool remained notoriously resistant to Chartist implantation,[92] but it occupies the largest single file in the Home Office Disturbance Papers for 1848. Its Irish population, calculated at 90 000 to 100 000, posed a serious physical threat, compounded by alarming intelligence reports from New York, pointing ominously to Liverpool as the landing-stage for the first squads of an 'Irish Brigade' equipped with American 'republican spirit and military science'. Convinced of the efficacy of physical force by events in revolutionary Europe, 'the springtime of the peoples', the Liverpool leadership cadre (studied in Chapter 5, below) readily embraced the direct action of John Mitchel's Irish Confederation, and duly prepared to assist nationalist revolution across the Irish Sea.[93] After Mitchel's arrest and conviction, Terence Bellew McManus promised the junta in Dublin that, come the day of the rising, his fellow Liverpool Confederates would seize a couple of the largest Irish steamers in Liverpool, load them with arms and ammunition taken from Chester Castle, and proceed to Ireland. As a diversionary ploy, the port of Liverpool was to be crippled by setting blaze at low tide to quayside cotton warehouses, 'filled with material as inflammatory as the dried grass of a prairie'.[94] To this end, the Liverpool Confederates – eschewing O'Connellite restraint and Chartist open agitation – developed in paramilitary fashion, revivifying the Ribbonite culture of secrecy (alas not immune to turn-coats and informers) to establish a network of armed clubs in sympathetic pubs, temperance hotels and private houses.

The local authorities, alarmed by the rapid spread of the clubs, placed the town under a state of siege. A specially-appointed committee of magistrates

91] John Belchem, 'Liverpool in the Year of Revolution: the Political and Associational Culture of the Irish Immigrant Community in 1848' in *Popular Politics, Riot and Labour*, ed. Belchem, 77. See also Takashi Koseki, 'John Donnellan Balfe and 1848: a note on a Confederate Informer', *Saothar*, Vol. 23 (1998), 25–32.

92] Kevin Moore, '"This Whig and Tory Town": Popular Politics in Liverpool in the Chartist Era', in *Popular Politics, Riot and Labour*, ed. Belchem, 38–67.

93] I cannot agree with Frank Neal's assertion that the Confederates were 'men of no standing in Liverpool, indicative of the lack of political or organizational "weight"'; F. Neal, *Sectarian Violence: The Liverpool Experience* (Manchester, 1988), 124.

94] Charles Gavan Duffy, *My Life in Two Hemispheres* (2 vols, London, 1898), Vol. I, 277–78. T.G. McAllister, *Terence Bellew McManus 1811(?)–1861* (Maynooth, 1972), 11–12. Diocese of Clogher Archives, Bishop's House, Monaghan: Clark Compendium, envelope D f.636.

reported that some 30 to 40 secret clubs were in existence by early July – I
have succeeded in identifying 23 of them (see Table 3.1) – each capable of
assembling 2000–4000 armed men, unannounced, on the streets. Armed
insurrection in Liverpool was 'very probable and indeed almost certain if
there be an Insurrection in Ireland ... though a political, might (in the
outset) be the ostensible motive - the real one would soon appear; a trium-
phant armed mob in a rich town would not respect property or life'.[95] A
number of emergency measures were taken: the police force was hurriedly
expanded (at the expense of usual standards as 'it was found impracticable
to take the usual precautions for enquiry into the Characters of the
Candidates'); some 12 000 special constables were sworn in (one of their
batons was displayed at the Historical Exhibition of Liverpool Antiquities
in 1907); military reinforcements were despatched to a vast tented camp at
Everton (financial responsibility for which was later a matter of considerable controversy); and, in the absence of a suitable warship, armed marines
were put aboard the *Redwing*, a government tender boat on the Mersey.[96]
Throughout the 'anticipated disturbances', John Bramley-Moore, Tory
chairman of the Dock Committee and the incoming mayor, had 'a bed placed
in the Albert Dock Warehouses that he might be ready for any emergency'.[97]

Within hours of the introduction of the Habeas Corpus Suspension Bill
in Ireland on 22 July, the mayor, magistrates and other leading citizens
petitioned for its provisions to be extended to Liverpool, where there were
fears of a rising that very night.[98] William Rathbone, a celebrated Liberal,
explained the circumstances to his daughter:

> 100,000 Irish in Liverpool unemployed, and Chartists to join, are
> fearful materials for mischief ... our open docks and warehouses leave
> us much at the mercy of the incendiary ... The English law is defective,
> we cannot search for arms when we know where they are; we cannot
> incarcerate the leaders, though preaching rebellion or virtually such,

---

95] Report of the Committee of Magistrates appointed at a General Meeting of
Magistrates held on 8 July 1848, HO45/2410B.
96] Horsfall, 25–26 July, HO45/2410B. See also, John Saville, *1848: The British
State and the Chartist Movement* (Cambridge, 1987), 154–55.
97] 'The Mayor at the Albert Dock warehouses', *Jones*, 18 Nov. 1848.
98] C.B. Banning, Post Office, Liverpool, 22 July, and Horsfall, 24 July, HO45/
2410B. *Liverpool Mercury* 25 July and 1 Aug. 1848, for the counter-petition of those
who thought suspension would be 'an unnecessary interference with the liberty of
the subject ... an indelible stain on the town of Liverpool'.

Table 3.1 Irish Confederate Clubs in Liverpool and Birkenhead, 1848

Name	Venue	Officer/Delegate
Liverpool		
1: Bermuda	Gt Howard Street	—
2: Oliver Bond	46 Naylor Street	—
3: Brian Boru	40 Gilbert Street	Patrick O'Hanlon
4: Byrne	—	—
5: Connaught Rangers	Addison Street	—
6: Davis (formerly Faugh a Ballagh)	—	Peter Ryan
7: Emmet	32 Rose Place	—
8: Lord Edward	—	—
9: Erin's Hope	—	—
10: Felon's Brigade	—	—
11: Felon's Hope	Ord's Temperance Hotel	Murphy
12: Bagenal Harvey	Bevington Bush	Dr O'Donnell
13: Liberator	Newsham Street	—
14: John Mitchel	47 Thomas Street	Ferrell and Perkins
15: Roger O'Moore	—	—
16: Owen Roe O'Neill	Ord's Temperance Hotel	Williamson
17: William Orr	—	—
18: Hamilton Rowan	—	—
19: St Patrick	New Bird Street	Martin Boshell
20: Sarsfield	—	Edward Murphy
21: Tom Steele	—	John Clifford
22: Wolfe Tone	—	—
23: '82 Club, Liverpool	—	T.B. McManus
	Eldon Place	—
	52 Hurst Street	—
	Milton Street	Dr Reynolds
	Limekiln Lane	Matthew Somers
	Dublin Street	Matthew Somers
Birkenhead		
John Frost	—	—
John Mitchel	Davis Street	Robert Hopper

Source: Reprinted from John Belchem (ed.), *Popular Politics, Riot and Labour: Essays in Liverpool History, 1790–1940* (Liverpool, 1992), 96.

though not legally; nor can we enter the houses where clubs we *know* meet, and the most inflammatory and rebellious language is used; yet Liverpool is the high road to and from Ireland, a post which a general would say the *country's safety* required to be guarded; yet her majesty's Ministers leave us very much to ourselves, and in some degree tie our hands by their reserve.[99]

Frustrated by Whitehall, the local authorities set legal objections aside to raid club premises. By chance, they stumbled across the Confederate minute book, a detailed record of committee membership and meetings. With its leaders in flight and most of its weapons seized – the major arms cache included 500 cutlasses and some canisters of gunpowder concealed in a cellar[100] – Confederate conspiracy was rendered powerless on the eve of the Irish rising. Bitterly disappointed, McManus (who had previously chartered three steamers to be on standby ready to sail to Wexford) made personal amends at Ballingarry, proving himself 'the boldest fellow among the entire body of insurgents'.[101]

The authorities remained on the alert, alarmed by intelligence reports from New York pointing ominously to Liverpool as the landing-stage for the first squads of the 'Irish Brigade', prototype Fenians with an officer corps drilled in the American militia, the latest firearms technology (including Colt revolvers) to supplement the native pike, and battle-hardened veterans of the Mexican war.[102] A couple of members of the advanced guard of the Brigade were spotted in Liverpool, tailed to Dublin, arrested and held without charge. Throughout the summer, the Liverpool authorities eagerly awaited the opportunity to apprehend the squads on arrival in British waters. When the *John R. Skiddy*, reportedly carrying the first contingent, crossed the bar, the mayor telegraphed her master and despatched three detectives by steam-tug to board and search the vessel off Crosby lightship. 'We have had a very rigid enquiry instituted', Horsfall reported to the Home Office, 'and there does not appear to be any person of a suspicious or even of a questionable character on board … or any supply

99] W. Rathbone to Mrs Paget, 23 July 1848, quoted in E.A. Rathbone (ed.), *Records of the Rathbone Family* (Edinburgh, 1913), 223–24.
100] Horsfall, 3 Aug., HO45/2410B.
101] For McManus's own narrative of events, see Denis Gwynn, *Young Ireland and 1848*, (Cork, 1949), Appendix 3.
102] For a full account, see John Belchem, 'Republican Spirit and Military Science: The "Irish Brigade" and Irish-American Nationalism in 1848', *Irish Historical Studies*, Vol. 29 (1994), 44–64.

of either arms or ammunition.'[103] Thereafter, Horsfall adopted a less conspicuous approach. Two specially-trained local police officers were stationed at the docks along with a detective from the Dublin force to watch all American arrivals, and work began on a special telegraph link to hasten communication with Clarendon in Dublin, with whom Horsfall was already in direct correspondence.[104] Occasionally, some suspicious types were spotted, as for example the 'two athletic Tipperary men', on the *Columbus*, 'whose conversation during the Passage shewed them to be interested in Irish affairs': they were kept under surveillance by a police officer as they crossed to Dublin. Most arrivals, however, were either old, infirm or lowly, 'that order of persons who appear incapable of taking any but the most subordinate part in a seditious or rebellious movement'. By the end of September, Horsfall began to doubt whether 'anything is to be apprehended of any arrivals from America worthy of consideration'.[105] It was not until March 1849, however, that Head Constable Dowling felt sufficient confidence in the restoration of tranquillity to dispense with the 55 additional officers (30 warehouse guards and 25 'armed Patrols on the outskirts') hastily added to the force when alarm was at its height.[106]

Several years later, the National Brotherhood of St Patrick, a legal cover for Fenianism, was launched at a fund-raising meeting in Liverpool for the funeral of the exiled McManus. The funeral in Dublin, a prototype exercise in Irish political/funereal art, brought the Irish Republican Brotherhood (IRB) to public attention.[107] After the experience of 1848, however, the Liverpool-Irish middle class, aware of the hardening of host attitudes to the Irish, were reluctant to place themselves at the head of physical force nationalism. Indeed, they endeavoured to sever links between nationalism, Ribbonism and the pub; hence, the emphasis shifted from bibulous conviviality, oath-taking rituals and collective mutuality to cultural nationalism. Through its central branch in Liverpool, the Brotherhood of St Patrick promoted a range of recreational and cultural projects: an athletics and

---

103] Horsfall, 2 Aug. 1848, HO 45/2410B. See also, 'Non-Arrival of the American Irish Brigade', *Isle of Man Times* 12 Aug. 1848.
104] Horsfall's daily reports, 3–18 Aug. 1848, HO 45/2410B. Bodleian Library, Oxford: Clarendon Papers, Box 16: Horsfall, 18 Aug. 1848.
105] Horsfall, 22, 23 and 25 Sept. 1848, HO 45/2410B.
106] Liverpool Record Office: Watch Committee 352 MIN/WAT 1/4, ff.614–48, Dowling's statistical returns for 1848.
107] 'The Remains of Mr. M'Manus', *Daily Post* 8 and 11 Nov. 1861. J. Newsinger, *Fenianism in Mid-Victorian Britain* (London, 1994), 26–27.

games programme to 'draw men from public houses' and render them 'more healthy'; a reading room (initially attached to the Manchester Arms in Stanley Street until more suitable premises were found in St Anne Street); and the Emmet Literary Club where individuals were assigned particular aspects of Irish history and literature to study for weekly discussion. Even so, the Brotherhood incurred the wrath of the Lancastrian Catholic hierarchy, who condemned it as another pub-based secret society – in Archbishop McDonald's words, 'just a new cloak, or rather a new name for Ribbonism'. The church put forward an alternative association, the Erin-go-bragh club which met at the Catholic Institute, Hope Street, an ill-attended and misjudged venture which antagonised the new local president of the Brotherhood, George Archdeacon, the veteran Manchester Confederate. Energised by Archdeacon, a relatively recent arrival in Liverpool, the Brotherhood kept the clergy at bay while drawing closer to the Fenians and to pub-based culture.[108] Liverpool Fenianism, its historian W.J. Lowe contends, was more important for its open-access pub-based conviviality, briefly shared with Irish-American officers, than for any military planning: 'the social significance of the Liverpool IRB outweighed its military or political importance'. Indeed, with its network of twenty or so pubs and beershops across the city, Fenianism was essentially a social affair which 'furnished a popular organisational foundation that helped to build the constitutional home rule movement'.[109]

In this new constitutional inflexion, home rule nationalism drew upon the combined and complementary (if still at times competing) resources of pub and parish, catering for second-generation (i.e. Liverpool-born) Irish, for whom the fate of Ireland was of less account than the immediate housing and employment needs of local Catholics.[110] Operating through pub-based personal contacts and priestly patronage, Irish nationalism served as an effective counterweight at the polls to the dominant Tory-

108] Gerard Moran, 'Nationalists in Exile: the National Brotherhood of St Patrick in Lancashire, 1861–5' in *The Irish in Victorian Britain: the Local Dimension*, ed. R. Swift and S. Gilley (Dublin, 1999), 212–35.
109] W.J. Lowe, 'Lancashire Fenianism, 1864–71', *Transactions of the Historic Society of Lancashire and Cheshire*, Vol. 126 (1977), 156–85.
110] Bernard O'Connell, 'Irish Nationalism in Liverpool, 1873–1923', *Éire-Ireland*, Vol. 10 (1975), 24–37; A. Shallice, 'Orange and Green and Militancy: Sectarianism and Working-class Politics in Liverpool, 1900–1914', *Bulletin of the Northwest Labour History Society*, Vol. 6 (1979–80), 15–32; and L.W. Brady, *T.P. O'Connor and the Liverpool Irish* (London, 1983). See also, P.J. Waller, *Democracy and Sectarianism: a Political and Social History of Liverpool, 1868–1939* (Liverpool, 1981).

Democratic electoral machine. As Don MacRaild notes, Sinn Fein struggled to gain a toehold in early twentieth-century Liverpool where home rule nationalism – as practised and perfected by T.P. O'Connor and the Harford brothers – was part of official municipal culture.[111] Behind the scenes (and awaiting proper historical research), the old Ribbonite ways and means persisted. The various schisms of the 'revolutionary underground' each had a pub-based presence in Liverpool, still looked to (with undue optimism) as the best venue to effect a rapprochement. James Murphy, the local IRB leader in the 1890s, was a barman at the Mitre Hotel, having previously been a publican in Scotland Road; the rival Irish National Brotherhood met in Dan Connolly's pub.[112] The Liverpool Company of the Irish Volunteers (IRA) protected itself in traditional manner behind the security framework of collective mutuality. Would-be recruits, new to Liverpool, had first to join the health benefit scheme of the Irish National Foresters:

> What the fellow didn't know was that when he handed his completed application form to Mr Moran's secretary, Nan Feeley, she made a copy of the applicant's name, birthplace, parents' names etc., and then sent a copy to IRA Headquarters in Dublin. Michael Collins would then send the information to the IRA intelligence officer in the area from which the applicant hailed and ask for it to be verified. Only when we received from Dublin a satisfactory report on the fellow would we consider accepting him into the company.[113]

* * * * *

While dismissed from the historical agenda of Irish studies in Britain, the complexities (and contradictions) of Irish nationalism require further research. Ethnic fade – the socio-economic process of assimilation by which Irish migrants identified, affiliated and integrated with host members of their particular class – seems not to have applied on the Mersey. In this large enclave, migrant adjustment operated through ethnic associational culture and nationalist sentiment. As an activist political project, nationalism was a minority creed, but it was embedded within a wider network of

111] Donald MacRaild, *Irish Migrants in Modern Britain, 1750–1922* (Basingstoke, 1999), 153.
112] National Archives, Dublin: Crime Department Special Branch, 3/716.
113] John A. Pinkman, *In the Legion of the Vanguard* (Boulder, 1998), 21–22.

convivial and collective activity, an ethnic ecology of sympathetic (if not always engaged and committed) affiliation that extended across the Liverpool-Irish enclave. Based alongside the associational, recreational and mutualist culture of the pub and parish, nationalism remained close to its constituency, better able than other formations to bridge the gap between the rarefied world of political activism and the everyday lives of ordinary people. While the Liverpool Liberal elite preserved its distance from the crude conviviality of working-class culture, Catholic priests and Irish nationalist politicians displayed a willingness to compromise with the street and the pub: regular intervention in such matters as fighting and drinking carried no expectation of permanent moral reform.

Liverpool's ethnic-sectarian nationalist formations, of which Ribbonism was among the first and most important, were at least as functional, popular and inclusive as the class-based movements and party structures privileged in conventional historiography.[114] By combining nationalism, ethnicity and sectarianism, pub and parish-based welfare services and collective mutuality were to extend across socio-economic, gender and other divisions within the Irish Catholic migrant community, providing a framework of inclusive cover probably unmatched by other forms of voluntary endeavour. Hence, no doubt, the belated conversion of Catholic workers to the labour movement, a major factor in Liverpool's proverbial 'backwardness' in labour history.[115]

114] Steven Fielding's study of *Class and Ethnicity: Irish Catholics in England, 1880–1939* (Buckingham, 1993), 5, dismisses Liverpool as a sectarian redoubt, 'marginal to the cultural and political life of the nation'.
115] For the best discussion of Liverpool's exceptionalism in labour history, see Sam Davies, *Liverpool Labour: Social and Political Influences on the Development of the Labour Party in Liverpool, 1900–1939* (Keele, 1996), 17–77.

4

Charity, ethnicity and the Catholic parish*

L iverpool's social problems, initially the consequence of exponential growth, have always claimed special attention. With characteristic inverted pride, the wretched early-Victorian reputation – 'the black spot on the Mersey' – has acquired metaphoric force in historiographical discourse: a damning indictment, it stands as the tidal-mark by which to measure (and applaud) Liverpool's subsequent pioneer role in social reform and its pre-eminence in philanthropy. While prejudice and sectarian tensions disabled political progress, 'squalid' Liverpool led the way in social amelioration, empowered by an innovative mixed economy of municipal and voluntary provision. This juxtaposition of backward politics with progressive social policy, a time-worn formulation of Ramsay Muir, requires careful interrogation.[1] No less than party politics, social policy (whether municipal or voluntary) was driven largely by ethnic and sectarian considerations and constructions. Local authority interventionism in health and housing was justified through denigration of the Irish 'other' in their midst, legitimising rhetoric which overrode laissez-faire sentiment and rate-payer retrenchment. Innovation in philanthropy, the specialism of the Unitarian liberal elite otherwise denied political influence, was spurred by the need · for business acumen, scientific rationality and trained professionalism to curb indiscriminate provision – the deformation of the gift – unduly

* This newly-written essay draws upon material previously published in my paper, 'The Immigrant Alternative: Ethnic and Sectarian Mutuality among the Liverpool Irish during the Nineteenth Century' in *The Duty of Discontent: Essays for Dorothy Thompson*, ed. O. Ashton, R. Fyson and S. Roberts (London, 1995), 231–50.
1] Ramsay Muir, *A History of Liverpool* (London, 1907), ch.16. I.C. Taylor, 'Black Spot on the Mersey: a Study of Environment and Society in 18th and 19th Century Liverpool', unpublished PhD thesis, University of Liverpool, 1976.

inflated in Liverpool by sectarian competitive rivalry and Catholic charitable largesse.[2] As this essay shows, Irish and Catholic were rendered synonymous in dispute over charity and social reform, an ethnic identity constructed in a complex process of host labelling and migrant affiliation.

In promoting interventionism, Dr Duncan, Liverpool's pioneering Medical Officer of Health, drew upon the anti-Irish rhetoric and prescriptions of the 'Condition of England Question'. The (necessary) underclass of early industrialisation, the Irish figured in the social engineering projects of the 1830s and 1840s as the internal 'other', a 'contaminating' presence within the unreformed and unprotected 'social body'.[3] Without sanitary and other social reforms, Liverpool, as Duncan demonstrated, was at highest risk of mass 'contagion':

> ... the native inhabitants are exposed to the inroads of numerous hordes of uneducated Irish, spreading physical and moral contamination around them ... By their example and intercourse with others they are rapidly lowering the standard of comfort among their English neighbours, communicating their own vicious and apathetic habits, and fast extinguishing all sense of moral dignity, independence and self-respect.[4]

The famine influx – accompanied by a typhus epidemic, 'Irish fever'[5] – added to the anxiety. Rushton, the stipendiary magistrate, calculated that within twelve hours of disembarkation, the famine Irish were to be 'found in one of three classes – paupers, vagrants, or thieves'.[6] According to his figures, 296 331 persons landed at Liverpool from Ireland between 13 January and 13 December 1847, of whom 116 000 were 'half naked and

2] Sectarian competition, however, was excluded from Margaret Simey's celebration of voluntary personal service, *Charitable Effort in Liverpool in the Nineteenth Century* (Liverpool, 1951), published (with Merseypride) as part of the contribution of the University of Liverpool to the Festival of Britain, and republished (to encourage 'our right to give as well as to get') as *Charity Rediscovered: A Study of Philanthropic Effort in Nineteenth-Century Liverpool* (Liverpool, 1992).
3] Mary Poovey, 'Curing the "Social Body": James Kay and the Irish in Manchester', *Gender and History*, Vol. 5 (1993), 196–211. D.M. MacRaild, 'Irish Immigration and the "Condition of England" Question: the Roots of an Historiographical Tradition', *Immigrants and Minorities*, Vol. 14 (1995), 67–85.
4] W.H. Duncan, 'On the Sanitary State of Liverpool' (1842) quoted in G. Kearns, P. Laxton and J. Campbell, 'Duncan and the Cholera Test: Public Health in Mid Nineteenth-Century Liverpool', *Transactions of the Historic Society of Lancashire and Cheshire*, Vol. 143 (1994), 98–99.
5] Frank Neal, *Black '47: Britain and the Famine Irish* (Basingstoke, 1998), ch. 5.
6] Quoted in Cannon Bennett, *Father Nugent of Liverpool* (Liverpool, 1949), 38.

starving'.[7] Hard-pressed Liverpool rate-payers pleaded in vain for central government assistance as the local poor law authorities adopted 'crisis management'. An efficient new system of vetting and visiting curbed the number of fraudulent claims, while tough new regulations to facilitate prompt removal back to Ireland deterred genuine claimants. The proportionate amount spent on the Irish rose considerably in 1847–1848, but as Frank Neal has shown, this was caused by earlier arrivals, unemployed Liverpool-Irish able to claim 'irremovable' status by the terms of the Five-Year Residency Act of 1846. As the presence of these long-stay Irish ensured low wages in the local labour market, Neal doubts whether they should be considered a net burden on rate-payer employers.[8] Nevertheless, the *Morning Chronicle* investigation of 'Labour and the Poor' in Liverpool in 1850 began by counting the cost – economic, moral and sanitary – of Irish in-migration: 'The town of Liverpool feels, through the sensitive medium of the pocket, that it has to pay a large price for the privilege of being the greatest port of the west, and that its advantages in being the outlet to America are nearly counterbalanced by the disadvantages in being the inlet from Ireland.'[9]

The Catholic church struggled to keep pace with demands for relief, aggravated by migrants trapped unintentionally in the human entrepôt of Liverpool, unable to proceed across the briny ocean. The resources of the Catholic Benefit Society were severely strained by 'the arrival from Ireland of many persons who intended to emigrate, but who were stricken down by sickness and want, and were thus compelled to remain'.[10] According to Father Nugent, an Irish-Liverpudlian himself, Irish migrants who thereafter remained in Liverpool were 'the dregs', the *caput mortuum*, unable, unsuited or unwilling to take advantage of opportunities elsewhere in Britain or the new world.[11] Portrayed in such pejorative terms – a trope that was to endure, setting Liverpool and its social problems apart – the

7] Cited in Frank Neal, 'Liverpool, the Irish Steamship Companies and the Famine Irish', *Immigrants and Minorities*, Vol. 5 (1986), 34.
8] Frank Neal, 'Lancashire, the Famine Irish and the Poor Laws: a Study in Crisis Management', *Irish Economic and Social History*, Vol. XXII (1995), 26–48.
9] 'Labour and the Poor: Letter 1: The Burdens upon Towns – Irish Pauperism', *Morning Chronicle*, 20 May 1850.
10] Liverpool Record Office (hereafter LRO) 361 CAT: Liverpool Catholic Benefit Society Minute Book, 1850–58, press cutting from *Liverpool Mercury*, 23 Dec. 1851.
11] Quoted in Taylor, 'Black Spot', 101. One of nine children, Nugent was the son of a first-generation Irish migrant with substantial interests in the fruit, poultry and game business in St John's market and other retail outlets.

Liverpool-Irish presented the fundamental challenge to social reformers and philanthropists alike. 'We were not prepared for the exodus from Ireland', Nugent reported to the Select Committee on Intemperance in 1877, 'and now we are punished by the children of those parents who came from Ireland, who have grown up in ignorance and neglect.'[12]

Confronted by the immovable Irish presence, the Catholic church – with Nugent to the fore – was compelled to redefine its local mission. The hierarchy remained English in composition and outlook, but there was a distinct 'hibernicisation' in philanthropic, associational and pastoral provision (ahead of Glasgow where the appointment of Irish priests – and other forms of 'Irishness' – were at first strongly resisted).[13] Claiming the depraved Irish as their particular concern – as their special mission for spiritual salvation and welfare protection – Catholics sought to outmatch Protestant philanthropic achievements. Along with other welfare networks – the Irish pub, court and core-street – the Catholic parish became a focus (particularly for women) for charity and 'cradle to grave' collective mutuality, adding to the infrastructure of 'ethnic' solidarity and social security which made the Irish reluctant to leave Liverpool. Seen in these terms, continued 'ghetto' residence in Liverpool, the port of entry, was quite as rational for Irish migrants as the peripatetic and uncertain quest for 'success' elsewhere. A form of cultural (and segregated) security, the community bonds of ethnicity and sectarianism – as in Boston – were to preclude movement outward and upward, away from the 'internal colony' and its culture of poverty.[14]

The impetus for Catholic social interventionism was essentially spiritual. Writing from Birkenhead in 1848, the Rev. Dr Miley lamented the spiritual deprivation of famine migrants:

> From the clergy and the nuns one hears the most heart-rendering accounts, not so much of the physical privations and miseries of every sort which form the ordinary lot of these exiles, but of the deplorable

12] 'Third Report from the Select Committee of the House of Lords on Intemperance', PP1877(418)XI, q.8314
13] P. Doyle, 'Bishop Goss of Liverpool (1856–1872) and the importance of being English', in *Studies in Church History 18: Religion and National Identity*, ed. S. Mews (Oxford, 1982), 433–47. M.J. Mitchell, *The Irish in the West of Scotland 1797–1848* (Edinburgh, 1998), 116–30 and 236–43.
14] M. Cross, 'Introduction: Migration, the City and the Urban Dispossessed' in *Ethnic Minorities and Industrial Change in Europe and North America*, ed. M. Cross (Cambridge, 1992), 1–16. M. Hechter, *Internal Colonialism* (London, 1975), xv.

effects which the woes of the last seasons seem to have had in almost utterly destroying the religious instincts of the Irish in England ... mass is neglected by multitudes, all kinds of profligacy, cursing and blasphemy in particular have fearfully increased within that period. There are in Liverpool alone a great many thousands who are said to have abandoned every religious practice with the exception of *abstaining on Fridays*.[15]

Prevention of 'leakage' from the faith was the overriding consideration, the obligation to win back the negligent and lapsed to a proper observance of their religion. Having left Ireland before its 'devotional revolution', migrants were unacquainted with the discipline of Tridentine conformism, the high standard of practice among the small indigenous Catholic community.[16] Furthermore, their parlous socio-economic plight made them continually vulnerable to Protestant proselytisation through dependence upon charitable and poor law agencies. For example, in the dire distress caused by the severe winter weather (and unwonted easterly winds) of February 1855, Irish Catholics took relief wherever they could get it: indeed, they constituted 78 per cent of the cases relieved by the District Provident Society and 82 per cent of the applicants for poor relief.[17] (The figures for those arrested in the February bread riots were no less instructive: 64 of the 84 men arrested were Irish-born as were 19 of the 22 women.)[18] However, there was another imperative for Catholic action: the need to eradicate the oath-bound, pub-based secret societies. As proscription proved of no avail, the church decided to outbid Ribbonism in its welfare services.

There were early indications of the new approach in the changing pattern of St Patrick Day processions. In the 1830s, the Hibernian Societies, exclusively Catholic but in the hands of the laity (and often covers for Ribbonism) dominated the proceedings: by the 1840s, various other

15] Dublin Diocesan Archives: Archdeacon Hamilton Papers. Dr Miley, Birkenhead, to Hamilton, 26 Oct. 1848.
16] G. Connolly, 'Irish and Catholic: Myth or Reality? Another Sort of Irish and the Renewal of the Clerical Profession among Catholics in England, 1791–1818' in *The Irish in the Victorian City*, eds R. Swift and S. Gilley (London, 1985), 225–54.
17] C.L. Scott, 'A Comparative Re-examination of Anglo-Irish Relations in Nineteenth-Century Manchester, Liverpool and Newcastle-upon-Tyne', unpublished PhD thesis, University of Durham, 1998, 36. The origins of Liverpool's pioneering Central Relief and Charity Organisation Society can be traced to the uncoordinated and 'indiscriminate' response to the 1855 crisis. See W. Grisewood, *The Poor of Liverpool and What is to be Done for Them* (Liverpool, 1899).
18] M. Kanya-Forstner, 'The Politics of Survival: Irish Women in Outcast Liverpool 1850–1890', unpublished PhD thesis, University of Liverpool, 1997, 28.

associations, mostly under clerical control, joined the procession. Dowling, the Deputy Head Constable, provided a detailed breakdown of the participants in 1842, when severe trade depression rather restricted the numbers: 'they are too poor to take their scarfs and other finery with which to bedeck themselves out of pledge; for it is the common habit of these men to pawn those articles together with their only decent suit of clothes from the 18th of March in one year until the 16th of the next'. Hibernian Societies were still to the fore: taken together, there were 400 marchers from the First and Second Hibernian Friendly Societies, the Third Hibernian Mechanical Society, the Fourth Philanthropy Hibernian Society and the Sixth Hibernian Industrious Society. Another separate society, the Hibernian Benevolent Society of St Patrick, was represented by a contingent of 150. The Irish Sons of Freedom mustered a similar assemblage, although Dowling calculated the total number of Ribbonmen as no more than 50, on the basis of those 'wearing shamrocks on the left breast with the stalk upwards' – it was Ribbonite custom to wear shamrocks in distinctive manner on 17 March, as instructed by their boards. Then there were groups under varying degrees of clerical patronage and control: 150 marchers from the Roman Catholic Total Abstinence Benevolent Society; 100 representing the Roman Catholic Teetotal Association (Cork Branch); two parish-based associations, 60 from St Anthony's Society, and 70 from St Anne's Society; and finally, 100 marchers from the Grand United Order of the Catholic Brethren of the Blackburn Unity in the Liverpool District.[19]

From its Blackburn base, as J.H. Treble has shown, the United Catholic Brethren 'sought to supersede all those secret societies which had hitherto ensnared innocent Catholics'. To match Ribbonism, however, it needed to construct a national framework, to offer not merely sickness and death benefits but also tramping relief. The necessary growth beyond the

19] Public Record Office, Kew: Colonial Office Papers (hereafter CO 904/9 ff. 203–06, Dowling, 18 March 1842. For this period, St Patrick's day should not be regarded as the Catholic equivalent of 12 July. While drunken disorder was frequent, sectarian riot was almost unknown. However, from 1853 all such processions were banned within Liverpool boundaries. See Ann Bryson, 'Riotous Liverpool 1815–1860', in *Popular Politics, Riot and Labour: Essays in Liverpool History 1790–1940*, ed. John Belchem (Liverpool, 1992) 118–20. Preachers such as Father Cahill sought to give the Catholic church credit for this 'sacrifice' intended to 'soothe political rancour' and increase 'social virtue and domestic happiness'. See D. Fitzpatrick, '"A Peculiar Tramping People": the Irish in Britain, 1801–70' in *A New History of Ireland, V. Ireland under the Union*, ed. W.E. Vaughan (Oxford, 1989), 654.

regional base, however, was impeded by the episcopate, which gave its blessing instead to local 'guilds' on the Bradford model, benefit societies strictly under the control of the local clergy and integrated into the spiritual life of the parish.[20] Having duly reminded his audience that members of secret societies could not be admitted to the sacraments, Bishop Sharples, speaking at the first anniversary of the Liverpool Holy Guild of Mercy in 1846, opined that Catholic guilds had more to offer than affiliated friendly societies like the Oddfellows:

> They aimed, he said, at providing for the mere physical wants of the members; but the guilds were preferable to any of them, as the members were bound together by the ties of religion, which united them the more firmly in the bonds of Christian charity, – whilst, at the same time, their physical necessities were provided for on a basis perfectly secure.[21]

By this time, however, most northern guilds had already collapsed, victims of the cyclical depression of the early 1840s. Thereafter, Treble contends, Catholic workers turned back to trade unionism towards which the clergy duly abandoned much of its former hostility.[22] In Liverpool, however, a different pattern prevailed. Catholic social welfare continued to expand, aided (particularly in educational provision) by the arrival in 1837 of the Christian Brothers.

From the early days of sectarian rivalry in Liverpool, the Catholics proudly asserted their supremacy in welfare provision. Protestant charity, the *Catholic Institute Magazine* critically observed, 'proceeds with a fixity of system, a calm calculation of practical results, a rigid economy of good works, which utterly destroy to Catholic eyes all that in Charity is most beautiful and most holy'.[23] Certainly, there were important differences in cultural style and strategy between what might be termed Protestant 'scientific charity' and Catholic 'alms-giving'. While the Liverpool Domestic Mission, founded by members of the Methodist Chapel on Renshaw Street, saw itself as an agency for moral reform rather than of relief distribution, the St Vincent de Paul Society (SVP) served – in Catholic Glaswegian fashion – as a 'General Purposes Society', granting generous relief in case

20] J.H. Treble, 'Attitudes of the Roman Catholic Church towards Trade Unionism in the North of England, 1833–1842', *Northern History*, Vol. 5 (1970), 104–11.
21] *Liverpool Mercury*, 25 Sept. 1846. At this stage, the boys' branch numbered 120, the girls' 150, and the men's about 120.
22] Treble, 'Attitude of Roman Catholic Church', 111–13.
23] 'Liverpool Catholic Charities: No. 1', *Catholic Institute Magazine*, Jan. 1856.

of need and where there was proof of minimal religious observance.[24] The best documented study of the Society relates to St Mary's, Highfield Street, a parish established in the eighteenth century close to the business quarter to serve the small Catholic population, but then overwhelmed by the famine influx of poor Irish immigrants into what became the 'most squalid part' of town.[25] In 'succouring the really deserving poor', the SVP gave immediate relief on the understanding – later articulated by Bishop Whiteside – that it was better to relieve a few 'imposters' than to reject a genuine case through zealous scrutiny.[26]

Instead of moral condemnation – such censure was reserved for duplicitous 'begging priests' from across the water[27] – Catholic leaders, clerical and lay, displayed a materialist understanding. Brought together in serious discussion of social issues at Nugent's Catholic Institute in Hope Street, leading local Catholics took an inverse pride, as it were, in the destitution of Irish migrants, 'the thousands of homeless, moneyless, raimentless, foodless creatures that call the Catholic Church their mother in Liverpool'.[28] In this 'sinkhole of sinfulness and depravity',[29] environmentalism extended to migrants seemingly lost to the faith:

> The best of the labouring classes do not emigrate. Those who do, are not treated on their coming, with kindness and considerateness – very much the reverse. They must descend to the worst work, and accept the worst pay ... they are on all sides treated with disrespect, and in many cases, unfortunately, they fail to respect themselves. Their new circumstances suggest brutal habits, and equally brutal enjoyments ... Those men of course are not Catholic, but they are not Protestant, and they are Irish.[30]

24] Bernard Aspinwall, 'The Welfare State within the State: the Saint Vincent de Paul Society in Glasgow, 1848–1920', in *Studies in Church History: Voluntary Religion*, ed. W.J. Sheils and D. Wood (Oxford, 1986), 445–59.
25] John Davies, 'Parish Charity: the Work of the Society of St Vincent de Paul, St Mary's, Highfield Street, Liverpool, 1867–68', *North West Catholic History*, Vol. xvii (1990), 37–46.
26] L. Feehan, 'Charitable Effort, Statutory Authorities and the Poor in Liverpool c.1850–1914', unpublished PhD thesis, University of Liverpool, 1987, 57.
27] There is much condemnation of such 'promiscuous begging' in Bishop Brown's pastoral letters; Lancashire Record Office: Archdiocese of Liverpool papers, RCLv: Box 40.
28] 'Church-Going in Liverpool', *Catholic Institute Magazine*, Nov. 1855. For the Catholic Institute, see Bennett, *Father Nugent*, ch.2.
29] 'Church-Going in Liverpool'.
30] 'Reformatories – Their Nature, Origin and Tendency', *Catholic Institute Magazine*, Sept. 1856.

Thenceforth, Catholics claimed the depraved Irish as their particular concern, their special mission for spiritual salvation and welfare protection. The poor, a pastoral letter explained, 'are a burden laid by God on the rich; but here it is no customary burden, but swollen out of all proportion by the most helpless classes of a neighbouring country, throwing themselves for support on the richer sister Island'.[31] The overwhelming concern, as Bishop Brown made clear to the local clergy, was not with the requirements of Ireland, but with the spiritual and material welfare of its migrants, 'the poor of the sister country, who are living among us and under our own eyes. These are a portion of that flock for which I and you have to be answerable to the Divine Lord of the Vineyard.'[32]

The cost of building (and maintaining) the Catholic parochial and charitable framework to accommodate the Irish influx was a constant drain on limited resources. 'In most of the other Dioceses [sic] of England', Bishop Brown noted enviously, 'there is a greater number of extensive landed proprietors *Catholics* than in this Diocess [sic].'[33] As it outstretched the generosity of the indigenous Catholic community, church provision depended on the goodwill of Irish merchants, prepared to donate money, resources and time. Pending proper premises, warehouses were used as places of worship – this was a variant on earlier practice when the original Edmund Street chapel, destroyed by a Hanoverian mob in 1746, was rebuilt under the disguise of a warehouse by the Irish merchant Henry Pippard.[34] Commercial business skills were put to use in organising subscription schemes and weekly penny collections for church building, a method pioneered by a group of newly-arrived Irish merchants in the south end where the first mission church, appropriately named St Patrick's, opened for worship in 1824. Thereafter the focus of attention switched to the north end, where most new (Catholic) Irish arrivals were to settle. St Antony's, a small chapel built by French refugees, was rebuilt in the early 1830s through the efforts of a subscription committee assisted by local Hibernian Societies and by a Ladies' Society 'established for the purpose of providing whatever is requisite and becoming for the service of the altar, and the decoration of the chapel'.[35] By 1870,

31] RCLv Box 40, Pastoral letter, 13 June 1854.
32] RCLv: Box 40, Brown 'To the Clergy Only', 23 May 1853.
33] Ibid.
34] J.A. Klapas, 'Geographical Aspects of Religious Change in Victorian Liverpool, 1837–1901', unpublished MA thesis, University of Liverpool, 1977, 24.
35] RCLv Box 40, Relation Status Missiorum in Diocesi Liverpolitana, and Box 28 for more material on St Anthony's.

there were 18 Catholic parishes in Liverpool served by 64 priests;[36] by 1914 the number of parishes had risen to 24 of which 16 were clustered in the Scotland, Vauxhall and Everton areas.[37]

On top of the mounting debt burden of the mission churches and parish-based schools (regarded as essential after the Tories brought an end in 1841 to the local Liberals' 'crucial experiment' of non-denominational public education on the Irish model),[38] funds were required for extra-parochial institutional and other forms of charity to meet Liverpool's special needs.[39] Through asylums and reformatories, the 'worst' of the famine poor, reduced to crime and depredation on the streets of Liverpool, were to be rescued for the faith. Particular attention was accorded to the growing number of street children. 'Save the Boy!' was Nugent's motto.[40]

In Victorian social pathology (derived from metropolitan social exploration into darkest and outcast areas), the streets were associated with licence and abandon, as the place where conventional distinctions of what was legal and illegal, moral and immoral, proper and improper, permissible and impermissible, did not prevail.[41] While London had clear boundaries (which flaneurs were wont to transgress), Liverpool lacked such segregation: respectable business was not insulated from the threat of street disorder. Commerce, the waterfront and the boisterous 'secondary economy' of the streets – domain of hawkers and costermongers, common lodging house keepers, bookies, pawnbrokers, prostitutes, petty criminals and others – were coterminous in central Liverpool. Catering for the needs of the city's poorest inhabitants and least wary visitors, the street economy, breeding ground of the 'scally scouser', was in constant territorial (and behavioural) conflict with the authorities. According to the *Liverpool Mercury*, street-wise children held their own 'markets' in Liverpool's 'Little Ireland' where

36] W.J. Lowe, *The Irish in Mid-Victorian Lancashire* (New York, 1989), 113.
37] Frank Boyce, 'From Victorian "Little Ireland" to Heritage Trail: Catholicism, Community and Change in Liverpool's Docklands' in *The Irish in Victorian Britain: the Local Dimension*, ed. R. Swift and S. Gilley (Dublin, 1999), 282–83.
38] J. Murphy, *The Religious Problem in English Education: The Crucial Experiment* (Liverpool, 1959). Mary Hickman, *Religion, Class and Identity: The State, the Catholic Church and the Education of the Irish in Britain* (Aldershot, 1995), 139–48.
39] National Library of Ireland, Dublin: Mss 32,483 Letter-book of Richard H. Sheil, ff. 351–52, Sheil to editor of the *Catholic Standard*, 1 Dec. 1853.
40] Bennett, *Father Nugent*, ch. viii.
41] Gertrude Himmelfarb, *The Idea of Poverty* (London, 1984), 366–68. J.R. Walkowitz, *City of Dreadful Delight: Narratives of Sexual Danger in Late-Victorian London* (London, 1992), ch. 1.

they disposed of 'swag' scavenged from the adjacent docks and warehouses.[42] Kept at a distance, away from respectable public view, street-trading was indispensable to the local economy, the point of consumption and/or income for many in-migrants, including single and deserted women, children and orphans.[43] Aware of the importance of this exchange economy, the SVP occasionally made grants to women to enable them to gain an income from street-selling. Nugent introduced a system of rewards and Christmas treats (clothing, geese and coal) for such 'basket-women' who 'could produce bank-books showing how they had saved some money during the previous twelve months'.[44] However, a double imperative prompted Catholic action to 'rescue' children from this corrupting environment.

First there was the need for intervention to counteract the baleful influence of the local authorities, to guard against the 'certain perversion' of poor Catholics taken off the streets and into care in official, thus Anglican, institutions. Such 'necessitous' children were denied proper Catholic religious instruction in the workhouse and the industrial schools, prior to their proselytisation and release.[45] Such manifold instances of bigotry and deficiency in civic social policy – Protestant sins of commission and omission – were later chronicled by Thomas Burke, a prosperous second-

---

42] *Liverpool Mercury*, 24 Feb. 1842, quoted in Kanya-Forstner, 'Politics of survival', 78.

43] M. Brogden, *The Police: Autonomy and Consent* (London, 1982), 43–73. Some participants in this exchange economy apparently sourced their goods from their own rented accommodation: 'In some streets, doors, stairs, and floors became the spoil of chip merchants, lead piping and iron, removed to marine store dealers, and we all ask where are the police!!' (evidence of H.E. Williams, *Full Report of the Commission of Inquiry into the Subject of the Unemployed in the City of Liverpool* (Liverpool, 1894), 103). The most organised criminal activity was cotton-stealing, described by Nugent as 'a very clever and well worked-out system', linked to dealers in Oldham and Rochdale; see 'Third Report on Intemperance', qq.8256–258. Street crime was sustained and promoted through various 'disreputable' premises: the Police report for 1860–61, for example, enumerated: 74 houses of receivers of stolen goods; 162 public houses, 78 beerhouses and 72 coffee-shops where thieves and prostitutes resort; 84 other suspected homes; 829 brothels and houses of ill-fame; and 331 tramps' and lodging houses; see 'The Police Establishment', *Daily Post* 25 Nov. 1861.

44] Bennett, *Father Nugent*, 112.

45] In 1860 a special committee was appointed 'for the location of Catholic children taken from the Industrial Schools' charged with preventing 'the alarming amount of proselytism that had been going on for years, by placing poor Catholic children in the families of Protestants ... This committee must find places for two hundred children annually, or certain perversion awaits them' (*Daily Post*, 3 July 1861).

generation Irish-Liverpudlian, and historian of Catholic Liverpool.[46] Then
there was Nugent's personal mission, his determination not merely to
counter but also to outmatch non-Catholic provision in social work,
preventive and reformatory, among the 'very lowest of the population':

> ... of late years the circumstances of Ireland have flung into the vortex
> of Liverpool low-life, innumerable creatures, without father, mother or
> friend. These are indeed, beings, whom to know, is to pity, and whom no
> Christian can desire to leave exposed to the temptations of the world. In
> their course of life, their normal condition is one of crime – and it is only
> in Reformatories they can, without the intervention of a special
> providence, become Christian. It is only thus these Arabs of society can
> be brought under the civilizing influences of citizenship.[47]

By enlisting the funds and support of the Catholic Club and of members of
the professional and business classes associated with his Catholic
Institute in Hope Street, Nugent established the Association of Providence.
This provided the finance for a number of schemes, extending from
emergency rescue provision at the Boys' Night Shelter and Refuge in Soho
Street, an attempt 'to deal more effectively with his street arabs', to
orphanages, industrial schools and, for those already tainted by street
crime, suitable reformatories.[48] As the agricultural training provided by
the Cistercians at the distant Mount St Bernard's Reformatory proved
inadequate and inappropriate, Nugent took the lead – as first president of
the Liverpool Catholic Reformatory Association – in promoting a ship
reformatory specially designed for adolescent Liverpool recidivists:

> Hitherto a fatal mistake has been made by sending so large a number of
> boys to Agricultural Reformatories. How few townsmen ever, either
> through choice or necessity, betake themselves to agricultural labour.
> The class of boys committed to reformatories have been accustomed to
> the streets of Liverpool from their childhood; they have their respective
> avocations, either begging, stealing or trading, and though young, theirs

46] T.N. Burke, *Catholic History of Liverpool* (Liverpool, 1910), 165 and passim. In
the provision of some services, the local authorities tried to be even-handed, as in
allocations for the first 80.5 acres at the new cemetery at Anfield Park: 40.25 acres
to the Anglicans; 22 acres to the Roman Catholics; and 18.25 acres to the
Nonconformists. Even so, the Catholics opened their own cemetery at Ford shortly
afterwards, see *Daily Post* 3,5, 6 and 9 Sept. 1861.
47] 'Reformatories', *Catholic Institute Magazine*, Sept. 1856.
48] Bennett, *Father Nugent*, 40–41.

has been a life of continuous excitement, and Liverpool's busy streets, quays, docks, ships and river are indelibly stamped upon their minds … Experience has further shown that Farm Reformatory and Industrial Schools have in no case proved as successful as a Ship Reformatory.[49]

The *Clarence* was brought into service in 1864 providing instruction in seamanship, carpentering, shoemaking, tailoring and other trades while religious instruction and practice was in the hands of a chaplain appointed by the Bishop of Shrewsbury.[50]

Where Nugent led, others followed. The local authorities introduced a licensing scheme to restrict juvenile street-trading to badge-holders (not surprisingly, most applicants were Catholic). A range of charitable organisations assisted these registered 'ragged urchins of the streets' – for example, the Clothing Society which called in 'the aid of the police to prevent drunken parents from pawning the clothes'. (The shame attached to wearing such clothes was to persist in the collective memory, as oral history projects in the docklands community have discovered.[51]) The worst cases were taken off the streets, assigned to the 'total' regime of reformatories (following the Catholic example) or despatched to Canada. Liverpool, Muir proudly recorded, was in the forefront of the movement for the prevention of cruelty to children, but street-trading (juvenile and otherwise) perforce persisted – Caradog Jones described it as a 'blight' in the 1930s.[52]

Similar factors prevailed in the Catholic rehabilitation of 'fallen women'. Many of Liverpool's prostitutes were Irish-born, forced into the trade by

49] Quoted in ibid., 53. For dissatisfaction with arrangements for delinquent girls sent to Arno's Court, Bristol, see RCLv Box 71, correspondence from Thomas Cookson, 1857–58, vicar-general at Liverpool.

50] The 'process of reformation' mirrored that on board the Protestant 'Akbar': 'Slummy boys, after batting aimlessly from alley to alley, are subjected five years to strict discipline; then, they are adjudged sailormen and given assistance in procuring berths on merchant ships. Only one ray of sympathy penetrates the harsh routine that is theirs, (welcomed usually with a lively distaste by the boys): the weekly visit of the pastor or priest with accompanying threats of hell-fire and damnation'; Pat O'Mara, *The Autobiography of a Liverpool Irish Slummy* (London, 1934), 8.

51] Pat Ayers, *The Liverpool Docklands: Life and Work in Athol Street* (Birkenhead, 1999 edn), 22.

52] Muir, *History*, 330–32. D. Caradog Jones, *Social Survey of Merseyside* (3 vols: Liverpool, 1934), Vol. ii, 231–32, and Vol. iii, 62. See also Revd J. Bell Cox, *Wage-Earning Children* (Liverpool, 1900); and F.J. Leslie, *Wasted Lives: The Problem of Child Labour* (Liverpool, 1910)

Table 4.1 Number of commitments to the Liverpool Borough Prisons, 1863–1876

Year	Total of all Denominations	Roman Catholics		Total number of Roman Catholics
		Male	Female	
1864	9913	2719	3067	5786
1865	7477	2099	2144	4243
1866	7746	2122	2253	4375
1867	8876	2757	2562	5319
1868	8909	2732	2799	5531
1869	10 503	3129	3578	6707
1870	12 719	3930	4461	8391
1871	11 724	3387	4326	7713
1872	13 723	3689	5334	9023
1873	12 420	3580	4742	8322
1874	13 239	4167	4855	9022
1875	13 683	4227	5170	9397
1876	13 313	4212	5098	9310
Total	144 272	42 750	50 389	93 139

Source: Based on paper handed in by the Rev. J. Nugent, Third Report from the Select Committee of the House of Lords on Intemperance, Appendix A, PP1877 (171) XI.

the inadequacy of other income opportunities on the streets.[53] As Catholic chaplain to the Borough Prison – 'the only prison in the world where the females exceed the males'[54] – Nugent came to a materialist understanding of their fate, and was duly strengthened in his determination to rescue them for the faith. Here again separate provision, however expensive, was essential, not least because the Liverpool Female Penitentiary permitted only Anglican services on Sundays. The timely arrival of the Good Shepherd Sisters in 1858 ensured that the women would be isolated and

53] Describing Liverpool in a paper presented to the National Association for the Promotion of Social Science in 1858, J.T. Danson claimed that 'our prostitutes (as our criminals and paupers) are nearly all Irish; and by far the great part of our female crime is committed in palpable connection with this sad "social evil"', quoted in Kanya-Forstner, 'The Politics of Survival', 186.
54] 'Third Report on Intemperance', q. 8337.

reformed within an exclusively Catholic culture, prior to despatch (as Nugent recommended) to the safety either of the adjacent manufacturing districts or distant Canada.[55]

As Nugent's career exemplifies, sectarian rivalry was no hindrance but the very spur to competitive charitable endeavour and innovation in Liverpool, 'the moral Waterloo of the nation'.[56] Excluded from the British 'master narrative' of Protestant constitutional liberty, Nugent and his fellow Catholics propounded an alternative concept of citizenship in which charitable provision held pride of place. Here, Catholic Europe with its charitable institutions set the example, offering the true solution to the 'Condition of England' question:

> ... England receives another lesson, that while in the Science of Government her knowledge is supreme, there are many social questions upon which her neighbours' knowledge is superior ... if we have triumphed through Representative Government, other countries who know not its advantages, have had their triumphs also; and have not neglected the interests of the poor. Again, it is a wholesome lesson that England should be taught, amid her pride of power and place, that she must draw the remedy for her social evils, and learn the means of reforming her seething population, from the wisdom and beneficence of that Church, which repudiating, she has never ceased to persecute.[57]

Catholic charity flourished in Liverpool, the *Catholic Institute Magazine* proclaimed, notwithstanding 'the restraints and confinements of countless obstacles to its natural development':

> The great bulk of the Catholic population is hopelessly poor, the number of our priests and religious is miserably disproportionate to the amount of labour they are obliged to undertake, and the watchful jealousy of our non-Catholic fellow-countrymen, excited by the incredible misrepresentations of a certain portion of their so-called pastors, clogs and impedes our every action ... in spite of the necessity under which we lay of expending a very great portion of our means in building churches to supply the stately edifices of which the ruthless injustice of

55] Kanya-Forstner, 'The Politics of Survival', ch. 5.
56] Revd Charles Garret quoted in *Daily Post* 11 June 1885, cited in I.D. Farley, 'J.C. Ryle – Episcopal Evangelist. A Study in Late-Victorian Evangelicalism', unpublished PhD thesis, University of Durham, 1988, 147.
57] 'Reformatories', *Catholic Institute Magazine*, Sept. 1856.

a tyrant had unscrupulously deprived us, England is already giving abundant proof that no persecution can stifle the Church of God, no pressure of poverty can destroy the Charity of her children.[58]

Indeed, as well as meeting the special needs of the local population, Liverpool Catholics were conscious of a wider national obligation, as in provision for the blind:

> Hitherto, no Catholic Asylum of this description has been established in these kingdoms; and, as Liverpool, on account of its great Catholic population, its central position, and ready means of communication with the Catholics of the Metropolis and other towns, offers many advantages for the commencement of such an institution, its founders trust that its formation here will prove a great and durable blessing to the Catholic Blind, and reflect a lasting honour upon its charitable supporters.[59]

By the late nineteenth century, there was a flourishing local *vereinskatholizismus*, to use the German term for the multiplication of organisations designed to meet the special needs – spiritual, economic and recreational – of every identifiable group within the Catholic population.[60] The *Catholic Family Annual and Almanac for the Diocese of Liverpool* (1884) accorded pride of place to the local orphanages, industrial schools and reformatories (by this time, the Liverpool Reformatory Association was responsible for the reformatory ship *Clarence*, a farm school at Ainsdale and a girls' reformatory in Old Swan), along with other charitable institutions, including the SVP; the Catholic School for the Blind; the Convent of the Good Shepherd where penitent women were occupied in laundry work; the Convent of Mercy which in administering to 'the corporal and spiritual wants of the poor' also admitted young women who were 'trained up to habits of virtue and industry'; the Home for the Aged Poor; the Liverpool Catholic Benevolent Society which provided the clergy with alms to relieve the sick poor; the Sisters of Bon Secours de Troyes who nursed the sick of all ages; and the Liverpool Catholic Children's Protection Society which found homes in Canada for 'Catholic children destitute or neglected, and in circumstances of danger and loss of their Religion' (an area where Catholics were in direct competition with Mrs Birt's Sheltering Homes, a

58] 'Liverpool's Catholic Charities: No. 1', *Catholic Institute Magazine*, Jan. 1856.
59] 'Catholic Blind Asylum', handbill in RCLv Box 28.
60] H. McLeod, 'Building the "Catholic Ghetto": Catholic Organisations 1870–1914', in *Voluntary Religion*, ed. Sheils and Wood, 411–44.

street-child emigration scheme enthusiastically supported by Ryle, Liverpool's first Anglican bishop).[61] The Little Sisters of the Poor, recent arrivals from a French order, were perhaps the most saintly and street-wise in balancing the books for this welfare provision. Preferring rather 'the regular weekly pennies of the people, to the occasional pounds of the well-to-do', the Sisters covered the building costs and capital expenditure for their home for the infirm elderly in Belmont Grove. Food was obtained by systematic daily begging trips in a sombre black van to city centre hotels, restaurants and refreshment rooms as well as collecting scraps from St John's Market, the best pickings being given to the inmates (some 138 in 1887) before the fifteen Sisters allowed themselves anything to eat.[62]

Nugent was the inspirational figure in this remarkable extension of philanthropic endeavour and preventive social work. Following a trip across the Atlantic in 1870–71, he sought to apply Irish-American techniques of temperance, collective mutuality and rational recreation to the Liverpool slums:

> I spent nine months in America, chiefly seeking openings for our surplus population ... I found attached to nearly every Catholic church in Canada and America total abstinence societies; they are of the characters of benefit societies as well as of total abstinence associations, and I found that those men were persevering in the work they did; it was the leaven of each congregation.

In pursuit of temperance, Nugent resolved to lure poor Catholics away from the pub and Liverpool's infamous dancing saloons, trusting to reverse Liverpool's reputation as the most drunken of towns (see Table 4.2). As penny readings were too 'dry', he promoted a more commercial repertoire at his popular Monday evening concerts: 'I always give them an address myself, but I think nothing of giving a person five guineas to sing a comic song ... I try to catch the taste of the people, and to elevate them':

> I give them entertainments of the same description as they would have at a public music hall ... I always sit on the platform myself, and those who attend the rehearsals take care that while the entertainment is of a character that pleases the people there shall be nothing vulgar, and of course nothing indecent ... there is nothing which the lower order of

61] Ryle considered emigration to be the most cost-effective means of rescuing the street children; see Farley, 'Ryle', 152–53.
62] 'Little Sisters of the Poor', *Liverpool Review*, 15 Oct. 1887, 11.

Table 4.2. Boroughs north of Birmingham with population of 50 000 and upwards, arranged in order of proportion of apprehensions for drunkenness and of licensed houses to population

Order in which each town stands (fewest apprehensions being No. 1)	Order in which each town stands (fewest licensed houses being No. 1)	Town	Proportion taken up for drunkenness	Proportion of licenced houses to population
1	19	Norwich	1 to 451	1 to 121
2	11	Leicester	1 to 205	1 to 203
3	14	Sheffield	1 to 200	1 to 179
4	5	Bradford	1 to 182	1 to 249
5	2	Leeds	1 to 164	1 to 316
6	1	Blackburn	1 to 142	1 to 340
7	9	Bolton	1 to 129	1 to 206
8	17	Birmingham	1 to 126	1 to 174
9	6	Huddersfield	1 to 118	1 to 247
10	15	Nottingham	1 to 116	1 to 178
11	13	Preston	1 to 103	1 to 187
12	12	Oldham	1 to 100	1 to 199
13	4	Hull	1 to 83	1 to 250
14	3	Halifax	1 to 74	1 to 252
15	8	Stockport	1 to 72	1 to 206
16	16	Newcastle-on-Tyne	1 to 54	1 to 174
17	10	Salford	1 to 45	1 to 201
18	18	Manchester	1 to 40	1 to 139
19	7	Liverpool	1 to 25	1 to 208

Source: Paper presented by Mr Rathbone, First Report from the Select Committee of the House of Lords on Intemperance, Appendix C, p. 335, PP1877(171)XI.

people like equal to dancing, so I take care to have a good Irish jig-dancer at least once in a fortnight; negro minstrelsy is also what the people like, and I take care there is something of that kind.

Other items on the bill included cookery demonstrations – undertaken by Nugent himself, having been instructed by his servant – and, as the high-point of the proceedings, the taking of the pledge in front of the audience. By such means, some 300–400 were won weekly to the temperance cause. Those who maintained such virtue for twelve months thereafter were entitled to progress to the 'League Veterans': 'I have a little short of 1,000 men and women in this association, and I give them an entertainment specially about Christmas or once or twice in the year, and as a large proportion of them are Irish, we clear the floor and allow them to dance'.[63]

Lacking such rapport with popular culture, Liberals were critical of Nugent's efforts, drawing attention to the inadequate housekeeping, poor sanitary standards and confessional exclusivism of his philanthropic institutions.[64] His co-religionist M.J. Whitty, editor of the *Daily Post*, disapproved of the showmanship, but Nugent was deservedly the most popular man in town, topping the poll in the *Liverpool Review* in July 1889.[65] He was the one Catholic to be included in the first album of leading civic personalities to be published by the *Liverpool Leader* in acknowledgement of his unmatched labours for 'promoting the social as well as the spiritual welfare of his co-religionists': 'Never did priest work harder or more disinterestedly, never did priest do better or holier work than this self-denying, never wearying minister has done, never did greater success reward such patient labour, and never was priest more greatly loved by all who came in contact with him than is the Rev. FATHER NUGENT'.[66] The inscription on his statue in St John's Gardens fittingly chronicles his achievements: 'Apostle of Temperance, Protector of the Orphan Child, Consoler of the Prisoner, Reformer of the Criminal, Saviour of Fallen Womanhood, Friend of All in Poverty and Affliction, an Eye to the Blind, a Foot to the Lame, the Father of the Poor.'[67]

Beneath these special provisions promoted by Nugent, the Catholic church provided a parish-based framework of spiritual and social welfare open to all Irish Catholic migrants, male and female – including penny

63] 'Third Report on Intemperance', qq. 8266–296.
64] See, for example, 'Ready to Perish: "Save the Boy"', *Liverpool Leader*, 16 June 1869.
65] Cited in Scott, 'Comparative Re-examination', 122.
66] 'The Rev. Father Nugent', *Liverpool Leader Album* (Liverpool, 1874).
67] Bennett, *Father Nugent*, 11 and 74–75. There is a full description of the statue in T. Cavanagh, *Public Sculpture of Liverpool* (Liverpool, 1997), 180–82. A forgotten figure, Nugent was to be rescued from historical neglect by Ray Dunbobbin's play, 'Black Spot on the Mersey', see 'Rescuer of the Ragged Children', *Daily Post*, 11 Mar. 1970.

banks (another of Nugent's enthusiasms) and 'clubs' for the poor who could not afford weekly subscriptions (and insignia) to the confraternities, sodalities, guilds and societies.[68] Liverpool's north end evolved as a distinctively Irish community in which new churches with Irish priests became the centre of associational life, not least for women, encouraging the tendency to residential propinquity.[69] In welfare and other functions, the Catholic parish co-existed in complementary rivalry with the local pub (where Irishness was given a more masculine expression – the heaviest manual labourers such as coal heavers and salt heavers were allowed six to ten pints of beer daily, 'permitted even under Father Nugent's temperance pledge')[70] and as a supplement to informal street-based female networks of mutual aid. Collective mutuality was complemented by cradle-to-grave sickness and welfare provision through parish-funded charitable organisations and the 'micro welfare-state' within the city, mainly administered by Irish nuns.[71] As in Dundee, another area of high Irish in-migration, the Catholic church created 'an entire way of life based upon the parish church, school and church-hall', a 'community within a community' in which 'religious, political, economic, educational and recreational elements were so fused as to form a culture from which total withdrawal was unlikely'.[72]

Interventionism by priests, nuns or 'plain-clothes' SVP visitors helped to mitigate some of the worst housing and social conditions in Liverpool (while ensuring against leakage from the faith). *Squalid Liverpool*, the shocking report published in 1883, accorded particular praise to the Catholic priest: 'the parson, the policeman, the doctor, the nurse, the relieving officer, the nuisance inspector, and the school board inspector all in one'. As the report made clear, there was no Protestant equivalent of this

---

68] St Francis Xavier, for example, ran a Girls' Club for the poorest school leavers who could not afford the penny weekly subscription or the cost of the cloak required by the Guild of St Agnes, see Feehan 'Charitable effort', p. 71 note 80. Feehan draws upon the parish magazine, *Xavierian*, to show how 'a whole host of spiritually orientated parochial organizations were developed to assist adults and children'.

69] J.D. Papworth, 'The Irish in Liverpool, 1835–71: Segregation and Dispersal', unpublished PhD thesis, University of Liverpool, 1982, ch. v. See also Frank Boyce, 'From Victorian "Little Ireland" to Heritage Trail', 277–97.

70] *Sir James Sexton, Agitator: an Autobiography* (London, 1936), 110.

71] Frank Boyce, 'Irish Catholicism in Liverpool: the 1920s and 1930s', in *The Irish in British Labour History*, ed. John Belchem and Patrick Buckland (Liverpool, 1993), 96.

72] H. McLeod, 'Building the "Catholic Ghetto"', 411–44.

impressive out-reach structure.[73] Some Anglicans denied the need on the grounds that 'squalid' Liverpool and 'Romish' Liverpool were coterminous (and alien) territory. Suburban 'clerkland', where the lower middle class were struggling to uphold respectability (and religious observance) against foreign (mainly German) competition, seemed more appropriate for Anglican concern.[74] Others, however, sought to adapt Catholic best practice in the central slums, most notably Abraham Hume, statistician, urban sociologist and, from 1847, Anglican vicar of the new district of Vauxhall. Born in County Down into a Presbyterian family, Hume renounced his religious upbringing and heritage on becoming an Anglican. Continued internal dispute with his family developed into strident repudiation of all forms of Nonconformity.[75] A great advocate of the territorial parish system, he condemned the dissenters in Liverpool for deserting the poor: based on the voluntary or congregational principle, Nonconformist churches had followed richer members of the congregation out into the suburbs.[76] Rich and poor were now 'practically as wide apart as if they resided in two separate quarters of the globe'.[77] To Hume's dismay, the parish system was weak in

73] *Squalid Liverpool*, 38. 'It is impossible to withhold admiration from these fearless men, whatever one's doctrines and religious beliefs may be. It is absolutely certain that they represent the one single influence for good which reaches the lowest depth of squalid poverty in Liverpool. The Protestant churches apparently have no sufficient machinery for penetrating so far beneath the surface of smug respectability. The poor of our churches and dissenting chapels are infinitely rich in comparison with these people. Your commissioners do not belong to the Roman Church, but they are compelled to bear witness to the fact that in squalid Liverpool there is scarcely any trace of the operation of any other religious organisation', ibid., 36.
74] Farley, 'Ryle', 237–40. Clerks complained of being replaced by cheap German clerks who 'can get along a little sausage and bread all day'. See the evidence of Howard Wright Moore, *Full Report of the Commission of Inquiry into the Subject of the Unemployed*, 59–60
75] See, for example, Hume to George Hume, 25 Jan. 1845, Letter-book 3, f.137, Public Record Office of Northern Ireland (hereafter PRONI): D2765 papers of the Hume Family. There is much similar correspondence in this large archive.
76] For similar criticism, see *Squalid Liverpool*, 87–88: 'What is the history of half the Protestant churches and chapels in Liverpool? The original position of the congregation has been rendered untenable by surrounding poverty and wretchedness, the old building has been sold – perhaps converted into a brewery – and the good people have erected for themselves a pleasant suburban place of worship. So religion is constantly trailing like a skirt behind prosperity, following it up step by step away from the region where its comforts, its enlightenments, and its humanising influences are most sorely needed.'
77] Rev. A. Hume, *Condition of Liverpool, Religious and Social* (Liverpool, 1858), 24.

Anglican Liverpool: much of the town council church-building of the eighteenth century had subverted the system; endowments were woefully inadequate; and richer parishes did little to help the poorer.[78] Undeterred, Hume sought to employ middle-class deaconesses to assist in the church's 'home mission to the poor', distinguishing their role from that of either 'Bible-women' or 'District-Nurses': 'From the former indeed our plan is distinguished by its embracing the official employment of women of the higher ranks, and by its organization being parochial, – from the latter by its aiming chiefly at spiritual ends while not forgetting the temporal'.[79] Hume was also an influential force in establishing Liverpool as a separate diocese, but under Ryle's tenure the enhanced status brought little addition to charitable donation or parochial welfare activity. Household visits were given new strategic importance in Ryle's evangelical mission, but were strictly restricted to spiritual purposes.[80]

Through its welfare provision, the Catholic church identified itself with Irish migrants, prompting a strong reciprocal reaction. Although higher than in other denominations, regular religious observance was a minority pattern in the Liverpool-Irish Catholic community. Indifference to Catholic ritual, however, should not be read as indifference to Catholicism itself. 'Nominal' Catholics as most of them were, the Liverpool-Irish maintained an exalted notion of their own religion and a sovereign contempt for the 'haythen' by whom they were surrounded. This loyalty owed much to the priest, a respected and revered figure – based in an adjacent humble abode – who displayed none of the condescending censoriousness of the Protestant clergy and other 'visitors to the poor'.[81] Denuded of 'wealth and worldly position', the Catholic clergy 'belonged to what was really and truly the church of the poor'.[82]

78] L.E. Bosworth, 'Home Missionaries to the Poor: Abraham Hume and Spiritual Destitution in Liverpool, 1847–84', *Transactions of the Historic Society of Lancashire and Cheshire*, Vol. 143 (1993), 57–83.
79] Hume Letter-book 10, f. 220, handbill, 'Female Parochial Agency for Liverpool' (n.d.).
80] Farley, 'Ryle', ch.3.
81] R. Samuel, 'The Roman Catholic Church and the Irish Poor', in *Irish in Victorian City*, ed. Swift and Gilley, 267–300. For an interesting comparison, stressing the key role of 'nominal' Catholics, see W. Sloan, 'Religious Affiliation and the Immigrant Experience: Catholic Irish and Protestant Highlanders in Glasgow, 1830–50', in *Irish Immigrants and Scottish Society in the Nineteenth and Twentieth Centuries*, ed. T.M. Devine (Edinburgh, 1991), 67–90.
82] Speech by John Yates at St Mary's Catholic Young Men's Society, *Daily Post* 20 Nov. 1861.

Dialectical developments in other denominations completed the process by which Irishness and Catholicism became synonymous (along with poverty) in Victorian Liverpool. Irish Protestant migrants merged (even to the point of anonymity) into the host mainstream. The Ulster-Scots (and their distinct Irish Presbyteries) disappeared quietly from view, denied any equivalent to the 'Scotch-Irish' identity of their compatriots in America. Anglo-Irish migrants were enthusiastic (often demagogic) advocates of Britishness, the populist Protestant identity which secured Tory hegemony in Liverpool until the Second World War and beyond.

Presbyterian migrants were cast adrift from their former home: links with Ulster were broken as they were brought within the British synod. The Irish Islington Church in Liverpool, formed in 1843 by Irish Presbyterian migrants, connected itself with the Presbytery of Belfast. A bitter dispute ensued with the Presbytery of Lancaster which was not resolved until the name Irish was deleted, and the General Assembly of the Presbyterian Church in Ireland had disclaimed 'any intention of invading the jurisdiction or territory of the English Synod'.[83] Members of the Reformed Presbyterian Congregation in Liverpool, part of the Eastern Synod of the Reformed Presbyterian Church in Ireland, tried to retain ministerial (and other) links with Belfast, but were finally compelled to transfer allegiance to the Reformed Presbytery of Glasgow in 1857 (under whose auspices a church was built in Shaw Street).[84] On an informal level, however, they continued to provide a reception service at Liverpool for emigrant Ulster Presbyterians en route to America.[85]

As the Catholics claimed the Irish as their own, Anglo-Irish evangelicals in Liverpool stood forward as the standard bearers of British Protestantism, led by the redoubtable Revd Hugh McNeile, 'eloquent even beyond Irish eloquence, Protestant even beyond Irish Protestantism'.[86] Samuel Holme, the Tory culture-broker, applauded the prominence of Irish Anglicans (often in search of a living) in local Protestant associations:

83] 'The Rise and Progress of Presbyterianism in Liverpool' in *Jubilee Memorial of Canning Street Presbyterian Church* (n.p., n.d), 119–20. *Minutes of the General Assembly of the Presbyterian Church in Ireland* (Belfast, 1850), 315 and 381.
84] PRONI: CR5/3, Reformed Presbyterian Church Records: Shaw Street, Liverpool. Presbyterian Historical Society of Ireland, *Minutes of the Annual Meeting of the Eastern Reformed Synod in Ireland at its meeting in Belfast 1857*, 20.
85] PRONI: D1835/27/5/3, Letter from Liverpool to James Staveley, 1 Dec. 1860 (on emigration database at Ulster-American Folk Park).
86] 'A Celebrated Ulster Divine', *Belfast News-Letter* 5 Apr. 1924, cutting in Bigger Collection, Belfast City Library.

We are deeply indebted to the Irish clergy ... Irish energy, and Irish vivacity, have assisted to kindle the latent warmth of England, and united, they emit a cheerful blaze ... on their fidelity, humanly speaking, the destiny and glory of this country mainly depends (hear): and I trust that every pulpit throughout England will ring with a sound and scriptural defence of Protestant principles (cheers).[87]

Fuelled by sensational and lurid stories of the horrors of Catholicism in Ireland, militant Protestantism was to resonate with the wider British public. Although an Irish implant, Protestant sectarianism drew upon an English narrative of libertarian struggle which recognised that 'it is to their qualities, derived from their religion, that Englishmen owe their liberties'. McNeile, a master of populist rhetoric, invoked the patriotic duty to defend 'the glory of England, her open bible, her liberty, her free press, her independence of mind in determining to stand by her law, and not to allow any man, sovereign or subject, to be absolute in the land'.[88] Militant Protestant sectarianism became the very symbol of British patriotism, integral to the 'common sense' of the working man.[89] McNeile's Operative Protestant Association was quickly incorporated within the panoply of local Tory organisations alongside the Operative Conservative Association and other militant Protestant voluntary groups, including the rejuvenated Orange Order which recruited strongly among workers with no Ulster connections. Thenceforth, Orangeism developed what Don MacRaild has described as 'an associational culture that echoed certain aspects of the impressive parish-level organizations of working-class Irish Catholics'.[90] Irish Protestantism was subsumed within a wider British membership and identity, upheld by an interlocking associational network (or 'pillar' to use Dutch terminology) – party, popular and sectarian – which facilitated ready interaction (and political mobilisation) between the classes.[91]

87] *Seventh Annual Report of the Liverpool Protestant Association* (Liverpool, 1842), 46–47.
88] Revd Hugh McNeile, *The Gunpowder Plot and the Revolution of 1688* (Liverpool, 1854), 12.
89] Joan Smith, 'Class, Skill and Sectarianism in Glasgow and Liverpool, 1880–1914', in *Class, Power and Social Structure in British Nineteenth-Century Towns*, ed. R.J. Morris (Leicester, 1986), 158–215.
90] Don MacRaild, *Irish Migrants in Modern Britain, 1750–1922* (Basingstoke, 1999), 103.
91] Sandra O'Leary, a PhD student in the School of History, University of Liverpool, is applying the Dutch concept of 'pillarisation' to an understanding of popular Toryism in Liverpool.

The Catholic hierarchy in Liverpool sought to disarm this Protestant populism by insisting on the Englishness of their religious practice. 'I am English', Bishop Goss repeatedly averred, 'I am a real John Bull, indeed I am a Lancashire man.'[92] While Goss studiously refrained from open embrace of the Irish cause, the 'hibernicisation' of Liverpool Catholicism perforce continued apace. Allied to its spiritual purpose, Catholic welfare provision – like its denominational education[93] – sought to prepare the Irish poor (as the hierarchy wished) for citizenship in conformity with dominant (English) notions of respectability. It was an uphill task. Although no longer seen as a contaminating and demoralising presence, the Liverpool Irish were perceived in terms of the late-Victorian anxiety over degeneration, a combination of racial genetics, colonial history and the urban slum. 'These people are what the conditions of their environment have made them', *Squalid Liverpool* concluded its Saturday night exploration into the most notorious area of Irish Liverpool:

> The wretches you see in Scotland-road inherit probably the proclivities of a dozen generations of degradation. Many of them come from Ireland, and bitterly has the sister country repaid us for centuries of wrong inflicted by our hands. Her poor, ground down from year to year to lower and lower depths of poverty, at length are driven by hunger from the sterile heaths and mountain sides, to find and to intensify in our great cities a squalour worse than they originally experienced. But the blame is not theirs. They have been born to ugliness and destitution, and with predispositions to vice transmitted from many a savage, ignorant ancestor.[94]

In seeking to reform the 'residuum', however, the Catholic church constructed a self-enclosed network of 'improvement' which, for all its commitment to Victorian 'respectability', served to underline Catholic apartness. Where Anglican and Nonconformist agencies came together in coordinated effort in philanthropy, 'scientific charity', and social work – often under encouragement from the Unitarian elite – Catholics kept apart, determined to look after their own (whether 'deserving' or

92] Doyle, 'Goss', 442.
93] Hickman, *Religion, Class and Identity*, chs 4 and 5.
94] *Squalid Liverpool*, 77. The ethnic inflexion was less pronounced in London in the shift in social concern from 'demoralisation' to 'degeneration'. See Gareth Stedman Jones, *Outcast London: a Study in the Relationship between Classes in Victorian Society* (Harmondsworth, 1976), ch. 16.

'undeserving').[95] Indeed, this self-sufficiency may well have engendered a dependency culture as the inverse pride in poverty and destitution, the initial register of Catholic middle-class social consciousness, was embraced by impoverished Irish migrants, by the poor recipients themselves. In Liverpool, as in Dundee, poverty was rationalised by the conflation of religious adherence and ethnic affiliation.[96] Sanctified by Catholicism, poverty – 'the ancient Catholic virtue of Holy Poverty' – became the proud hallmark of being genuinely Irish. In Liverpool, as throughout the diaspora, Irish migrants constructed their own 'culture of poverty'. Some Irish-Australians chose to eschew the Australian narrative ethic of individual material advancement in favour of the communality and solidarity – and welfare benefits? – available only at the bottom of the social, but not the spiritual, scale.[97] A similar mentality seems to have applied in parts of Irish-Liverpool.

Despite its importance in the construction of ethnic identity, the extent (and influence) of Catholic provision in Liverpool should not be exaggerated. Welfare was a competitive imperative, a matter of confessional honour and pride in the prevalent sectarian rivalry. Beyond its provision, there was no distinctive Catholic social philosophy or social movement, 'European' features which took root on the Clyde, but not on the Mersey.[98] Furthermore, it was neither comprehensive nor inclusive. The workhouse and other official institutions loom large in Pat O'Mara's autobiography of a 'Liverpool Irish Slummy' – as do pawnshops and money-lenders, the infamous "Fish and Money" people, who relied less upon collateral than upon their reputation for administering physical beatings to recalcitrant debtors'. Accepting the Catholic church's teachings on marriage, his much-

95] Philanthropy apart, there was little co-ordination between Nonconformist denominations as the son of a Baptist minister was to attest: '… between Orthodox Dissent and the Unitarians, a wealthy, and from a civic point of view, a most useful and influential sect, there was a great gulf fixed. My father, I am convinced, would sooner have seen me a pious convert to the Church of Rome than sitting at the feet of that pre-eminently Christian philosopher and eloquent divine, James Martineau, then the minister of Hope Street Unitarian Chapel', Augustine Birrell, *Some Early Recollections of Liverpool* (Liverpool, 1924), 8.
96] W.M. Walker, 'Irish Immigrants in Scotland: their Priests, Politics and Parochial Life', *Historical Journal*, Vol. 15 (1972), 649–67.
97] Patrick O'Farrell, *The Irish in Australia* (Kensington, NSW, 1986), 299.
98] T. Gallagher, 'The Catholic Irish in Scotland: In Search of Identity' and B. Aspinwall, 'The Catholic Irish and Wealth in Glasgow', in *Irish Immigrants and Scottish Society*, ed. Devine, 19–43 and 91–115.

abused mother was unable to turn to the priest and the parish at times of greatest need, when compelled to leave her drunken and violent husband.[99]

While some 'soupers' may have profited from competing charitable provision, playing one agency (or denomination) off against another,[100] there were those who fell outside any safety net, victims of the uncoordinated expansion of social intervention in Victorian Liverpool. In the early 1860s, for example, there were a number of clashes between the Health Committee and the poor law authorities over the non-interment of corpses left to putrefy in the slums. Among the most notorious cases was that concerning an elderly couple, Mr and Mrs M'Cann of number 7 court, Upper Henderson Street, who had taken in Biddy Malew's illegitimate child for a small weekly payment. According to the M'Canns, payment stopped after the first fortnight, as Malew got married and deserted the sickly infant. On its death a few months later, the destitute M'Canns were unable to pay for the baby's burial, and left the corpse in the house in a soapbox begged from a shopman as a makeshift coffin. The Toxteth Board of Guardians were unmoved, claiming that the M'Canns had continued in receipt of income for the child (and hence had earlier refused to allow its removal to the care of the workhouse) supplemented by charitable aid from St Patrick's. Despite his appearance in police court as 'the very embodiment of poverty and misery', the septuagenarian M'Cann was not apparently without resources or reserves: according to the relieving officer, he 'got his living by begging and sent money to Ireland; he also kept a donkey and cart'. The Board were prepared to bury the child – legally the responsibility of the M'Canns as householders – by taking the donkey and cart to cover costs, an offer flatly refused. Although ordered by the court, on application by the Health Committee, to bury the putrefying corpse, the Board condemned such ill-judged (and increasing) intervention in its affairs:

It would continue as heretofore to exercise its discretion as to who should be buried at the expense of the ratepayers. It was much easier for a board of guardians to be lavish of the public money than to resist attempts at imposition. By resisting them, they often got the character of being stern and hard-hearted, but cases were constantly occurring in

99] O'Mara, *Liverpool Irish Slummy*.
100] 'It was the willingness of the poor to turn elsewhere which encouraged Catholic leaders to provide more generous and varied forms of relief for their less fortunate parishioners', Kanya-Forstner, 'The Politics of Survival', 247.
101] 'Police Court', *Daily Post*, 20 Aug., and 'Toxteth Guardians', *Daily Post*, 23 Aug. 1861.

which it was necessary for them to be firm and to refuse relief.[101]

Significantly, poor law 'discretion' was later to be exercised in a more generous fashion – with a considerable increase in out-relief in Irish districts – following reform of the vestry in the 1890s and the application of Irish nationalist political pressure.[102]

Seen from the perspective of an Irish nationalist in the early years of the twentieth century, there was much welfare work still to be done in the 'Irish Colony' in Liverpool. While friendly society membership of the Irish National Foresters should be encouraged among 'all people of Irish birth or descent' in the city, the most pressing need was the establishment of 'a non-political and non-sectarian Irish society of social workers in Liverpool to improve the conditions of slum life'. No less urgent than welfare, however, was the need to recover and project a sense of 'Irishness', to embrace an identity beyond loyalty and allegiance to the local Catholic parish. Here other forms of associational and political culture were recommended: the Gaelic Athletic Association, the Gaelic League, the Liverpool Irish Society, the Liverpool Irish Literary Society, and the prompt formation of a Liverpool branch of Sinn Fein.[103]

102] Feehan, 'Charitable effort', 409–10 and 447.
103] Anon., *The Liverpool Irishman, or Annals of the Irish Colony in Liverpool* (Liverpool, 1909).

5

Micks on the make on the Mersey*

Inspired by the methods and paradigms of historical geography and urban sociology, studies of Liverpool have tended to concentrate on spatial and socio-economic factors, ignoring cultural and associational aspects of ethnic identity and collective mutuality. Census statistics have been deployed as 'hard' evidence for a positivist case study in the paradigmatic 'urban transition'. Liverpool was ahead of other cities in its 'modern' spatial segregation, a pattern already established on Merseyside by 1871. Distinct areas took their character and identity from the socio-economic status of the residents, although choice of residence was influenced by subsidiary variables such as position in the family life cycle, and ethnic affiliation. In this model, Irishness was reduced to the lowest socio-economic level, an ethnic stigma that clung to the worst housing areas adjacent to waterfront casual labour markets, recourse of the impoverished famine migrants. Predominantly unskilled, the Irish tended to congregate around 'core-streets' in the 'instant slum' of the north end with its purpose-built court housing, and in the failed middle-class suburb of the south end, hastily 'made down' into overcrowded and cellared street housing. The persistence rate was remarkably low as the Irish, lacking attachment to particular jobs or buildings, favoured short-distance movements within familiar territory. Few, however, moved outwards and upwards. Considerably smaller in numbers, the Irish middle class, a longer-established and mainly Protestant mercantile presence, rapidly

* This essay draws upon material in two recently published papers: 'Class, Creed and Country: the Irish Middle Class in Victorian Liverpool' in *The Irish in Victorian Britain: the Local Dimension*, ed. R. Swift and S. Gilley (Dublin, 1999), 190–211; and 'The Liverpool-Irish Enclave', *Immigrants and Minorities*, Vol. 18 (1999), 128–46.

distanced themselves from the 'core' areas, abandoning any identification with such Irishness to seek socio-economic integration in the more desirable residential location of outer suburban Merseyside.[1] Isolated and segregated in the city, the Liverpool-Irish poor were simply assumed to lack the resources for associational culture – other than the 'muscle' to defend disputed residential boundaries.[2]

This crude assumption, at odds with post-modernist emphasis on cultural identities, has remained unchallenged despite the burgeoning interest in the Irish in Britain. Dismissed as a sectarian redoubt marginal to the cultural and political life of the nation, Liverpool has no place in the emergent orthodoxy, focused on assimilation, small-town studies and ethnic fade.[3] Given its size, however, the Liverpool-Irish 'colony' compels attention. It is perhaps best approached through comparison with large migrant communities overseas, enclaves within which 'ethnic' culture was not only retained but rewarded, a pattern which continues among some contemporary Hispanic and Asian migrant communities.[4] Indeed, much could be gained by cross-chronological comparative analysis with Puerto Ricans in the present-day United States. Both groups are technically citizens, not

1] R. Lawton and C.G. Pooley, 'The Social Geography of Merseyside in the Nineteenth Century', Final report to the SSRC, July 1976 (Department of Geography, University of Liverpool); R. Lawton, 'The Population of Liverpool in the Mid-Nineteenth Century', *Transactions of the Historic Society of Lancashire and Cheshire*, Vol. 107 (1955), 89–120; and C.G. Pooley, 'The Residential Segregation of Migrant Communities in Mid-Victorian Liverpool', *Transactions of the Institute of British Geographers*, Vol. ii (1977), 364–82; 'Migration, Mobility and Residential Areas in Nineteenth-Century Liverpool' (unpublished PhD thesis, University of Liverpool, 1978); and 'The Irish in Liverpool *circa* 1850–1940' in *Ethnic Identity in Urban Europe*, ed. M. Engman, F.W. Carter, A.C. Hepburn and C.G. Pooley (Aldershot, 1992), 71–97. For a critique of Lawton and Pooley, see Richard Dennis, *English Industrial Cities of the Nineteenth Century* (Cambridge, 1984), 4, 205–65. See also J.D. Papworth, 'The Irish in Liverpool 1835–71: Segregation and Dispersal' (unpublished Ph.D. thesis, University of Liverpool, 1982).
2] Frank Neal, *Sectarian Violence: The Liverpool Experience 1819–1914* (Manchester, 1988).
3] Steven Fielding, *Class and Ethnicity: Irish Catholics in England, 1880–1939* (Buckingham, 1993), 5. However, even in small towns where their numbers were low, Irish in-migrants developed distinctive patterns of association within the wider framework of local social networks, see Louise Miskell, 'Custom, Conflict and Community: a Study of the Irish in South Wales and Cornwall, 1861–1891', (unpublished PhD thesis, University of Wales, Aberystwyth, 1996).
4] For a critical introduction to the 'enclave-economy hypothesis' of Alejandro Portes and colleagues, see J.M. Sanders and V. Nee, 'Limits of Ethnic Solidarity in the Enclave Economy', *American Sociological Review*, Vol. 52 (1987), 745–67.

immigrants, but paradoxically this status seems not to have been advantageous in securing upward social mobility.[5] The comparative analysis attempted here is less ambitious. Restricted to the Irish in the nineteenth century, it seeks to apply the ethnic functionalism displayed by Irish-Americans (under the control of middle-class culture brokers) to their compatriots in Liverpool.

Across the Atlantic, the 'Gaelic-Catholic-Disability variable' came into play, to use Don Akenson's iconoclastic terminology. Individual 'success' and ambition may have been hindered, but this cultural construction was by no means dysfunctional: it provided the 'ethnic' base for considerable 'resource mobilisation' at collective level.[6] Unskilled Irish-Americans came to acquire uniformed status, pensions and 'lace-curtain' economic security, tangible benefits secured by 'Irish' control of local machine politics, public construction projects, the Catholic church and labour unions. The Irish also established ethnic niches in particular sports, entertainment and organised crime (most notably, labour racketeering and the 'politics-gambling' complex). Irish-Americans were anchored in the urban structure by a network of associations, formal and informal, religious and political, respectable and unrespectable, all proudly affirming their hyphenated identity.[7] Once implanted, ethnic associational culture provided a means by which successful middle-class Irish-Americans could guard against social radicalism while keeping a check on violent inflexions of nationalism.[8] Was there an equivalent leadership cadre in Irish-Liverpool? Comparative

5] 'Introduction: Ethnic Life in Chicago' in Melvin G. Holli and Peter d'A. Jones, *Ethnic Chicago* (4th edn, Grand Rapids, MI, 1995), 10.
6] D.H. Akenson, *The Irish Diaspora* (Belfast, 1996), 237–42.
7] L.J. McCaffrey, *Textures of Irish America* (Syracuse, NY, 1992). See also the section on 'Ethnic Institutions' in *Ethnic Chicago*, 503–639; and Hasia Diner, '"The Most Irish City in the Union": The Era of the Great Migration 1844–1877' in *The New York Irish*, ed. R.H. Bayor and T.J. Meagher (Baltimore, 1997), 87–106. There is little evidence, however, that the Irish in Liverpool (or elsewhere in Britain) developed an ethnic niche in serious organised crime, see Frank Neal, 'A Criminal Profile of the Liverpool Irish', *Transactions of the Historic Society of Lancashire and Cheshire*, Vol. 140 (1991), 87–111; and Roger Swift, 'Heroes or Villains?: The Irish, Crime and Disorder in Victorian England', *Albion*, Vol. 29 (1997), 399–421.
8] Kerby A. Miller, 'Class, Culture and Immigrant Group Identity in the United States: the Case of Irish-American Ethnicity' in *Immigration Reconsidered*, ed. V. Yans-McLaughlin (New York, 1990), 96–129. D.B. Light, Jr, 'The Role of Irish-American Organizations in Assimilation and Community Formation' in *The Irish in America: Emigration, Assimilation and Impact*, ed. J. Drudy (Cambridge, 1985), 113–42. See also, T.N. Brown, *Irish-American Nationalism* (Philadelphia and New York, 1966).

research into large migrant communities throughout late nineteenth-century Europe has shown how ethnic associations 'tended to be related to social class, to be bids for group leadership'.[9] Does Irish-Liverpool conform to the pattern? Was there an Irish-Liverpudlian middle class able to construct, implant and uphold a distinctive ethnic Irishness against competing and alternative identities and affiliations?

The middle-class presence in the Irish diaspora has been rescued from neglect by revisionist interest in what Roy Foster has called 'Micks on the make.'[10] As the census analysis suggests, some middle-class migrants favoured 'ethnic fade', distancing themselves from all things Irish to effect the quickest route out of the Liverpool 'ghetto' into economic success and assimilation. A significant number, however, having identified their best interests (or market niche) in servicing the migrant community, chose to accentuate their Irishness. In Irish-Liverpool, as in other large migrant enclaves, there was considerable internal stratification, but socio-economic success was often legitimised through ethnic leadership, both cultural and political. Thanks to these middle-class culture-brokers, 'Irishness' was to span socio-economic and spatial boundaries.

By their very weight, census statistics tend to obscure the minority of Liverpool-Irish above the adverse variables and lowly occupations. Factor analysis of the (pre-Famine influx) 1841 census, by which time there were already 49 639 Irish-born in Liverpool, some 17.3 per cent of the population, has highlighted three main clusters of interrelated variables, a three-class model with an Irish/unskilled/lodging/industrial service/court house cluster at the base. Comparative analysis confirms the picture: all migrant groups were under-represented in the unskilled stratum, except the Irish; all migrant groups, except the Irish, were of a higher socio-economic status than the locally born.[11]

Nationalist leaders, however, proffered a different perspective, stressing the socio-economic importance and success of their compatriots against the

9] A. C. Hepburn, 'Ethnic Identity and the City' in *Ethnic Identity in Urban Europe*, ed. Engman et al., 4. See also, J. Rex and B. Drury (eds), *Ethnic Mobilisation in Multi-cultural Europe* (Aldershot, 1994); J. Rex, D. Joly, and C. Wilpert (eds), *Immigrant Associations in Europe* (Aldershot, 1987); and M. Cross (ed.), *Ethnic Minorities and Industrial Change in Europe and North America* (Cambridge, 1992).
10] Roy Foster, 'Marginal Men and Micks on the Make: The Uses of Irish Exile c.1840–1922' in *Paddy and Mr. Punch* (London, 1995), 281–305.
11] I.C. Taylor, 'Black Spot on the Mersey: a study of environment and society in 18th and 19th Century Liverpool', unpublished PhD thesis, University of Liverpool, 114–15. Pooley, PhD thesis, 178–79.

odds. In his written report on the Liverpool-Irish to the Council of the Irish Confederation in Dublin in 1848, George Smyth, a successful hat manufacturer in Paradise Street, stressed their crucial contribution to the local economy:

> The Irishmen in Liverpool perform nearly all the labour requiring great physical powers and endurance. Nine-tenths of the ships that arrive in this great port are discharged and loaded by them; and all the cargoes skilfully stowed. Out of 1,900 shipwrights 400 are Irish, or of Irish parents; and although Liverpool is a port rather for repairing than building vessels, there is one Irishman of the three or four master builders of the town, and many Irish foremen. In almost every branch of trade Irishmen, notwithstanding the many prejudices with which they have to contend, have risen to the highest promotion ... a large majority of the boot and shoemakers and tailors of the town are Irish, and I know that Irish skill is recognised in the various foundries. Many Irishmen are distinguished for their ability as architects, draftsmen [sic], and clerks of the works.[12]

Reporting on the Irish in Britain for *The Nation* in 1872, Hugh Heinrick calculated that between one-fifth and one-sixth of the Irish in Liverpool, broadly defined and estimated at 180 000 in total, were 'above the ranks of ordinary toil'. By his 'approximate estimate' there were 300 merchants of the 'first class'; 1500 merchants and factors of the 'second class'; 800 in the professions; 3500 clerks; 3500 shopkeepers; and 2000 commercial assistants. 'Of the Irishmen who have attained to wealth and position in Liverpool', Heinrick asserted, 'there is not one in fifty who has not risen from the ranks of labour – and risen, too, in opposition to prejudices and various hostile circumstances such as no other member of the community has had to encounter and endure'.[13]

Such figures and claims served a political purpose and must be read with caution. Prejudice and discrimination apart, upward mobility proved difficult to effect and was not always appealing (given the ethnic solidarity and conviviality at the bottom of the hierarchy). Restricted to 'niche' occupations, Irish labourers remained labourers, protected against undue adversity by Ribbonite and other ethno-sectarian networks of collective

---

12] *Nation*, 15 Jan. 1848.
13] Heinrick's letter, dated 24 September 1872, is reprinted in *A Survey of the Irish in England, 1872*, ed. Alan O'Day (London, 1990), 87–95. A Wexford-born journalist, Heinrick's career later included a spell in Liverpool on the *United Irishman*.

mutuality. Evidence presented to Cornewall Lewis's 1835 report on the state of the Irish poor in Britain suggested that the Liverpool-Irish, whether in construction, warehousing or the merchant marine, were ill-disposed towards apprenticeship or training in mechanics. Those with ambition, the Revd Fisher noted, 'rise to be small-shopkeepers, provision-vendors and public house keepers'.[14] As the Irish 'colony' grew, so such opportunities expanded. For those with enterprise, Irish-Liverpool held out the prospect of upward mobility into the petite bourgeoisie (and beyond) by catering for the migrant community itself, a socio-economic advance topped off by ethnic political prominence. In the Ribbonite period, pub-licans and shopkeepers, many of whom had risen from the ranks, provided a conduit between the higher ranks of the middle-class 'nationalist' leadership cadre – shipping agents, doctors, tradesmen – and the wider migrant community. Account should also be taken of those who operated at the disreputable and parasitic end of the ethnic economy and displayed no political ambition or conscience. Such, for example, were the Irish runners, 'infamous land pirates' who fleeced their innocent migrant fellow country-men in transit in Liverpool. The Liverpool 'man-catchers', the *Morning Chronicle* reported, were 'principally Irishmen themselves, and knew both the strength and weakness of the Irish character – many of whom, poor and miserable as they look, have sovereigns stitched amid the patches of their tattered garments – and persuade them into the purchase of various articles, both useful and useless'.[15] Irish women were later to the fore in the money-lending business in the Liverpool slums, as for instance Mary Ellen Grant, the 'Connaught Nigger' with an Irish mother and West African father. The technique deployed by Grant and the other 'fish and money people' was to tour the slums with 'baskets of putrid fish and inquire who

14] PP1836(40)XXXIV: Royal Commission on the Condition of the Poorer Classes in Ireland: Appendix G, The State of the Irish Poor in Great Britain, 8–41. Signifi-cantly James Muspratt – father of the British heavy chemical industry, who left Dublin in 1822 to produce soda by the Leblanc process on Merseyside – spoke favourably of the work application of his Irish workforce, as did the soap and sugar manufacturers, also large employers of Irish labour in the kinds of job which native workers preferred not to do. The most disparaging comments came from Irish merchants in linen and other imported goods at Liverpool, commercial men with little workplace contact with their fellow-countrymen.

15] 'Emigration – Emigrants and Man-Catchers', *Morning Chronicle* 15 July 1850. One Irish migrant, wise by experience, wrote that 'if a man had 7 senses, it would take 500 senses largely developed to counteract the sharpers of Liverpool', Thomas Reilly to Kelly, 19 June 1848, National Library of Ireland Mss 10,511 [2].

among the men had "got on" down at the dock … if any of the men's wives were courageous enough to borrow four shillings in cash, they would also have to take two shillings' worth of this putrid fish. The debt would therefore stand at six shillings to be paid on the following Saturday – or else.'[16]

Standing forward as political activists, nationalist leaders were a visible minority within the Irish middle class in Liverpool, an opaque, complex and diverse grouping.[17] Differing considerably in background – in wealth, income and resources – middle-class migrants displayed a bewildering gamut of political, cultural and 'ethnic' attitudes towards Ireland and Irishness. Research in progress suggests a division between the charitable and cultural Irish projects sponsored by those at the apex (those members of the middle class whose business interests and commercial practices extended above and beyond Ireland and the Irish-Liverpool enclave) and the ardent nationalist politics pursued by Catholic merchants in the Irish trade and members of professions in daily contact with poor Irish migrants.

Unlike more distant migrant enclaves, Liverpool was generally perceived as stepwise entrepôt, not as place of destination. As the 'second metropolis', Victorian Liverpool was an important staging-post in career development for the Irish middle class – forerunners of today's brain-drain 'Eirepreneurs'[18] – a convenient testing-ground for their journalistic, legal, medical, clerical, entrepreneurial and other talents. When Justin McCarthy came to Liverpool as a 'stepping-stone on my way to London', he found that most of the staff on the *Northern Daily Times* were also Irish.[19] What happened to those who remained in Liverpool, whose onward metropolitan career ambitions were thwarted? How did their embitterment translate into political terms? Considerable numbers seem to have adjusted to permanent residence with little difficulty. A satirical survey of the local medical profession, written by a second-generation Irish-Liverpudlian journalist, identified a number of long-established Irish practices (replenished by

16] Pat O'Mara, *The Autobiography of a Liverpool Irish Slummy* (London, 1934), 66–67.

17] For a wider analysis of the 'Liverpolitan' middle classes, see John Belchem and Nick Hardy, 'Second Metropolis: the Middle Class in Early-Victorian Liverpool' in *The Making of the British Middle Class?*, ed. A. Kidd and D. Nicholls (Stroud, 1998), 58–71.

18] Mary P. Corcoran, 'Emigrants, *Eirepreneurs* and Opportunists: a Social Profile of Recent Irish Immigration in New York City' in *New York Irish*, ed. Bayor and Meagher, 461–80.

19] J. McCarthy, *Story of an Irishman* (London, 1904), 102. Irish artisans were similarly mobile: Dublin, Liverpool and Manchester formed an inner triangle within a wider circle from London to Glasgow, Belfast to Cork, Bristol to London.

professional chain migration) located both in fashionable areas and in the north end Irish 'ghetto'.[20] As the *Liverpool Weekly Mercury* observed: 'Many of the most prosperous men in England, and more especially in Lancashire, are of Irish birth, who have found here a larger and richer field for their talents and energies than they were able to meet with in their own country'.[21]

The Irish were well represented in merchant ranks, reflecting the crucial significance of Irish trade in Liverpool's development. In his 1848 report, George Smyth calculated the value of the 'Irish trade, with or through, Liverpool, import and export' at 'between eleven or twelve millions a year ... greater than that of any other country of the world, the United States of America alone excepted'.[22] Economic historians have focused on the more exotic (and financially less secure) trans-oceanic trade, but Liverpool's prosperity was underwritten by its near-hegemony in the movement of goods and people within and around the 'inland' Irish Sea, trade which attracted and required a significant Irish mercantile presence.[23]

Liverpool was Ireland's most convenient point of access to distribution networks in Britain and overseas. Channelled through Dublin, the Irish export economy was overwhelmingly agrarian: Ireland supplied over 75 per cent of the cattle, pigs, oats, oatmeal, butter, eggs, lard and preserved meats imported coastwise at Liverpool.[24] The Anglo-Irish cattle trade was dominated by the Liverpool firm of Cullen and Verdon, comprising Michael and James Cullen – brothers of Cardinal Paul Cullen of Dublin – and their brother-in-law, Peter Verdon. During the famine, the Liverpool-based branch of the Cullen family, noted for their wealth and charity, set up temporary hospital facilities on their premises for Irish migrants.[25] Although overshadowed by Dublin, Belfast served as outlet for linen and other industries increasingly concentrated in the Lagan valley. By 1839, fierce competition

20] J.F. McArdle, *A Patient in Search of a Doctor* (Liverpool, 1872). The author was the son of the publican, John McArdle.
21] *Liverpool Weekly Mercury* 23 Mar. 1867, quoted in C.L. Scott, 'A Comparative Re-examination of Anglo-Irish Relations in Nineteenth-Century Manchester, Liverpool and Newcastle-upon-Tyne', unpublished PhD thesis, University of Durham, 1998, 82–83.
22] *Nation* 15 Jan. 1848.
23] See the interesting portrayal of 'Liverpool and the Celtic Sea' in Robert Scally, *The End of Hidden Ireland* (New York, 1995), ch.9.
24] Valerie Burton, 'Liverpool's Mid-Nineteenth Century Coasting Trade' in *Liverpool Shipping, Trade and Industry*, ed. Valerie Burton (Liverpool, 1989), 26–66.
25] Peadar Mac Suibhne, *Paul Cullen and His Contemporaries* (5 vols, Nass, 1967–77), Vol. iv, 28.

in cross-channel steamship services had effected what the local Chamber of Commerce described as 'an entire change in our foreign commerce, which instead of being carried on as formerly by means of vessels sailing direct from Belfast at long and uncertain intervals is now conducted entirely through Liverpool from whence the valuable manufactures of the North of Ireland are transmitted almost daily to their ports of foreign destination'.[26] There were mutual benefits in this entrepôt arrangement, the basis for subsequent close links between Liverpool shipowners and Belfast shipbuilders.[27] In the 1830s, Liverpool merchants invested heavily in the Ulster Railway (a director was appointed specially to safeguard their interests), and in the new Ulster Bank, 46 of the 56 British shareholders were Liverpool-based, including William Brown.[28]

Brown was a merchant prince in the Atlantic trade, a major figure in flax, linen, cotton, and then in merchant banking. Born near Ballymena to Alexander Brown, a linen merchant of the 'smaller class', William was taken to Baltimore and thence to Liverpool, gaining considerable experience and wealth in the wider family business. W. and J. Brown, however, fell into serious difficulties in 1836–37, from which it was rescued by the coordinated support of three Belfast banks. Brown's ancestral links were an important factor (no doubt it was in the banks' self-interest to prevent the collapse of a major Liverpool finance house involved in the Atlantic trade). Thereafter, Brown seems to have forsaken his Ulster heritage to secure his position (and a baronetcy) within the Liverpool mercantile elite and the Lancashire establishment. Presbyterianism was abandoned in favour of Anglicanism, and his benefaction was expended, much to the annoyance of Irish nationalists, not on his native Ballymena but on funding the magnificent Liverpool museum, an immortalising symbol of the culture of commerce in the 'Florence of the north'.

Across the sectarian divide, wealthy Irish Catholic merchants in Liverpool followed a different assimilationist path, quickly acculturating themselves to the modern Tridentine norms and political alignment of the small

26] Belfast Chamber of Commerce to Morpeth, quoted in L. Kennedy and P. Ollerenshaw (eds), *An Economic History of Ulster* (Manchester, 1985), 64. See also, R.C. Sinclair, *Across the Irish Sea: Belfast-Liverpool Shipping since 1819* (London, 1990).
27] These links were often mediated by G.C. Schwabe, Liverpool merchant and financier, personal friend of Edward Harland and uncle of Harland's assistant, Gustav Wolff. See Kennedy and Ollerenshaw, *Economic History of Ulster*, 89–91.
28] E.R.R. Green, *The Lagan Valley 1800–50* (London, 1949), 51–54. P. Ollerenshaw, *Banking in Nineteenth-century Ireland: The Belfast Banks, 1825–1914* (Manchester, 1987), 48–51.

and socially exclusive indigenous Catholic community – high levels of church attendance, and unquestioning support of rich local Liberal (often Unitarian) merchants, progressive friends of Catholic emancipation. Henceforth, energies were expended on imposing these confessional and political norms on the ever-growing number of their impoverished co-religionists and fellow countrymen in Liverpool. At the time of the famine influx, the most prominent and influential Irish Catholic merchant was Richard Sheil, cousin of the Irish Liberal MP and orator of the same name. Born in Dublin in 1790, Sheil travelled extensively, particularly in the Caribbean, promoting the Liverpool-based import and export agency of which he was a partner. The principal Catholic layman in Liverpool, and for long the only Catholic member of the council (where he sat as a Liberal), Sheil was a founder member of the Protector Society established in 1839 to register Catholic voters, and of its important successor, the Catholic Club.[29] Intended as a counterweight to Hugh McNeile's Protestant Association in the fierce controversy over the schools issue, the Catholic Club was to extend and solidify the Liberal alliance. Prosperous middle-class Catholics, Irish and otherwise, were brought together in continuing support of Liberal candidates drawn from Unitarian and progressive ranks within the mercantile elite.[30]

A pillar of mercantile respectability who had acquired the 'solid and practical character of Englishmen', Sheil did not conceal his 'rich, mellifluous brogue' or his Irishness:

> Ireland has not a son who loves his country better ... He is ever to be found at the head of any movement which, in his opinion, is calculated to promote her political or religious welfare, and his enthusiasm on such occasions shows with what heartiness and zeal he spouses the cause of Ireland.[31]

29] In 1857 he was joined on the Liberal benches in the council chamber by his Catholic business partner, J.C. Corbally. Sheil's public prominence was in marked contrast to the low profile adopted by Edward Smith (c.1808–1880) of 6 Abercromby Square, a penniless migrant from Co. Down, who made a fortune through colliery ownership. Despite his staunch Catholicism, the wealthy Smith appears not to have donated to charitable (or political) causes, personal information kindly provided by Cornelius Smith, Blackrock, Co.Dublin.
30] L.W. Brady, *T.P. O'Connor and the Liverpool Irish* (London, 1983), 27–28.
31] H. Shimmin, *Pen-and-Ink Sketches of Liverpool Town Councillors* (Liverpool, 1866), 87–91, which observed: 'Some think that the honourable gentleman mistook his profession when he became a merchant, and that he would have achieved great distinction had he been an ecclesiastic'. See also the obituary notice in *Porcupine* 4 Mar. 1871.

However, there was a pronounced social conservatism to his political and public life. An intense Catholic, deeply distressed by the spread of 'philosophical unbelief' and social radicalism, Sheil's abiding concern was to prevent leakage from the faith among the ever-growing numbers of Irish in Liverpool. A private letter written in 1854, in the wake of parliamentary attempts to intervene in the management of Catholic convents, gives an indication of his outlook and fears:

> It is almost appalling to hear the lengths to which the bulk of non Catholic young men will go in denying the essential truths of Christianity, and as among the working classes there appears to be a perpetually encreasing [sic] spirit of opposition to the classes above them, I can not help thinking that we are living upon a half concealed volcano which will before many years elapse burst into an eruption as will not be very easily restrained.[32]

A communicant at St Oswald's, Old Swan, the most fashionable of local Catholic churches, Sheil took particular delight, as his letter-book attests, in arranging elite charity functions within the social 'season': in June and July 1853, for example, he organised a fancy dress ball and a soirée in aid of Catholic charity schools.[33] Other aspects of his considerable charitable work were more tiresome:

> The entire task of collecting subscriptions for the maintenance of the Catholic Chaplain to the industrial schools has been allowed to fall upon me and as you will easily conceive this circumstance not only causes very serious inconvenience to me but is also attended with much danger to the charity, for nothing but the great stagnation of business could have enabled me to spare the amount of time which I have already devoted to going about in search of subscriptions.[34]

Fund-raising was a never-ending task given the Catholic commitment to a

---

32] National Library of Ireland, Dublin, Mss 32,483: Letter-book of Richard H. Sheil, 1850–56, ff. 365–66, letter dated 9 June 1854.
33] Sheil Letter-book, f.318, Sheil to Runge, 15 Apr. 1853, one of many letters on such matters. For the 'elite' at St Oswald's, see Dublin Diocesan Archives: Cullen Papers, 353/2/101, Fr McGinity to Dr Cullen, 3 Dec. 1852.
34] Sheil Letter-book, f. 392 to President of the Irish Catholic Club, 19 Dec. 1854. See also, f. 393 to Bishop of Liverpool, 27 Jan. 1855; f. 400 to James Whitty, 15 June 1855; f. 414 to Rev. R. Shea, 29 Oct. 1855; and f. 415 to Canon Newsham, 30 Oct. 1855.

self-enclosed welfare network from cradle to grave. The Catholic cemetery
at Ford – an essential requirement as Catholics 'naturally shrank from
having their bodies laid by the side of persons who had never known the
efficacy of the sacraments' – imposed a 'heavy debt on the church', the
ground having been 'purchased at great expense and great risk'. In solicit-
ing subscriptions from Sheil and other wealthy merchants at the consecration service, Bishop Goss appealed to both commercial Merseypride and
Christian salvation:

> In the distance was the town in which they lived, with its docks not to
> be surpassed in the world – with its magnificent Free Library – its gor-
> geous St George's Hall – its splendid Town Hall – a city rivalling in its
> splendour the gorgeous places of Pagan antiquity, where the merchants
> toiled to obtain fortunes to hand down to prosperity; but how long
> would they enjoy it? – 'here to-day and gone to-morrow' ... let them live
> ever mindful of this, and at the same time let them order their lives so
> that they might make their future end happy. Why strive for accumu-
> lated wealth? Why not dispense it now to appease the wrath of God? For
> by fasting, prayer and alms deeds, we were told the Lord was appeased.[35]

Creed was placed before country for wealthy Irish merchants like Sheil,
sponsors of the Catholic project. For such Catholic 'protectionists', to use
Ryan Dye's terminology, nationalism was at odds with Catholic ultramon-
tanism and assimilationist loyalty to Britain.[36]

Commitment to Irish nationalism as the prime loyalty was found in
different quarters, in lower ranks of middle-class (predominantly Ulster-
born) Catholic migrants. Two groups were particularly prominent: those
whose commercial interests still centred on the Irish Sea (and took them
regularly across to Ireland)[37] and those whose professional practices
brought them into everyday contact with the Liverpool-Irish community.
Terence Bellew McManus, leader of the Irish Confederates in Liverpool in
1848, the year of European revolution, was a forwarding and commiss-
ioning agent prominent in the Irish trade who passed £1.5 million in goods
per annum. An Ulster-Catholic by birth, he was a friend of Charles Gavan

35] 'Consecration of the Cemetery Chapel at Ford', *Daily Post*, 9 Sept. 1861.
36] Ryan Dye, 'Catholic Protectionism or Irish Nationalism? The Associational and
Political Culture of Liverpool Catholicism, 1829–1845', *Journal of British Studies*,
forthcoming.
37] Informers such as E. Rorke and P.H. McGloin were also recruited from these
two-way commercial travellers. See above 73–74.

Duffy from early business days together in Monaghan.[38] McManus was assisted by his second cousin, Dr Patrick Murphy, whose professional duties had brought him into direct contact with the famine influx. In recognition of his heroic exertions, Murphy was invited to preside at a meeting in February 1848 to raise a memorial to the monks of St Benedict who had given up their lives in the typhus epidemic, the 'Irish fever', of 1847.[39] Significantly, two other members of the medical profession, Francis O'Donnell and Lawrence Reynolds, were among the most militant of the Liverpool Confederates in 1848.[40]

Having abandoned O'Connellite restraint in the 'springtime of the peoples', nationalist leaders in Liverpool (and throughout the diaspora) were soon forced into embarrassing retreat, shamed by the humiliating turn of events in Ireland (where 'revolution' collapsed in farcical confrontation in Widow McCormack's cabbage patch in Ballingarry, County Tipperary). The events of 1848 confirmed the diagnosis of the 'Condition of England' question: an alien presence, the Irish were the 'internal other' incapable of political and cultural conformity – an identity subsequently elaborated (on both sides of the Atlantic) by pseudo-scientific racialism. Paddy was henceforth depicted in cartoons and other representations as racially inferior, more ape-like than man, a despised simian with ludicrously exaggerated prognathous features.[41]

The hardening of attitudes was first apparent in the Liverpudlian satirical press, ahead of the events of 1848. Amiable amusement at Irish

38] T.G. McAllister *Terence Bellew McManus 1811(?)–1861* (Maynooth, 1972), draws extensively on the Clark Compendium, Diocese of Clogher Archives, Bishop's House, Monaghan (hereafter Clark Compendium). R. Carleton, a Waterford trader, praised McManus's 'character for great integrity – so high his character that most of the Irish business was transferred to him'. See National Library of Ireland (hereafter NLI), Mss 812, Briefs for the counsel in the trial of T.B. McManus.
39] T.N. Burke *Catholic History of Liverpool* (Liverpool, 1910), 95.
40] For details of the leaders and events of 1848, see John Belchem, 'Liverpool in the year of revolution: the political and associational culture of the Irish immigrant community in 1848' in *Popular Politics, Riot and Labour: Essays in Liverpool History 1790–1940*, ed. John Belchem (Liverpool, 1992), 68–97. My conclusions differ significantly from two earlier studies: W.J. Lowe, 'The Chartists and the Irish Confederates: Lancashire 1848', *Irish Historical Studies*, Vol. 24 (1984), 172–96; and Louis R. Bisceglia, 'The threat of violence: Irish Confederates and Chartists in Liverpool in 1848', *Irish Sword*, Vol. 14 (1981), 207–15.
41] Note the attention accorded to 1848 in the revised edition of L. Perry Curtis, Jr, *Apes and Angels: the Irishman in Victorian Caricature* (Washington, 1997), charting (p. xxii) 'the emergence of a bestialized or demonized Paddy, bent on murder and mayhem, in cartoons after the rather farcical rebellion of 1848'.

Table 5.1 List of Irish Confederates indicted for seditious conspiracy, Liverpool, August 1848

Name	Occupation	Sentence
T.B. McManus	Shipping Agent	Transportation
Lawrence Reynolds	Surgeon	Not tried
Patrick Murphy	Surgeon	Not tried
Francis O'Donnell	Surgeon	2 years
P.H. Delamere	Coal-agent	Acquitted
Joseph Cuddy	Porter	1 year
Matthew Somers	Provision dealer	2 years
Robert Hopper	Joiner	2 years
Edward Murphy	Bookkeeper and collecting clerk	3 months
James Laffin	Tailor	Not tried
Martin Boshell	Clerk	1 year
Thomas O'Brien	Labourer	Not tried
George Smyth	Hat manufacturer	2 years
Patrick O'Hanlon	Labourer	Not tried
James O'Brien	Linendraper	6 months
James Campbell	Labourer	Not tried

Source: Reprinted from John Belchem (ed.), *Popular Politics, Riot and Labour: Essays in Liverpool History 1740–1940* (Liverpool, 1992), 97.

arrivals – the *Picturesque Hand-Book to Liverpool* recommended the entertainment to be derived by a visit to the Clarence Dock when the Irish packets docked – gave way to harsh stereotyping as the famine influx intensified. Noting the arrival of 'Irish Pauper, Esq. and family, attended by his suite, including Messrs. Fever, Starvation, Taxes, Impudence and Knavery, etc.', the *Liverpool Lion* chronicled Mr Dennis Bulgruddery's brazen prowess and blarney in cheating relief agencies, fraudulent begging, inner-city pig-keeping, heavy drinking and fisticuffs.[42] However, it was not until the political events of 1848 – satirised as *'Pat-riot-ism'* – that the liberal

42] 'Mr Dennis Bulgruddery's Correspondence with his Relations in Ireland' began in *Liverpool Lion* 8 May 1847. See also, 'Unfashionable Arrivals at the Clarence Dock', ibid., 11 Dec. 1847.

press fanned such anti-Irish prejudice. The *Liverpool Mercury*, outraged by the political ingratitude (and unconstitutional extremism) of the Irish in their midst, sought to banish them from local labour markets, and called for publication of the names of all known Confederates. Attitudes hardened on discovery that charitable funds, intended for the Irish poor, were diverted to assist the restoration of the Pope in Rome.[43]

The harsh response to 1848 prompted the Liverpool-Irish middle class to rethink their ways and means. Nationalist leaders did not abandon the physical force option, but they sought to elevate nationalism as a cultural project, located beyond and above oath-bound Ribbonism, violence and the pub. Middle-class Catholic merchants, shocked by the liberal backlash and continued conflict over Italian affairs and threats to the temporal power of the papacy, began to question their traditional political alignment.[44] Here were the beginnings of a new conjuncture: constitutional home rule nationalism, a 'new departure' in Irish-Liverpool which could draw upon the combined resources of the middle class, the pub and the parish.

Established during 'a lull in Irish politics', the Emerald Minstrels exemplified the new cultural emphasis. Having gained instruction from Nugent's Catholic Institute ('the great centre of Catholic education and talent'), its founders sought to make the Liverpool Irish 'both respectable – in the best sense – and respected'. Significantly, the Minstrels' cultural agenda – the 'cultivation of Irish music, poetry and the drama; Irish literature generally, Irish pastimes and customs; and above all, Irish Nationality' – excluded Irish language.[45] There were vestigial clusters of Irish speakers in some of the poorer districts (sufficient numbers to prompt Abraham Hume to learn gaelic to improve his 'mission'),[46] but language retention and/or retrieval was at a discount in Irish Liverpool. In this respect (as in several others), the Irish migrants differed significantly from their Welsh counterparts. Relatively dispersed across the city, the Welsh

43] *Liverpool Mercury* 1 and 11 Aug. 1848, cited in Scott, 'Comparative Re-examinations', 77. *Jones*, 10 Mar., 5 May and 14 July 1849.
44] 'The Papacy was the centre of civilisation in Europe – the corner-stone of the whole of European society – and without that corner-stone the whole edifice would fall to ruins', speech at the Holy Cross Young Men's Society, *Daily Post* 18 Dec. 1861.
45] John Denvir, *The Life Story of an Old Rebel* (Dublin, 1910), 118–22.
46] Scott, 'Comparative Re-examination', 242. Significantly, there was a thriving Liverpool branch of the Irish Society, a Protestant proselytising body in Ireland for promoting scriptural education among Irish-speaking Catholics chiefly through the medium of their own language. The Rev. Canon McNeile took the chair at the 1861 annual meeting of the branch, *Daily Post* 17 Dec. 1861.

displayed a strong sense of ethnic 'community', bonded together by strong cultural-linguistic ties: families travelled long distances to worship together in Welsh-speaking Calvinist chapels; Welsh newspapers circulated in the city; and the National Eisteddfod was held there on several occasions. By contrast, 'Irishness' was able to flourish without a specific 'celtic' language, undermining the efforts of a later generation of nationalist leaders in Liverpool (as throughout the diaspora) to promote a 'gaelic revival'.[47]

The cultural project of the Minstrels, subsequently embraced by the National Brotherhood of St Patrick, sought to contest English stereotyping. Nationalist culture-brokers encouraged the Irish to take control of their own ethnicity, to stand above the curious compound of political stigma and commercial caricature imposed upon them. To the despair of nationalists, 'Irishness' – in depoliticised and ersatz form – was a marketable commodity, enjoyed by respectable Liverpool audiences in need of vicarious saturnalian release at Paddy's expense.[48] 'We were doing good work', John Denvir observed of his fellow Minstrels, 'by elevating the tastes of our people, who had, through sheer good nature, so long tolerated an objectionable class of so-called Irish songs, as well as the still more objectionable "stage Irishman"'.[49]

To this end, the National Brotherhood of St Patrick, a legal cover for Fenianism, launched at a fund-raising meeting in Liverpool for the funeral of the exiled McManus, offered a range of cultural activities, located (where possible) away from the pub.[50] Here their efforts coincided with those of Nugent and the Catholic temperance agencies, whose counter-cultural provision – including the engagement of professional Irish jig-dancers – sought to keep pace with developments in the licensing trade, thrown open to 'free trade' by the magistrates in 1862.[51] However, tensions still persisted between the nationalists and the church, prompting the former into closer engagement with pub-based Fenianism.

47] On the absence of a 'gaelic' perspective, see Anon., *The Liverpool Irishman, or Annals of the Irish Colony in Liverpool* (Liverpool, 1909).
48] Scott, 'Comparative Re-examinations', 230–31.
49] Denvir, *Life Story*, 118–19. Among the most successful of the 'stage Irishmen' was John Drew, 'one of the first delineators of Irish character with a Liverpool audience', who acquired international celebrity for his portrayal of 'The Irish Emigrant' and 'The Happy Man'. See 'Mr John Drew', *Daily Post* 8 Nov. 1861.
50] See above, 97
51] Canon Bennett, *Father Nugent of Liverpool* (Liverpool, 1949), 109–13; and see above, 117–19.

Table 5.2 Number of licensed public houses and beer-houses in Liverpool, 1850–1899*

Year	Public houses	Beer-houses	Total
1850	1480	700	2180
1857	1493	897	2390
1862	1667	1005	2672
1866	1933	873	2806
1876	1919	334	2253
1899	1865	244	2109

* A free trade system of open licensing was introduced in 1862 and abolished in 1866. Note the decline in the number of beer-houses (regarded as more disorderly) following legislation in 1869 transferring their licensing from the Excise to the magistrates.
Source: Morning Chronicle 2 Sept. 1850; Paper presented by Mr Rathbone, First Report from the Select Committee of the House of Lords on Intemperance, Appendix C, p. 334, PP1877(171)XI, covering 1857–1876; and *Daily Post*, 21 Aug. 1899.

Rumours of serious involvement abounded, notably the claim that the highly respectable Liverpool Irish Rifle Corps of Volunteers, commanded by the Catholic Peter Bidwell, a corn importer and Liberal councillor, provided military training for Fenian recruits. According to the *Mercury*, 'many men of Irish descent, who hold their heads high on 'change, are strongly suspected of coquetting with this new idée Irlandaise'.[52] Police and intelligence reports, however, suggested otherwise, pointing to a middle-class withdrawal from active leadership of insurrectionary nationalism. John Ryan was the exception who proved the rule: the son of a prosperous Liverpool merchant, he was to devote his life to Fenian military service as 'Captain O'Doherty'.[53] While eschewing active involvement or leadership, the Liverpool-Irish middle class were prepared to offer 'cover', assistance and bail surety to Irish-American officers and other Fenians on military duty, in flight or under detention. For example, Michael Breslin, a leading Fenian, posed as a traveller in the tea trade, having been specially supplied with samples and other credentials by the Liverpool tea merchant James

52] *Liverpool Weekly Mercury* 3 and 24 Feb. 1865, quoted in Scott, 'Comparative Re-examinations', 196.
53] Denvir, *Life Story*, 74, 77–78 and 111–12.

Lysaght Finigan, later MP for Ennis (1879–82).[54] Liverpool Fenianism, W.J. Lowe contends, was more important for its open-access pub-based conviviality, briefly shared with Irish-American officers, than for any military planning. With its network of twenty or so pubs and beershops across the city, Fenianism was essentially a social affair which 'furnished a popular organisational foundation that helped to build the constitutional home rule movement'.[55]

The first hesitant move towards a new political formation can be traced back to the Irish Catholic Club. Established in 1851 amid the controversy surrounding the restoration of the Catholic hierarchy, it represented the first tentative step away from the Liberal alliance and mainstream party politics: the club aimed to return an independent Catholic MP for the city within twenty years. However, in social composition and political practice it differed little from the Catholic Club. The leading figure was the Wexford-born merchant James Whitty, who came to Liverpool in 1848, established business as a woollen draper and entered local politics via membership of the Select Vestry (1853–65), thence as Liberal councillor for Vauxhall (1863–73). He was the cousin of M.J. Whitty, another County Wexford man. Originally from farming stock, he progressed through trade and journalism in Dublin and London to enjoy a long and varied career in Liverpool as its first head constable (the appointment of a Catholic to this sensitive post was one of the more imaginative and successful aspects of the Liberals' brief tenure of office in the 1830s), proprietor-editor of the *Liverpool Journal* and founder of the *Daily Post*.[56] For the most part, the Catholic Club and the Irish Catholic Club worked amicably together as middle-class representatives of the Irish-Catholic community. On a fund-raising trip for a Catholic University of Ireland, Father McGinity endeavoured to inject some competitive rivalry between the two societies, but the tactic misfired. He was politely informed by the Bishop that he had out-stayed his welcome in Liverpool: 'The wants of religion in the town are

54] Ibid., 124.
55] W.J. Lowe, 'Lancashire Fenianism, 1864–71', *Transactions of the Historic Society of Lancashire and Cheshire*, Vol. 126 (1977), 156–85.
56] Brady, *T. P. O'Connor*, 28. Biographical details can be found in the appendices to C.D. Watkinson, 'The Liberal Party on Merseyside in the Nineteenth Century', unpublished PhD thesis, University of Liverpool, 1967, and B. O'Connell, 'The Irish Nationalist Party in Liverpool, 1873–1922', unpublished MA thesis, University of Liverpool, 1971.

numerous and pressing indeed I may say greater than can be *adequately* supplied and you know that *Charitas bene ordinata* begins at home'.[57]

From the 1860s, the leading protagonist of home rule was John Denvir, a second-generation, upwardly-mobile Irish-Liverpudlian, an 'Emerald Minstrel' turned full-time political activist. Much to his delight, he could claim Irish birth, having entered the world in County Antrim when his parents briefly returned to the homeland on a work contract. Having followed in his father's footsteps as an apprentice joiner with a Liverpool firm of builders, Denvir established his own business in the trade. Thereafter, Nugent's patronage carried him upward, in recognition perhaps of his prowess as an evening class student at the Catholic Institute and of his enthusiastic adoption of the temperance cause (Denvir was the first to take the pledge at Nugent's League of the Cross). Presumably ignorant of Denvir's Fenian connections, Nugent appointed him as Secretary of the Catholic Boys Refuge, the showpiece of Catholic institutional charity, and then put him in charge of the *Catholic Times*. From his new printing and newsagency business in Byrom Street, Denvir turned his talents to full-time promotion of the nationalist cause: as well as his famous 'Irish Library' publications, he was responsible for the *United Irishmen*, organ of the new Home Rule Confederation, of which he was a founder member and later its national agent and organiser. As secretary of the Catholic Club, Denvir hoped to carry its rich merchants and Liberal councillors into the home rule camp. Soon disabused by such 'anti-Irish Irishmen', he devoted his energies to securing the return of independent Irish National councillors.[58]

Efforts were concentrated on the Scotland and Vauxhall wards, where the extensive parish and pub-based ethnic infrastructure facilitated an effective challenge to the traditional Liberal alignment. Aided by some enthusiastic electioneering by a local priest, Father McGrath, Denvir secured Lawrence Connolly's return for the Scotland Ward in 1875. Further electoral successes were to follow: Connolly was the first of 48 Irish Nationalists to sit on the council between 1875 and 1922. Furthermore, the Scotland Division became T.P. O'Connor's parliamentary fiefdom from 1885 to 1929, secured by the same ethnic electoral machinery. O'Connor's contribution to Liverpool-Irish politics was minimal, however: a carpet-bag

---

57] See the correspondence between McGinity and Brown, 12 and 13 Jan. 1853, in Cullen papers 325/8/1.
58] Denvir, *Life Story*, passim.

national political figure, he rarely visited the city and was a poor constituency member.[59]

Although a new departure, home rule drew upon the traditional leadership cadre. The mixture of continuity and change is perhaps best exemplified by the fate of the McArdle cousins, prosperous cotton merchants originally from Monaghan. Charles gained a Vauxhall seat for the Irish nationalists in 1876, while his cousin John, standing on the old Liberal-Catholic Club platform, was unseated in the Scotland ward by Dr Bligh, the Irish National candidate. Biographical details of the Irish National Party councillors show three major groups, the first two of which had previously been prominent in the Liberal-oriented Catholic Club.

First, there were the lawyers, doctors (including Bligh and his brother, close friends of Parnell) and other professionals whose practices covered the Irish community. There were no less than four INP councillors in the office of Irish-born solicitor W. Madden (O'Hare, Lynskey, Flynn and Madden himself, who represented the Scotland ward, 1885–87). In the upper professional echelons, the Liberal affiliation tended to persist. Thus, Charles Russell (later Lord Russell of Killowen), the most distinguished Irish barrister on the Liverpool-based Northern circuit, and the first choice of Denvir and Crilly to chair the local home rulers, declined to abandon the Liberals. However, his fellow barrister, the patrician Dr Andrew Commins, a pronounced anti-Fenian, served in his place: a member for the Vauxhall ward (1876–92), he acted as leader of the group on the council.[60]

The second major group consisted of traders who prospered and/or diversified as they took responsibility for the Liverpool end of Irish businesses. Connolly, the first to be elected, was a good example. A farmer's son from County Dublin, he came to Liverpool in 1857 in connection with his brother's Dublin-based business. Branching out from the family firm, he established his own business as fruit-broker and commission merchant, and then moved into property speculation, gaining a fortune from resort development at New Brighton (he left £78 000 in his will). Others included Limerick-born Patrick De Lacy Garton, wholesale fish dealer and owner of

59] Strictly speaking there was not an Irish National party, but five official home rule organisations which succeeded each other. However, there are good reasons to use the portmanteau term as O'Connell's thesis (indispensable for electoral and biographical detail) shows.

60] Commins's anti-Fenianism doubtless accounts for his disparaging (and inaccurate) recollections of McManus. See Commins to Clark, 12 May 1894, Clark Compendium: Envelope F.

a large herring fleet at Howth and Kinsale, and O. O'Hara, undisputed 'king' of the Irish egg trade. In typical Irish-Liverpudlian fashion, business success carried O'Hara (who came to Liverpool from Ireland in the early 1860s) into politics: a generous donator to party funds (he also made his Scotland Road premises available for party meetings), he was rewarded with a seat in the South Scotland ward (1895–98).

The final group, new to political leadership, included shopkeepers and others who attended to the daily needs of the Liverpool-Irish (these included the undertaking service provided at branches throughout the city by Dundalk-born J. Daly, member for North Scotland, 1895–1902). Here there were some genuine 'rags to riches' stories, retail entrepreneurs who made their fortune supplying basic pleasures within the ethnic 'enclave' – for example, J. Clancy (St Anne's, 1904–5; North Scotland, 1911–25) who began as a 'hotel boots' and then developed a lucrative tobacconist business, worth over £25 000 on his death; and 'Dandy' Pat Byrne (Scotland 1883; Vauxhall, 1884–90) who started work as a dock labourer, before acquiring a string of public houses, a remarkable wardrobe and a fortune estimated at £40 000. Only two of the Irish National councillors could be considered working-class, the first to serve on Liverpool council: J.G. Taggart (Vauxhall, 1888–1908) who rose from trade union office to become an estate agent (and thenceforth vehemently anti-Labour); and T. Kelly (Vauxhall, 1890–95) a salary-less commission agent.

The emergence of this new group reflected an on-going pattern of fissure and radicalisation in home rule nationalism in Liverpool. Division over Parnell and Irish policy was accentuated by local concerns: the desire to eradicate all vestige of patrician Liberal dependence, and the determination to protect the interests of the Catholic working-class community against the dominant Tory political machine. As local leadership of the Irish National Party passed steadily into the hands of second-generation (i.e. Liverpool-born) Irish, it displayed less interest in the fate of Ireland than in the immediate needs of the local Catholic community in housing and employment. Even so, the leadership remained distinctly middle-class. The new social radicalism owed much to the Harford brothers, Austin and Frank, scions of a prosperous Liverpool-Irish mercantile family in the woollen and cloth trade. Liverpool-born and educated, they successfully combined business and politics (Austin left £76 686 in his will). Having entered the council for South Scotland in 1898 and 1899 respectively, they developed a form of community politics which depended first on a large network of confidants able to produce the goods, and second on the continued estrangement of the Liverpool Irish from other (class-based) political formations. The slow advance of Labour in Liverpool was a tribute to their success.[61] Home rule matured into what Sam Davies has described as 'Nat-labism', a cross-class political formation which proved more resonant and enduring than conventional Lib-Labism elsewhere.[62]

A party of social inclusion, this ethno-sectarian political formation exemplified Liverpool exceptionalism. Elsewhere, as Alan O'Day has shown, middle-class Irish migrants, while generous with contributions to religious and humanitarian causes, were generally unwilling to engage in nationalist politics.[63] Glasgow was perhaps the nearest comparison, but despite the presence of a significant number of 'ghetto professionals' and sympathetic priests, the Irish vote carried little impact. The Catholic 'machine' extended no further than single-issue politics, mobilised only in defence of denominational education. As 'Red Clydeside' entered its second and more inclusive phase in the years after the First World War, the Irish were swiftly subsumed into working-class Labour.[64]

Although seemingly deviant, Irish nationalism in Liverpool represented a bid for wider inclusion in British politics. In similar manner to Irish-American nationalism, the Liverpudlian inflexion displayed increasing obeisance to host political and constitutional norms. No less chastened by the events of 1848, Irish-Americans – *in* the republic but not *of* it – had successfully pursued a number of strategies to legitimise their hyphenated

61] See the articles by A. Shallice, 'Orange and Green and Militancy; Sectarianism and Working-Class Politics in Liverpool, 1900–1914', and 'Liverpool Labourism and Irish Nationalism in the 1920s and 1930s', *Bulletin of the North West Labour History Society*, Vol. 6 (1979–80), 15–32, and Vol. 8 (1981–82), 19–28.

62] Sam Davies, '"A Stormy Political Career": P.J. Kelly and Irish Nationalist and Labour Politics in Liverpool, 1891–1936', *Transactions of the Historic Society of Lancashire and Cheshire*, Vol. 148 (1999), 147–89. See also his *Liverpool Labour: Social and Political Influences on the Development of the Labour Party in Liverpool, 1900–39* (Keele, 1996), 69–73.

63] Alan O'Day, 'Political Behaviour of the Irish in Great Britain in the Later Nineteenth and Early Twentieth Centuries', paper presented to the Irish and Polish Migration in Comparative Perspective Conference, Bochum, 6–10 Oct. 1999.

64] Iain McLean, *The Legend of Red Clydeside* (Edinburgh, 1983), 176–201. Tom Gallagher, 'The Catholic Irish in Scotland: In Search of Identity', B. Aspinwall, 'The Catholic Irisna and Wealth in Glasgow', and John McCaffrey, 'Irish Issues in the Nineteenth and Twentieth Century: Radicalism in a Scottish Context' in *Irish Immigrants and Scottish Society in the Nineteenth and Twentieth Centuries*, ed. T.M. Devine (Edinburgh, 1991), 19–43, 91–115 and 116–37.

identity: urban machine politics; institutionalised St Patrick's day display; Catholic conservatism; and a programme of Celtic cultural ethnicity promoted through middle-class-led organisations which conformed to the associational norms and values of the host society.[65] There was a similar conformist trajectory in Liverpool: violence was excluded, socialist radicalism was marginalised, while the poor were instructed in respectability and citizenship. Hence the Catholic church gave Irish nationalism its blessing, setting aside a previous range of objections: the need to place creed above country; the fear of a Protestant backlash by identification with the 'unEnglish' Irish; and Ultramontane repudiation of competitive national identities. However, the desired pluralist outcome was not achieved. In acculturating their own kind, nationalist culture-brokers and Catholic agents constructed a self-sufficient network which, to the eyes of the host population, served only to emphasise Irish-Catholic apartness. Ironically, the Liverpool-Irish bid for inclusion in the wider society served to confirm Irish 'difference': they remained the internal 'other' against whom the otherwise 'non-ethnic' English defined themselves. Where their compatriots in America were to enter the mainstream and enjoy the 'wages of whiteness', the Liverpool-Irish remained segregated in their enclave, as yet unable to align with a racial hierarchy that would reduce their ethnic difference (and disability) to insignificance.[66]

65] John Belchem, 'Nationalism, Republicanism and Exile: Irish emigrants and the revolutions of 1848', *Past and Present*, Vol. 146 (1995), 119–23.
66] David Roediger, *The Wages of Whiteness: race and the making of the American Working Class* (London, 1991), ch. 7; and Noel Ignatiev, *How the Irish became White* (London, 1995).

Part Three
TORY TOWN

6
Protectionism, paternalism and Protestantism: popular Toryism in early Victorian Liverpool*

L iverpool, a veritable stronghold of popular Toryism for much of the nineteenth and twentieth centuries, stands apart from the main-stream narrative of Conservative party history. Caradog Jones was struck by the 'independence' of Liverpool Toryism and the absence of national party leaders among its representatives: 'It is remarkable that few eminent members of the Tory and Conservative parties have ever sat for a city so staunch in its adherence to those faiths'.[1] Beneath the national leaders, personalities and politicians, the electoral success of popular Toryism depended on the organisational and rhetorical skills of 'culture-brokers', political activists who could forge alliances among heterogeneous (but exclusively male) social groups, adjusting the language according to audience and context.[2] No study of popular Toryism in Liverpool can ignore the demagogic oratory – 'eloquent even beyond Irish eloquence, Protestant even beyond Irish Protestantism'[3] – of the Rev. Hugh McNeile and his

---

* This is an amended version of a paper previously published as '"The Church, the Throne and the People: Ships, Colonies and Commerce": Popular Toryism in Early Victorian Liverpool', *Transactions of the Historic Society of Lancashire and Cheshire*, Vol. 143 (1993), 35–55.
1] D. Caradog Jones, *Social Survey of Merseyside* (3 vols: Liverpool, 1934), Vol. I, 44.
2] For the importance of 'culture-brokers', see James Vernon, 'Politics and the People: a Study in English Political Culture and Communication, 1808–68', unpublished PhD thesis, University of Manchester, 1991, ch. 7. On the wider historiographical debate, stressing the importance of cultural-political identities rather than socio-economic differentiation, see Dror Wahrman, 'National Society, Communal Culture: an Argument about the Recent Historiography of Eighteenth-Century Britain', *Social History*, Vol. 17 (1992), 43–72.
3] 'A Celebrated Ulster Divine', *Belfast News-Letter* 5 Apr. 1924, cutting in Bigger Collection, Belfast City Library.

'Irish Brigade' of stridently sectarian Ulster in-migrant Protestant preachers.[4] However, I want to draw attention to a less dynamic and more prolix orator, Samuel Holme – or Samivel Loquitur as he was known in the satirical press[5] – a local builder and first president of the Liverpool Tradesmen's Conservative Association. A talented organiser, Holme helped to construct a popular Tory identity based not only on Protestantism but also on protectionism, on a progressive 'one nation' philosophy sensitive to material circumstances and needs. It was a tribute to Holme's efforts that temporary perception about material advantage was transformed into lasting political habit, producing what John Vincent has described as the deepest and most enduring Tory 'deviation' among Victorian workers.[6]

Liverpool was an unlikely site for popular Toryism. A commercial seaport with a large casual labour market and proliferation of 'pitch-pot' masters, it lacked the large manufacturing plants in which Tory employer paternalism was to flourish best: 'In Liverpool, almost alone amongst the provincial cities of the kingdom, the intercourse between masters and men, between employers and employed, ceases on payment of wages'.[7] As a freeman borough, however, it possessed a pattern of liberties and endowments which sustained the Tory allegiance of riverside artisan trades, a continuous alignment from the early years of George III, perhaps best explained in terms of 'the autonomy of the political'.[8] Holme served his apprenticeship in this traditional system. Born around the turn of the century (his obituary notice in *Liverpool Celebrities* is imprecise on this vital detail),[9] Holme

4] 'McNeile has been called "the real creator" of Liverpool Conservatism. He made it unremittingly sectarian in character by condemning Popery both "as religious heresy ... and as political conspiracy"' (P.J. Waller, *Democracy and Sectarianism: a Political and Social History of Liverpool 1868–1939* (Liverpool, 1981), 11.
5] See, for example, the cartoon in *Jones* 14 July 1849.
6] J.R. Vincent, *Pollbooks: How Victorians Voted* (Cambridge, 1967), 61.
7] W.S. Trench and C. Beard, *Workingmen's Dwellings in Liverpool* (1871), quoted in M. Simey, *Charitable Effort in Liverpool in the Nineteenth Century* (Liverpool, 1951), 12. For the classic study of employer paternalism in the nearby industrial districts of Lancashire, see Patrick Joyce, *Work, Society and Politics: the Culture of the Factory in Later Victorian England* (Hassocks, 1980).
8] John Belchem, 'The Peculiarities of Liverpool' in *Popular Politics, Riot and Labour: Essays in Liverpool History 1790–1940*, ed. John Belchem (Liverpool, 1992), 3–7.
9] *In Memoriam of Liverpool Celebrities*, 114–17. The obituary notice in *Porcupine*, 9 Nov. 1872 gives no date of birth. H. Shimmin, *Pen-and-Ink Sketches of Liverpool Town Councillors* (Liverpool, 1866), 29–34 states that Holme 'was born, about the year 1800, "within gun-shot of the Town Hall", as we remember him to have once stated in public'.

entered politics in the 1820s, the last decade of the unreformed system. In this popular *ancien regime*, Tories and the freemen trades negotiated within a framework of mutual advantage. Political support was exchanged for economic protection. The Tories, as Holme appreciated, generally ran parliamentary candidates from the West India trade, merchants who were also shipowners and hence major local employers: 'I have always been of opinion that a West India merchant in Liverpool is rather a formidable opponent at an election, for they employ so many shipwrights, and so many in the ramification of those trades, that I believe that the person that opposes a West India merchant stands a very poor chance'.[10] Similarly, at local level Tory mayors recognised their electoral obligations by judicious intervention in waterfront trade disputes, according the shipwrights, as Kevin Moore has shown, considerable power at the workplace.[11] In the early 1830s, however, reform and the threat of freeman disfranchisement undermined the smooth operation of this time-honoured system.

True to his Tory colours, Holme stood forward to defend traditional liberties, upholding the independence, integrity and virtue of the Liverpool freemen in evidence to parliamentary select committees investigating corrupt practices. Although clearly distinguished from the merchants by his tradesman status, Holme was one of the largest employers in Liverpool. Proud of his origins as the son of a self-made tradesman, he enjoyed a ready rapport with working-class freemen, particularly in the St Andrew's Street area where he spent the fortnight before elections canvassing the 'very lowest generally living in courts'. 'Being well known among the lower classes', he explained, 'I have always considered that I should do much more good by taking an out-of-doors department.' During such canvassing, he was occasionally asked for a little 'allowance' for drink, but these were casual requests, he insisted, not political bargains: 'I am pretty well known in Liverpool by employing so many operatives, and I am frequently stopped in the street by those men, saying to me, in a jocular way, "Cannot you give us something to drink?" but that is at other times as well as the elections'. Among his own workforce, normally around 300 strong, there were some 40

10] Select Committee on Liverpool Borough Elections, Parliamentary Papers, 1833 (583), x, q. 4658. By contrast, merchants specialising in American trade tended to use American ships and to be Whigs and reformers in politics.
11] K.C. Moore, 'Liverpool in the "Heroic Age" of Popular Radicalism, 1815–20', *Transactions of the Historic Society of Lancashire and Cheshire*, Vol. 138 (1989), 137–57.

or so freemen, whom he expected 'to poll which way they pleased; but I advised them to vote for the party that I was canvassing for'.[12]

Although disfranchisement was avoided, the prompt registration of propertied electors in the wake of parliamentary and municipal reform rapidly reduced the significance of the freeman vote. The old 'out-of-doors' style of politics as practised by Holme – employer influence, bonhomie and beer – lost much of its purchase:[13] in 1835, indeed, the Tories were ejected from local office, their hereditary hold on power seemingly at an end. With Holme to the fore, the Tories promptly readjusted, pursuing a number of strategies – involving a range of cultural styles – to construct a wider constituency of support beyond the diminishing freeman vote.

Sectarianism proved the most successful of the new approaches, sweeping the Tories back into municipal office by 1841.[14] Previously the preserve of Ulster migrants and the hitherto diminutive Orange Order, sectarian rhetoric was readily appropriated by the Tory establishment when the newly-reformed liberal council introduced the non-denominational Irish system in the corporation's two elementary schools, restricting religious instruction to a selection of passages taken partly from the Catholic Douai version of the Bible.[15] Once again, the Tories posed as defenders of traditional liberties, upholding the Englishman's right to the Protestant Bible, open and entire, the very symbol of English religious and constitutional liberty. Holme, a prominent member of McNeile's Liverpool Protestant Association, spread his energies across an interlocking network of new sectarian and party organisations to condemn the 'double evil' of popery:

It is a political evil, for it enslaves instead of giving liberty. It is a religious evil, for its creed is false and it withholds the scriptures from

12] Select Committee on Liverpool Borough Elections, Parliamentary Papers, 1833 (583), x, evidence of Holme, qq. 4658–4745; and Select Committee to inquire into the Petition on Liverpool Borough, Parliamentary Papers, 1833 (139), x, evidence of Holme, qq. 4436–4527. Holme admitted to giving his own workmen 'a little allowance, perhaps on Saturday night a little to drink'.
13] On the general decline of the old outdoor electoral culture, see Frank O'Gorman, 'Campaign Rituals and Ceremonies: The Social Meaning of Elections in England 1780–1860', Past and Present, Vol. 135 (1992), 79–115.
14] 'The clergy have done it all', Holme proclaimed after the election victory. See Liverpool Mercury 29 Apr. 1842.
15] Frank Neal, Sectarian Violence: the Liverpool Experience, 1819 to 1914 (Manchester, 1988), chs 1 and 2. James Murphy, The Religious Problem in English Education: the Crucial Experiment (Liverpool, 1959).

the people, for the Pope knows well that popery and the free circulation of God's holy word cannot be co-existent.[16]

In supporting McNeile, the scourge of 'Romish devotion' and continental absolutism, Holme's purpose was essentially conservative: radical Dissent, the *real* threat to the liberty and property of the Anglican establishment in church and state, was condemned by association with the Catholic cause.[17] Speaking to the Operative Conservative Association in 1836, Holme castigated the 'fanciful theories' of the new Liberal council, trusting that the electors would soon 'return men who were not mere party men, but who would most zealously maintain those institutions which it was their duty to hand down unimpaired to the latest posterity'.[18]

Sectarianism drew upon a narrative of libertarian struggle, invoking an inclusive rhetoric of patriotic duty to defend what McNeile described as 'the glory of England, her open bible, her liberty, her free press, her independence of mind in determining to stand by her law, and not to allow any man, sovereign or subject, to be absolute in the land'.[19] When allied to ethnicity, Protestant sectarianism provided a solid base for popular Tory support, addressing workers' fears not of Rome or reform but of Irish migration. Through detailed knowledge of the local labour market, Holme appreciated the viability of a popular Toryism identified with defence of the 'marginal privilege'[20] of the English Protestant worker. Confined to the

16] Report of a meeting to form a branch of the Protestant Association in Toxteth, *Liverpool Standard* 30 Sept. 1840, quoted in Neal, *Sectarian Violences*, p. 65. See also Holme's speeches in the Annual Reports of the Liverpool Protestant Association for 1838 and 1839, pamphlets held in the British Library at 1608.733.
17] Barbara Whittingham-Jones, *The Pedigree of Liverpool Politics: White, Orange and Green* (Liverpool, 1936), 34–39. There were also close business ties between Holme and McNeile: Holme's firm built St Paul's, Toxteth, McNeile's new church, financed by grateful middle-class subscribers; Holme and his brother James were the architects for McNeile's new 'large and elegant' house in Aigburth, see Neal, *Sectarian Violence*, 63.
18] *Liverpool Courier* 26 Oct. 1836, quoted in Murphy, *Religious Problem*, 83–84. Holme took a leading role in the establishment of the Collegiate Institution, of which he was subsequently a director, to 'provide the commercial, trading, and working classes with an education in which secular instruction should be combined with religious instruction in the doctrines of the Established Church', ibid., 223, and Shimmin, *Pen-and-Ink Sketches*, 34.
19] Rev. Hugh McNeile, *The Gunpowder Plot and the Revolution of 1688* (Liverpool, 1854), 12.
20] See E.W. McFarland, *Protestants First: Orangeism in Nineteenth-Century Scotland* (Edinburgh, 1990), 87.

bottom of the labour market, the Irish, he explained to Cornewall Lewis's inquiry into the state of the Irish poor, found a niche in the kind of labouring jobs which native workers wished not to do themselves:

> At the chemical manufactories nearly all the dirty work is done by the Irish, under an overseer, who is generally not Irish. In soaperies and sugar-houses the common dirty work is usually done by them. All the low departments of industry are filled by the Irish ... I consider the Irish are of great value to the town; if it were not for the influx of them, the almost unlimited number at our command, and their willingness to do the dirtiest and the meanest work, the wages of common labour would rise considerably.

Following the long-established practice of his father, Holme relied heavily on such cheap labour in his building business, having some 130 Irish labourers on his books, mainly Catholics from Ulster and Leinster:

> I have never employed any one as a server of bricklayers but Irishmen ... Invariably those who come bricklayers' labourers remain bricklayers' labourers. I scarcely ever knew them wish to get higher ... We could not do very well without the Irish for hodmen. Englishmen will not carry the hod. The hoisting of large buildings may be done by machinery: I am now doing the new Custom-house in this way; but for small buildings the expense would be too great, and the labour of hodmen is indispensable.[21]

As he moved between the new sectarian and party organisations of the 1830s, Holme sought to construct a popular Toryism which would protect the English worker not only from political-religious enslavement but also from demeaning labour. An indispensable economic presence, Irish migrants were no less essential for the construction of a Tory identity in Liverpool: they were the internal 'other' against whom the English worker defined (and elevated) himself.

Holme's efforts to organise the Tory vote, however, were by no means restricted to the Protestant working class. Partisan sectarianism was the defining characteristic of the Liverpool Tradesmen's Conservative Association, of which he was the founder-president. Here master tradesmen,

---

21] Royal Commission on the Condition of the Poorer Classes in Ireland, Parliamentary Papers, 1836 (40), xxxiv, Appendix G, The State of the Irish Poor in Great Britain, evidence of Holme, 27–30.

shopkeepers and other members of the middle classes were enrolled in active support of:

> loyalty to the King, attachment to the House of Lords, as one strong bulwark of the real liberties of the people, and an increasing desire to return to the Commons' House of Parliament men of conservative principles, men who will resist the rash innovations of theoretical statesmen, and, above all, will secure to the people of Great Britain and Ireland, undiminished and unimpaired, those means of instruction in the Protestant Religion which they now so freely possess.[22]

A different cultural style was on display, with respectability and deference taking the place of the populist conviviality exhibited towards working-class freemen. Leading party figures, local members of the landed gentry and other dignitaries were regularly invited to grace the society's dinners and meetings. Judging by the collection of autograph letters in the Liverpool Record Office, few such invitations were accepted. George Hamilton, MP for Dublin, sent his apologies with requisite tact and politeness, stating his conviction that 'the political regeneration of the Country will be attributable mainly to the revival of sound Constitutional feeling and principles – and to the union of all classes of Society – effected by means of Societies like yours'.[23] Others, such as Hesketh Fleetwood, were less courteous, condemning the impact of party organisation on true conservatism and gentlemanly independence:

> Amongst the ill effects of party it always appeared to me that the banding together of societies such as yours has had the effect of promoting the private interests of second and third rate Parliamentary adventurers for it has become proverbial in political life that party like an eel generally has its head pushed forward by the wriggling of the body and tail. Political party has tended and especially now does tend, to prevent the best public men in the country from cooperating with each other.[24]

22] *Rules of the Liverpool Tradesmen's Conservative Society* (n.p, n.d).
23] Liverpool Record Office 920MD 394, Autograph letters from MPs, f. 46. G.A. Hamilton, 15 Oct. 1836.
24] Hesketh Fleetwood, ibid., f. 55. Viscount Sandon, the local MP, accepted Holme's invitation to join 'your *select* party in the amphitheatre' to celebrate the second anniversary of the Society, Sandon, 3 Oct. 1837, ibid., 395 f. 7a.

Undeterred by such haughty rebuffs, Holme continued his efforts to construct a broad-based popular Toryism, concentrating his energies on municipal improvements. As a tradesman, he did not belong to the elite institutions of polite culture, the preserve of merchant princes and the professions, but he participated prominently in the more practical and applied local societies, such as the Lyceum (of which he was president in 1839 and 1842)[25] and the Polytechnic Society, where 'the active and vigorous character of the commercial and trading community can be inseparably united with the graces and accomplishments which distinguish the man of literature and of science'. In 1843, the year following his first election to the town council, he addressed the Polytechnic Society on the need for public improvements in Liverpool, the start of a sustained campaign to boost civic pride, commercial efficiency and public health through 'width of streets – beauty of elevation – harmony of parts – ventilation and drainage'.[26] As a builder and Tory, Holme's multi-faceted urban improvement project bore a distinctive political imprint, embracing the latest technology while repudiating laissez-faire political economy with its 'inordinate love' of cheapness and competition.[27]

It was this 'mistaken economy', most evident in the adjacent cost-cutting manufacturing districts, which threatened the commercial efficiency of the port, where the necessary replacement of the old timber warehouses by fire-proof brick and iron structures required regulation and control:

> The warehouses throughout the town are generally loaded most heavily, and any error in construction will soon be discovered ... hence the necessity of throwing overboard that unwise economy which saves an architect's commission at the risk of the building, and of subjecting builders to a competition, which practically, in the majority of cases, obliges many men to execute their work in the cheapest manner, or

25] See list of Presidents, *Laws of the Lyceum* (Liverpool, 1849).
26] Samuel Holme, *The Public Improvements of Liverpool. An Essay, Read at the Monthly Meeting of the Polytechnic Society ... 15 March 1843* (Liverpool, 1843), 5 and 26.
27] Some observers were perplexed by this combination of technological progressivism and political conservatism: 'It has been a matter of surprise to many that a gentleman possessing so much perception, and who has been a man of progress, should have continued so steadily attached to a political party which has almost become fossilised; and that one who has been foremost in the race of mechanical science should yet attach himself to the megatheriums of extinct Toryism', *Pen-and-Ink Sketches*, Shimmin, 31.

otherwise submit to loss, instead of living by their labour. Unqualified competition, however, is now a favourite theme. It sounds well in theory, but it is vicious in practice.[28]

This false competition not only put safety at risk, it also sacrificed 'judgement and taste', thereby hindering the efforts to enhance Liverpool's image and identity. Here Holme addressed a pervasive desire among Liverpool gentlemen. Proud of its rapid promotion to 'second metropolis', Liverpool merchants sought to upgrade the town's physical fabric and cultural provision: unlike industrial Manchester, Liverpool, the 'western emporium of Albion', was to rival London as a centre of commerce, finance and culture.[29] Guided by Roscoe, its most distinguished scholar, Liverpool looked to Renaissance Italy, aspiring to establish its provincial supremacy as the Florence of the north.[30] No less than the local Unitarian intelligentsia, Holme was an admirer of 'that enlarged spirit which existed among the commercial princes of Italy, and which have rendered their cities the admiration of travellers, and the models from which the man of taste may draw the most important instruction'. However, while looking to the 'great works of antiquity ... for grandeur of architectural *design*, for just proportion and harmony of parts', Holme based his proposals on the application of the latest British engineering skill and architectural talent to ensure quality, durability and taste.[31] The same methods and principles, he insisted, should be applied to sanitary reform and public health. Liverpool pride required the active exercise of civic duty:

> When he looked at the magnificence of Liverpool, its splendid structures, and at the vast wealth of its public bodies, – when he found such was the enterprise of its merchants, that if a new port was opened in

28] *Report of William Fairbairn, Esq., C.E. on the Construction of Fire-Proof Buildings with Introductory Remarks by Samuel Holme* (Liverpool, 1844). Holme was also keen to improve commercial efficiency by widening the streets: as Mayor in 1853, he banned processions through 'our crowded and too narrow thoroughfares'. See Public Record Office, Kew: Home Office Papers (hereafter HO) 54/5128, ff. 560–02, Holme, 26 Aug. 1853.
29] See the description of Liverpool in *Mitchell's Newspaper Press Directory* (London, 1847), 161; see also, *Liverpool Repository of Literature, Philosophy and Commerce*, Jan 1826; and *Liverpool Literary and Scientific Register*, 1 July 1835.
30] *Address delivered by the President at the Opening of the Sixth Session of the Liverpool Philomathic Society* (Liverpool, 1830), 55–56.
31] Holme, *Public Improvements*, 6–7. Soon afterwards, Holme had to resign his council seat as he gained a contract to undertake work on St George's Hall.

the furthest verge of the world, a Liverpool ship was the first to go to that port, and that Liverpool was the port at which the first cargo arrived, – when he thought of our magnificent Town-hall, and our splendid Assize Courts, and then went, in imagination, to Crosbie-street, it did appear to him most strange and anomalous that, though wealth poured in upon us, and we were in the very midst of civilization, there should be at least 30,000 of the population of this town, – a town which gave a tone to the whole world, – living in a state in which he would be sorry to place his horses.[32]

To eradicate the social (and moral) evils of unsewered streets, pent-up courts, want of water and neglect of ventilation, Holme was obliged to advocate municipal collectivism as 'competition' had undermined the paternal supervision previously exercised by employers like his father:

Every thing was done in the present day by 'public competition' ... The result had been that capital was brought into competition with labour – that the small employers (he spoke more particularly of the trade he was connected with) had diminished in numbers – business had been gradually concentrating into fewer hands ... the result had been that, where his father employed, comparatively, a few men, he was obliged to employ a great number; and whereas his father knew every man in his employment, understood their domestic circumstances, and was a parent to them, to whom they clung in their distresses, he having become a sort of monopolist – he confessed it – by the force of circumstances over which he had no control, might at that moment be addressing a great number of workmen in his employment, living in the wretched habitations he had described, and in perfect ignorance of their domestic circumstances.[33]

Once committed to municipal intervention, Holme was undeterred by heated polemics with ideologues of private provision, laissez-faire and 'cheap government', again taking pride in his socio-occupational status – 'Having a considerable number of workmen in my own employment, and

32] Holme's speech in *Report of the Proceedings at a public meeting of the friends of the Liverpool Health of Towns' Association, held at the Music-Hall, Bold Street ... September 29, 1845, for the purpose of adopting measures towards the establishment of a Working Men's Society for Promoting the Health of the Town* (Liverpool, 1845), 18.
33] Ibid., 16–17.

being from my peculiar engagements, brought into daily contact with all classes, from the highest to the lowest, I can speak from experience upon some subjects on which men can only theorise'.[34] Private water companies were inadequate and inappropriate for the task, given that 'self-interest is the ruling motive and the smallest supply at the highest rate produces the most satisfying dividends':

> This town will never be supplied as it ought to be while we are depen-
> dant on private companies ... it is about as wise to permit a private
> company to supply us with air for respiration, as in crowded and
> densely populated towns to permit them to supply us with the equally
> essential element of water. It ought to be copious and free to all, and it
> never will be, so long as it is in the hands of those who make a profit by
> its sale.[35]

Active intervention, he insisted, was sensible pre-emptive politics: 'We ought not to neglect the social condition of the poorer classes; if we do, we are laying materials for an explosion which, depend upon it, will shatter our social system to atoms'. Furthermore, proper provision, based on long-term planning and the latest technology – as in his controversial proposals of water supply from Rivington Pike – made economic sense:

> I believe that wide thoroughfares, well-ventilated dwellings, well-
> sewered and well-cleansed streets, with abundance of water, will even-
> tually cause a diminution of those rates of which you justly complain,
> and on the principles of real economy, and on the higher and holier prin-
> ciples of humanity, I commend the matter to your serious consideration.[36]

As practised by Holme, the politics of improvement were an exercise in 'one nation' Toryism, stressing the links, economic and organic, between the classes:

34] 'Report of Mr Samuel Holme of Liverpool, to the Health of Towns Commission: Replies to Questions', printed as appendix in Samuel Holme, *Want of Water: A Letter to Harmood Banner, Esq., in Reply to his Pamphlet Entitled 'Water'* (Liverpool, 1845), 77–78; see also, Appendix to First Report of the Commissioners of Inquiry into the State of Large Towns and Populous Districts, Parliamentary Papers, 1844 (572), xvii, 185–95.

35] Holme, *Want of Water*; and *Public Improvements*, 30–31. See also, Harmood Banner, *Water: A Pamphlet* (Liverpool, 1845).

36] *Speech of Samuel Holme, Esq. at the Music Hall, Liverpool, on the 15th of October, 1849* (Liverpool, 1849), 19–21.

I stand here acknowledging that I am deeply indebted to the working classes of Liverpool, and I am not ashamed to acknowledge it. (Applause) I am desirous, and will be while I have life, of forwarding every measure which may ameliorate the hard condition of those who by the stern laws of nature are compelled to earn their daily bread by their daily labour (Applause).[37]

He looked upon the local Health of Towns' Association as 'a chain of communication and a link between ourselves and this community of our fellow-creatures whom we desired to reach':

We wanted, too, all men rich and poor, the merchant, the tradesman, and the working man, to know and feel that physical benefit was most closely connected with the morals of the people; that it was impossible for us to have either a happy or a healthy community, so long as one-tenth of the population – our fellow-men – were living like pigs, and dying in despair, and misery and degradation.[38]

Holme's unrestrained interventionism, in particular his commitment to the controversial Rivington Pike scheme, temporarily cost him his council seat.[39] It also brought him under the critical gaze of *Jones*, the leading local satirical journal which gave voice to fears that high local taxes would prompt an exodus from Liverpool (even to barren Birkenhead). The self-professed champion of the rate-payers and tradesmen ('or what he calls "his order"'), Holme was expected to uphold retrenchment and probity, not to promote costly schemes or to consort with merchant princes, the 'municipal fungi' who squandered civic wealth through jobbery, corruption and extravagance. As mayoral ambitions drew him closer to these 'pseudo-

---

37] Ibid., 20.
38] *Report of Proceedings... towards the establishment of a Working Men's Society for Promoting the Health of the Town*, 16 and 20. Holme's name appears first in the list of the General Committee; see 'First Annual Report of the Liverpool Health of Towns' Association', *Liverpool Health of Town's Advocate*, No. 8, 1 Apr. 1846. He was appointed to four sub-committees: Lecture; Apparatus and Diagrams; Health of Tenements; and Water and Sewerage.
39] Derek Fraser, *Urban Politics in Victorian England* (Leicester, 1976), 160–66 provides a useful analysis of the controversy. For an example of anti-Pike retrenchment, seeking 'to show the cumbrous, useless, expensive, clogging and clumsy nature of the machinery by which the business of this large and otherwise highly intelligent parish, is worked; and to suggest a system of management, simple, cheap and easy of attainment', see *Liverpool Burgesses and Ratepayers Magazine and Tradesmen's Advertiser* 2 June 1851.

aristocrats' and their pretensions – 'the fluid which runs in the veins of these aristocratic "Gentlemen" is a strange mixture of rum, palm oil, molasses and nigger blood' – Holme was a frequent target for attack, condemned for 'intrinsic snobbishness' (and vainglorious circumlocution):

> *JONES* would advise you too, friend Samuel Holme, but fears that inflated vanity and self-esteem render you proof against the council of your best friend, and there is no alternative but to let you 'oxydise upon the surges of an ephemeral popularity' (to use your own *beautiful* trope).[40]

The Rivington Pike controversy cut across socio-economic divisions, cultural spheres, and normal party lines – Holme's fellow Pikists included many of the wealthy Liberal elite such as William Rathbone, George Holt and William Earle. On national issues, however, the fundamentals still applied. Indeed, after the repeal of the Corn Laws in 1846, free trade and protectionist positions became more extreme in Liverpool, an ideological polarisation yet to be incorporated into British historiographical discourse.

Having progressed beyond the sectional demands of the Liverpool Association for Reduction of Duty on Tea, the Liverpool Financial Reform Association advocated abolition of *all* indirect taxes and 'the transfer to direct taxation of those imposts which interfere with the industry and limit the subsistence of the people'.[41] A thorough agenda of retrenchment and reform, this was far in advance of the free trade associated with Manchester and the Anti-Corn Law League which meant no more than repeal of duties on manufactured goods and their raw materials. Committed in principle and programme to complete free trade, the mercantile elite in control of the new Association refused to endorse partial reform, tactical alliance or pragmatic compromise: on a point of (self-defeating) principle, cooperation with popular London-based parliamentary reformers was decisively rejected. The Financial Reform Association antagonised influential opinion (not least *The Times*) by relentless anti-aristocratic and penny-pinching attacks on governmental extravagance, the Civil List and Army expenditure, but failed to attract workers to public meetings. Financial reform was too negative: bewilderingly, the form of direct taxation to replace the unjust and inefficient taxes on commerce and industry remained unspecified. Based on the demand for a reduction of government expenditure to 1835 levels, Cobden's 'National Budget', read to a public

---

40] *Jones*, 21 Oct., 18 Nov. 1848, 24 Feb. and 8 Sept. 1849.
41] *Economist* 22 Apr. 1848.

meeting of the Association in December 1848, seemed to offer an attractive starting-point on which to launch a popular national campaign. Neither side, however, displayed much enthusiasm: the Association continued to uphold its purist maximalist stance while Cobden soon joined John Bright in a dual campaign for parliamentary and financial reform. The Liberal merchant elite were left in isolation to pursue their ultimate goal which, as Francis Boult averred, would only be realised when 'the [customs] building at the bottom of South castle-street, which prevented shipping from coming into port, was shut up, or turned to some better purpose'.[42]

On the other side of the divide, Holme and the Tories fought hard to maintain the Navigation Acts. 'In the minds of many', Clarendon observed, 'they are an institution, a bulwark, bound up with Church and State, and as Ricardo says, 40th article of the National Creed'.[43] Despite strong support for 'laws so vitally important to the shipowners, ship-carpenters and mariners of this port',[44] the local protectionist campaign began inauspiciously with the defeat of both Tory candidates at the general election of 1847. Cardwell, the Peelite candidate of 'Commercial Freedom and Religious Toleration', displayed skilful political dexterity, outmanoeuvring the protectionists in an election address of studied ambiguity, promising to 'support no change in the Navigation Laws calculated to interfere with the growing prosperity of the shipping and commercial interests'.[45] Furthermore, the Tories were hampered by their unfortunate choice of candidates. Lord John Manners had impeccable protectionist credentials, but embedded within the organic idealism of his 'Young Englandism' was a penchant for Puseyite tractarianism. Such 'Romish' ritualism aroused the wrath of McNeile and his followers, who brought forward Sir Digby Mackworth, an uncompromising Orange zealot, a 'No Popery' candidate pledged to the repeal of the Emancipation Act and the exclusion of Catholics from public office.[46] The electoral debacle of 1847 was an early warning of subsequent tension and dysfunction within sectarian politics. The rhetoric of 'No

42] W.N. Calkins, 'A Victorian Free Trade Lobby', *Economic History Review*, 2nd series, Vol. XIII (1960–61), 90–104.
43] Clarendon to Grey, 9 Jan. 1847, quoted in A.C. Howe, 'Free Trade and the City of London, c. 1820–1870', *History*, Vol. 77 (1992), 402.
44] *Second Annual Meeting of the Liverpool Constitutional Association* (Liverpool, 1850), 5.
45] Sarah Palmer, *Politics, Shipping and the Repeal of the Navigation Laws* (Manchester, 1990), 109–10.
46] Charles Whibley, *Lord John Manners and his Friends* (2 vols: London, 1925), Vol. i, 238–42. Thomas Burke, *Catholic History of Liverpool* (Liverpool, 1910), 90–92.

Popery', introduced to defend the Tory-Anglican establishment, was later to be stood on its head: with populist flourish, militant Dissenters were to take to the streets to condemn the ritualism prevalent in the Anglican church and the upper echelons of the Conservative party.[47] Sectarian organisations like the Orange Order were 'Protestants First', placing religious allegiance above partisan affiliation.

Chastened by defeat in 1847, the Tories reorganised in January 1848 as the Liverpool Constitutional Association, of which Holme was a committee member, and from which the modern party traces its origins. Adopting the motto, 'The Church, the Throne and the People. Ships, Colonies and Commerce', the Association established a set of principles which placed protectionism above Protestantism, the essential aim being 'to vindicate the principles of the British Constitution, as generally held by "WILLIAM PITT AND GEORGE CANNING", securing for commerce, agriculture, manufactures, shipping and railways, due encouragement, thereby procuring for the artizan, the peasant, the operative, and the merchant-seaman, that fair reward for his labour which Englishmen have been used to enjoy'.[48] Registration of voters was the main function, but the Association turned to extra-parliamentary agitation when the Protectionists at Westminster, having secured temporary delay, failed to prevent the final repeal of the Navigation Laws in 1849.

The campaign highlighted the distinctive features of Liverpool Toryism. In terms of policy, Liverpool protectionists were 'constitutional' Tories, under which proud label H.C. Chapman, a local merchant and shipowner, promoted an alternative Bill, removing the vexatious restrictions on 'long voyage' shipping, but otherwise leaving protectionism untouched.[49] Toryism of this order – the politics of Chatham and Pitt, of Liverpool, Huskisson, Canning, Grey and, until his treachery, Peel – looked to economic management through a strong and responsive executive, arbitrating between the needs of government and of society in taxation and tariffs, and recognising

47] John Bohstedt, 'More than One Working Class: Protestant and Catholic Riots in Edwardian Liverpool', in *Popular Politics*, ed. Belchem, 173–216.
48] 'The Liverpool Constitutional Association', handbill in British Library, 8364 b. 24; and *Rules and Regulations of the Liverpool Constitutional Association* (Liverpool, 1848).
49] H.C. Chapman, *A Letter on the Subject of the Navigation Laws, Addressed to the Chairman of the Committee of the Liverpool Shipowners' Association* (Liverpool, 1847); and idem, *Suggestions for the Improvement of our Navigation Laws* (Liverpool, 1848). Palmer, *Politics, Shipping*, 144.

the interdependence of classes and interests in the distribution of national income.[50] By contrast, ideological free traders, 'the restless politicians of the Manchester school of economists', stood condemned for their 'anarchistic' and divisive politics. Free trade, the Liverpool Constitutional Association regretted, 'has placed in hostile array class against class – the factory against the field – the Colonies against the mother country'.[51] Holme gave this Toryism a 'one-nation' inflexion in which protectionism, a register of patriotism and Protestantism, stood in proud defiance of the false political economy of cheap competition. The policy which had carried England forward to supremacy, protectionism was the necessary guarantee of liberty and property, ensuring the continued prosperity and security of the providential Protestant nation. Holme and his fellow Liverpool Tories propounded an inclusive rhetoric of national pride, welfare and enterprise as they drew attention to 'the very important position which has been gained by the enemies of the British Constitution in the abrogation of those time-honoured Navigation Laws which fostered the commerce of England – secured for its flag the dominion of the seas – guarded its colonies in every quarter of the globe – made it the exalted missionary of civilization, and rendered its prosperity the envy and wonder of the world'.[52]

At a public meeting in June 1850, jointly convened by the Liverpool Constitutional Association and the National Association for the Protection of British Industry and Capital, Holme applauded and flattered the national character of the audience, a true Tory gathering of all classes:

There he saw assembled the peer of the realm, a large number of the merchant princes of Liverpool, whose names were honourably known in every part of the world; – (hear, hear.) – he saw himself surrounded by many tenant farmers, by many of that important class, with whom he had himself the honour to be identified – he meant the tradesmen of the town. (Bravo, and hear, hear.) He saw, too, a number of spectators from amongst those men who earned their bread by their daily labour, and who were relatively as much interested in the prosperity and glory of England as the noble chairman and his family, who were the possessors of untold acres. (Great applause.) He (Mr Holme) thought that out of

50] Angus Macintyre, 'Lord George Bentinck and the Protectionists: a Lost Cause?', *Transactions of the Royal Historical Society*, fifth series, Vol. 39 (1989), 154.
51] *Second Annual Meeting of the Liverpool Constitutional Association*, 8–10.
52] Ibid., 4.

England it would be impossible to witness such an assembly as that. (Great applause).

Protectionism was the cement of this patriotic interdependence and social harmony:

> It was the duty of England to connect all classes in a mutual phalanx of support. (Hear, hear.) No one class was to prosper on the fall or ruin of another; and, if it were so, then it appeared strange they should be placed in unjust competition with foreigners, who paid no part of the national burdens.

As he moved the first resolution, a comprehensive indictment of free trade, Holme condemned the reckless pursuit of cheapness and competition which, in failing to acknowledge England's historic burdens and duties, threatened to undermine its hard-won constitutional liberty and prosperity:

> With one swoop the legislature swept away the navigation laws, and on which he had asserted previously and again repeated it, the maritime glory of England was built (Cheers). This prevented their operative classes competing with the ill-fed and worse paid classes of the Baltic: but they must meet unprotected labour such as this, and this was called forsooth, 'the spread of liberal opinions'. (Laughter and cheers) ... Had we no taxes to pay, no poor-rates to raise, no colonies to maintain, no army and navy to support, and would other nations indeed reciprocate with us, then he said frankly he should be a free trader to the full extent of the term. Then would the skill and indomitable industry of Englishmen, placed in fair competition, be victorious over the world. But there was unfairness in the present competition, and it was that unfairness which they objected to.[53]

Such agitation, however, was to no avail, serving only to embarrass and antagonise the Tory parliamentary leadership, for whom protectionism was a lost cause.[54] However, its local force should not be denied: indeed, its ability to attract broad support probably accounted for the halting progress of the local free trade lobby. In its Liverpudlian inflexion, protectionism was not a matter of social stasis, nostalgia or mercantile self-interest. As in

---

53] *Report of the Speeches delivered at the great meeting held in the Liverpool Amphitheatre, Thursday, June 6, 1850, for the Protection of British Industry and Capital. Published by the Liverpool Constitutional Association* (Liverpool, 1850).
54] Palmer, *Politics, Shipping*, 173.

London, where 'gentlemanly capitalists' with shipping, timber, tea and sugar interests preferred to reap the benefits of monopoly rather than rush headlong into an open and risky market, Liverpool's merchant princes in the West India trade were staunchly protectionist.[55] Some of the best debating points were scored by McNeile and other protectionist orators who exposed the double standards of liberal free traders whose policies condemned the West Indian colonies to the unfair competition of 'Slave Labor versus Free Labor Sugar':

> The free traders idolize cheapness, and exalt it as a motive of action, far beyond all moral, social and political principles. In order to save one penny in the pound of sugar, these avaricious hucksterers sacrifice the transcendant glory of negro emancipation.[56]

The distinctive feature of Liverpool protectionism, however, was its extension beyond old, previously-privileged, mercantile interests to incorporate the riverside artisan trades. Indeed, it was the last expression of the old, once dominant, Tory-shipwright alliance.

By defending freeman rights, the marginal privilege of Protestant workers and the Navigation Laws, the Tories retained the overwhelming support of the shipwrights. Young shipwright apprentices were the most conspicuous participants in sectarian violence against the Irish, ritualised clashes which developed into an adolescent vendetta with a dynamic of its own. In disrupting meetings of the Anti-Monopoly Association – gatherings which attracted large numbers of Irish dock labourers for whom free trade meant more trade through the docks – they were joined by bricklayers' apprentices working for Holme.[57] The rejection of free trade, or rather the retention of the Navigation Laws, was essential for the riverside artisan trades. With the rapid growth of the docks, fuelled by the expansionist fervour of Bramley-Moore and Hartley in eager anticipation of the freeing of trade,[58] shipbuilding had been squeezed out of the Liverpool waterfront,

---

55] Howe, 'Free Trade', 396–404.
56] *Slave Labor versus Free Labor Sugar. Speech of the Revd Dr McNeile, delivered at a public meeting held at Liverpool, 13th June 1848* (London, 1848). *Second Annual Meeting of the Liverpool Constitutional Association*, 8.
57] Kevin Moore, ' "This Whig and Tory Ridden Town": Popular Politics in Liverpool, 1815–1850', unpublished MPhil thesis, University of Liverpool, 1988, 367–85. In the political excitement of 1848, there were rumours that the local Irish Confederates intended to take Holme's life. See Dowling's report, 24 Aug. 1848, HO 45/2410B ff. 1245–46.

leaving the shipwrights to concentrate on ship-repair. An erratic business at the best of times, this had reduced them to the somewhat anomalous position of a skilled trade with an employment pattern similar to that of the casualism of the docks. Repeal of the Navigation Laws was a devastating blow, since foreign ships made minimal use of local repair facilities.[59] 'If it were not for the colonial-built ships, our men would be in a state of starvation', the officers of the Liverpool Shipwrights' Association testified to the special committee appointed by the town council in 1850 to consider the state of the shipbuilding trade in Liverpool: 'We should be a good deal better off if you never let a foreign ship come into this port, for they do us no good.'[60] In a letter to Edward Molyneux, president of the Liverpool Constitutional Association, William Dalton, a ship's carpenter, calculated that foreign vessels, Prussian and otherwise, had reduced income in the graving docks to one-tenth of the level previously generated by the regular caulking and overhaul of colonial-built vessels.[61] The decline soon spread to allied riverside trades. Betteley, one of the largest manufacturers of chain cables and anchors in the country, presented a bleak report to the annual general meeting of the Liverpool Constitutional Association in 1850:

> In the year 1846 he was manufacturing 50 tons per week; in 1849 the quantity was reduced to 40 tons per week; and now they were only making 20 tons per week … he was obliged to propose a reduction in the wages of the workmen, and many of them were thrown out of employment. If this was to be the result of free trade, we should find our workhouses becoming enlarged and our poor rates increasing.[62]

For all their economic, political and symbolic importance, repeal of the Navigation Acts did not presage a new Liberal ascendancy in Liverpool. Merchant groups soon set former differences aside to cooperate in the

58] *Report of the Speech of J. Bramley-Moore … on the Subject of Dock Extension addressed to the Liverpool Town Council* (Liverpool, 1846).
59] 'Labour and the Poor: Liverpool. Letter xvii: Ship-Building and Repairing', *Morning Chronicle* 9 Sept. 1850.
60] *Shipbuilding in Liverpool. Evidence taken before the Committee appointed by the Town Council to consider the present state of the Shipbuilding Trade in Liverpool, and the best means which can be adopted for encouraging it* (Liverpool, 1850), 113–50, evidence of Linacre and Neill.
61] *Report of the speeches at the great meeting … for the Protection of British Industry and Capital*, 47–48.
62] *Second Annual Meeting of the Liverpool Constitutional Association*, 19.

newly-established Liverpool Chamber of Commerce, in defiance of predictions that 'it was impossible for gentlemen of different political opinions,
having different commercial interests, and different commercial views, to
meet and act for a common object and a common good'.[63] In politics,
Liverpool remained a Tory town, much to the consternation of merchants
like George Melly, 'a Liberal of the most advanced principles of social
science', who bemoaned the enduring Tory hegemony in 'the largest
commercial port in the world – and commerce is another word for free
trade – commerce is another word for radicalism – commerce is another
word for free and enlightened opinion'.[64]

Protestant sectarianism doubtless contributed to the continuing Tory
success, but cultural style, the persistence of the convivial populism
introduced by Holme, was probably a more important factor. The Tories,
the *Daily Post* observed, owed their mastery in municipal matters to their
ready rapport with the electorate. Being assured of their position, the
Tories were 'affable, kind and conciliating. There is about them what is
called *bonhommie* [sic]. The leading Liberals, on the other hand, are somewhat imperious. They are not conciliatory; they repel rather than attract.
In fact, they are more exclusive than the Tories.'[65] Unable to bridge the
social gap, the Liberals were locked in what William Rathbone described as
'mutual ignorance, the incapacity to understand one another, which want
of intercourse has produced in rich and poor'.[66]

Having served as mayor in 1852 and become an alderman a year later,
Holme retired to the magisterial bench to indulge his propensity for
lengthy and homely speeches, subjecting prisoners, *Porcupine* observed, to
a veritable 'tongue-thrashing'.[67] Toryism, however, continued to thrive in
the interlocking associational network – party, popular and sectarian –
which facilitated ready interaction between the classes. Local notables

63] Liverpool Chamber of Commerce, *First Annual Report of the Council, presented
to the Chamber at the General Meeting, held February 3, 1851* (Liverpool, 1851), 6.
64] *Northern Daily Times* 28 Oct. 1857, newspaper cutting in Danson Archive,
National Galleries and Museums on Merseyside.
65] 'Conservatism in the Town Council', *Daily Post*, 23 Oct. 1861.
66] W. Rathbone, *Social Duties considered with reference to the Organisation of
Efforts in Works of Benevolence and Public Utility* (London, 1867), 1–2.
67] 'Mr Samuel Holme is Instructed', *Porcupine* 10 Aug. 1861; and 'Justice Holme',
Porcupine 27 Sept. 1862. Holme died in 1872 but his estate was not wound up until
the auction in 1948 of shops he had built in Renshaw Street and Benson Street in
1850, ' a rather remarkable case of property remaining in the family of the original
builder for nearly 100 years', *Daily Post* 30 Jan. 1948.

continued to monopolise political positions – there was no working-class Conservative councillor before 1914 – but as need arose, they were able to mingle at ease within the network, displaying a Holme-like common touch. Indeed, this soon became the distinguishing (and essential) characteristic of local Tory leadership, a style perfected in Archibald Salvidge's electoral machine, perhaps the most remarkable example of British 'boss politics'.[68] While Liverpool Toryism displayed the characteristics of a party of 'social integration', the Liberals remained socially exclusive (and hence politically disabled), safeguarding the integrity of their advanced principles from contaminating contact with drink, ignorance and vulgar prejudice.[69]

Furthermore, the Tories continued to honour the obligations which Holme had acknowledged, placing the needs of their working-class supporters above the policies and practices of mainstream middle-class conservatism and orthodox political economy. Forwood was drawn beyond the rhetoric of 'Tory democracy' into a Tory version of municipal socialism.[70] Salvidge, his successor, defied local 'business conservatism' to uphold Tariff Reform, championing local working-class interests against the 'lower middle-class fraud, called Liberalism or "Free Trade"'.[71] 'Faithfulness to constitutional fundamentals does not rule out progress', Alderman Shennan declared as he celebrated the centenary of the Liverpool Constitutional Association in 1948 in words echoing (but not specifically acknowledging) Holme's achievements:

> Indeed, in many respects, such as public health, water supply, development of electric power, and practical encouragement of industrial

---

68] Waller, *Democracy and Sectarianism*, 16–17 and passim. Joan Smith, 'Labour Tradition in Glasgow and Liverpool', *History Workshop Journal*, Vol. 17 (1984), 32–56.

69] John Garrard, 'Parties, Members and Voters after 1867' in *Later Victorian Britain 1867–1900*, ed. T.R. Gourvish and A. O'Day (Basingstoke, 1988), 127–50; and Waller, *Democracy and Sectarianism*, 12–16. See also B.D. White, *History of the Corporation of Liverpool* (Liverpool, 1951), 28 for an interesting contrast between the cultural styles of Holme and Sir Joshua Walmsley, chair of the Tradesmen's Reform Association.

70] Ibid., ch.13. In 1870, however, Holme wrote from retirement to condemn the extravagance of municipal interventionism, a consequence of the uncoordinated proliferation of council committees and sub-committees. As a builder, White notes, his objections to the construction of St Martin's cottages 'were perhaps not based only on a zeal for economy', ibid., 93 and 104.

71] Waller, *Democracy and Sectarianism*, 210–13.

enterprise, this Tory city has deservedly won fame as a pioneer of civic progress ... There is, believe me, more solid substance in Liverpool's famous Tory Democracy than the scoffers have realized.[72]

72] *Liverpool Constitutional Association Centenary. Official Souvenir* (Liverpool, 1948), 11.

Part Four
COMPARATIVE PERSPECTIVES

7
Ethnicity, migration and labour history[*]

E thnicity, a form of cultural belonging, is a relatively recent addition to the conceptual vocabulary of history and the social sciences: its first recorded use in the *Oxford English Dictionary* is 1953. For the most part, it has been deployed negatively, applied only to the 'other', to migrant and minority groups: in Britain, for example, Englishness has been assumed as a superior non-ethnic norm over and above the 'ethnic' characteristics of others.[1] While such usage may be traced back to the Greek *ethnos*, a synonym of gentile, its current application in the sociology of migration is more historical and inclusive. Eschewing the 'new racism' of ethnic absolutism – the process of constructing essentialised groups, of reifying cultural differences as absolute differences and bases for social mobilisation[2] – sociological studies locate ethnic affiliation within a complex interactive process, a socio-historical dialogue between dominant and subordinate groups. Put bluntly, there can be no ethnic 'other' without an ethnic 'us'.[3]

* This essay draws upon papers presented at two recent European conferences: 'Ethnicity and Labour History: with Special Reference to Irish Migration', presented to the foundation conference of Labnet (European Network of Labour Historians), Amsterdam, 17–18 Feb. 1997; and 'Irish and Polish migration: Some Preliminary Analysis', opening lecture at the conference on Irish and Polish Migration in comparative perspective, Bochum, 6–9 Oct. 1999.
1] Catherine Hall, '"From Greenland's Icy Mountains ... to Afric's Golden Sand": Ethnicity, Race and Nation in Mid-Nineteenth Century England', *Gender and History*, Vol. 5 (1993), 212–30.
2] Anne-Marie Fortier, 'Ethnicity', *Paragraph*, Vol. 17 (1994), 213–23.
3] For an introduction to the vast amount of theoretical and conceptual writing on ethnicity, see J. Hutchinson and A.D. Smith (eds), *Ethnicity* (Oxford, 1996). As the Project Director conceded, research funded by the European Science Foundation on 'Comparative Studies on Governments and Non-dominant Ethnic Groups in Europe, 1850–1940' concentrated on ethnic minorities, see F.M.L. Thompson,

Thus, while giving a voice to the other, to previously excluded marginal and minority groups, a focus on ethnicity (as on gender) should also encourage critical deconstruction of dominant formations.

A cultural construction, ethnic identity is defined and projected in two main ways: through opposition to an 'alien' other and by the invocation of deep-rooted, self-referential myth. The project of intellectuals and cultural nationalists, this 'invention' of ethnicity is outside the scope of this essay. Migrant workers, however, were often the first to embrace the 'collective fiction' ahead of the vernacular mobilisation of the people – the crucial transition from Miroslav Hroch's phase B to phase C – back in the homeland.[4] A relational identity, ethnicity seems to have acquired added salience at a distance, strengthened in dialogue between host-ascription – generally in the form of crude labelling and stereotyping – and migrant response. 'Irishness', for example, was in part an imposed and host-invented stigma, but was also a creative response, an act of migrant self-imagination to facilitate adjustment to new surroundings.

For labour historians, Irish migrants are an interesting case study. According to functional analysis, migrant labour needs to be not only a quantitative addition (to allow expansion of production when lack of domestic labour might impose constraint), but also a qualitatively different source of supply (low-level labour prepared to accept conditions below normal standards).[5] In the case of the Irish, there were no linguistic, pigmentary or other phenotypic means of distinguishing and defining them as alien and hence more exploitable. Their position in this respect would seem more favourable than that of 'German' Poles on the Ruhr, yet alone that of later guestworkers, illegal immigrants or colonial migrants from a distant 'dark' continent.[6] Furthermore, as David Fitzpatrick has observed,

'Series Preface', in *Ethnic Identity in Urban Europe*, ed. M. Engman, F.W. Carter, A.C. Hepburn and C.G. Pooley (Aldershot, 1992), xix. See also, Richard Williams, *Hierarchical Structures and Social Value: the Creation of Black and Irish Identities in the United States* (Cambridge, 1990).

4] Eric Hobsbawm, *Nations and Nationalism since 1780* (Cambridge, 1990) provides a useful introduction to the theoretical frameworks of Hroch, Gellner and others.

5] Stephen Castles, 'Migrants and Minorities in Post-Keynesian Capitalism: the German Case' in M. Cross (ed.), *Ethnic minorities and industrial change in Europe and North America*, Cambridge, 1992, 36–54.

6] R.C. Murphy, *Guestworkers in the German Reich: a Polish Community in Wilhelmian Germany* (New York, 1983); Ulrich Herbert, *A History of Foreign Labor in Germany, 1880–1980* (Ann Arbor, 1990).

Irish migrants were unusually well-tailored for the role of servicing other people's industrial revolutions (allowing Ireland itself to remain 'green', an emerald isle relatively unpolluted by industrialisation). Young unmarried adults with an even sex balance, they left home without question, entering the labour markets of their new lands of residence with low expectations of comfort and without the burden of accompanying dependants – the age-selectivity, sex balance and low return home rates distinguish the Irish from other 'moving Europeans'.[7] Bred to migrate, they readily withstood the 'shocks' of displacement, displaying 'ethno-cultural and other 'coping capacities' which the Chicago School failed to appreciate.[8]

Along with the Poles, Irish migrants occupy a pioneer (if unenviable) status in the historiography of migration and ethnicity. Thomas and Znaniecki's multi-volume study of *The Polish Peasant in Europe and America* (1918–20) was the foundation text of positivist sociology, an exposition of disorganisation and dysfunctionalism as migrants moved from traditional mechanisms of social regulation to the modern world of individualisation. Primitive peasants in provenance, Polish migrants were studied simply as objects of social processes: atomised, cultureless and normless, they exemplified general laws of social change and individual social behaviour. This Chicago school methodology (with its roots in German sociology) was soon extended backwards by Handlin's study of the 'uprooted' Irish transplanted in America. Early arrivals, the Irish were the first to undergo the alienation and individualisation subsequently experienced by Poles and other 'new' immigrants from eastern and southern Europe. As the respective archetypes of the two main waves or 'generations' of migrants – an historiographical perspective which still applies – the Irish and the Poles figured prominently in subsequent studies of assimilation, a uniform (upward) process perceived (and celebrated) in individualised terms of personal attributes and achievements.[9]

7] David Fitzpatrick, *Irish Emigration 1801–1921* (Economic and Social History Society of Ireland, 1984), 32.
8] For a useful introduction to historiographical developments, see David Ward, *Poverty, Ethnicity and the American City 1840–1925* (Cambridge, 1989), ch. 6; and Leo Lucassen, 'The Gulf between Long Term and Short Term Approaches in Immigration. A Reassessment of the Chicago School's Assimilation Concept', paper presented to the European Social Science History Conference, Noordwijkerhout, 9–11 May 1996.
9] D.A. Gerber, 'The Immigrant Letter between Positivism and Populism: the Uses of Immigrant Personal Correspondence in Twentieth-Century American Scholarship, *Journal of American Ethnic History*, Vol. 16 (1997), 3–34. R.A. Kazal, 'Revisiting

Positivism and assimilation have long since fallen from fashion. In the pluralism and post-modernism of recent scholarship, ethnic fade is no longer the inevitable fate of Irish, Polish and other migrants. As is now appreciated, ethnicity was to persist – at times to flourish – within hyphenated and multiple migrant identities. Once characterised as pre-modern peasants, nineteenth-century migrants are now acknowledged as pioneers in the modernisation of consciousness, among the first to adapt to multinational or 'distanciated' (to use Antony Giddens' terminology) space and time in the global economic system.[10] Information networks and mobility channels were acutely sensitive to 'niche' market opportunity, in a manner not always discernible, however, to the panel-regression indices and cliometrics which now supplement the old 'push-pull' analysis of mass migration.[11] Irish migrants, David Fitzpatrick has observed, 'might be restricted to the worst jobs, but they clustered in regions of expanding employment. In effect, they occupied the worst seats in the best theatres.'[12] Sensitivity to the international labour market, however, was generally accompanied by commitment to traditional values back in the homeland. Remittances sent home by migrant workers facilitated the survival of large families on otherwise 'uneconomic' holdings. Emigration wages in America and elsewhere were a crucial factor in the final solvency of the Polish countryside: one assessment for Galicia set the amount at 24 to 30 million US dollars annually.[13] Fertility remained high in nineteenth-century Ireland as married couples reared children to migrate, a form of insurance policy offering a pension or lump sum from the grateful offspring once they gained employment in the diaspora.

    Given such favourable 'human capital' factors for industrial development – not least their readiness to speak English and to undertake tasks which native workers preferred not to do – why did Irish migrants encounter prejudice in their new lands of residence? In the absence of phenotypic

---

Assimilation: the Rise, Fall and Reappraisal of a Concept in American Ethnic History', *American Historical Review*, Vol. 100 (1995), 437–71. Ewa Morawska, 'The Sociology and Historiography of Immigration' in *Immigration Reconsidered*, ed. V. Yans-McLaughlin (New York, 1960), 187–238.

10] Gerber, 'Immigrant Letter', 26.

11] For the latest cliometrics, see T.J. Hatton and J.G. Williamson, *The Age of Mass Migrations: Causes and Economic Impact* (New York, 1998).

12] Fitzpatrick, *Irish Emigration*, 34.

13] D.A. Pacyga, *Polish Immigrants and Industrial Chicago. Workers on the South Side 1880–1922* (Columbus, 1991), 123.

distinction, ethnic stereotyping provided the requisite labelling to identify an underclass, to facilitate labour market segmentation. Through 'ethnic' portrayal of 'Paddy' as drunken and feckless, fit only for the most menial physical labour, Irish migrants were kept confined to the bottom of the labour market. The stereotype soon entered the 'common sense' of lowly native workers, enabling them to exercise options, to lift themselves above the least desirable occupations. Thereafter, a harsh self-fulfilling logic prevailed: set off from society by the type of work they did, the Irish were identified with the roughest of rough labour, performed by the lowest of the low. Stigmatised by ethnic stereotype as more suited to strenuous work than their Anglo peers, Irish migrants endured a rationalisation of labour exploitation reminiscent, Peter Way notes, of the assertion that blacks were built to work under a broiling sun or in fetid rice swamps.[14]

The gender implications of this stereotyping merit deconstruction. As the heaviest and hardest manual labour was undertaken by Irish migrants and blacks, physical abilities were at a discount in the construction of mainstream working-class masculinity. Emphasis was placed on craft skill and discipline. This construction, with its emphasis on masculine 'property in skill', was subsequently adopted (and privileged) by labour history which has tended to idealise such artisan culture as the plebeian prototype of working-class consciousness.[15] Conflict over skill and control of production has dominated the conventional narrative, closing off the real history from below, the struggle over material conditions which preoccupied women, the unskilled and ethnic migrant communities.

At this level of struggle and survival, ethnicity can prove a functional means of mobilising resources. Indeed, for some present-day migrant groups (the Cubans and the Chinese in the United States are the best-studied examples), 'ethnic solidarity' can empower self-sufficient 'enclave economies'. In seeming defiance of ecological models of assimilation (and labour market segmentation theory), newly-arrived workers can gain parity with the primary labour market outside, without linguistic or other extra-ethnic interaction: in the enclave economy, earning-returns are

14] Peter Way, *Common Labour: Workers and the Digging of North American Canals 1780–1860* (Cambridge, 1993), 90.
15] David Roediger, 'Race and the Working-Class Past in the United States: Multiple Identities and the Future of Labour History', *International Review of Social History*, Vol. 38 (1993), Supplement, 135–37. Anna Clark, *The Struggle for the Breeches: Gender and the Making of the British Working Class* (Berkeley, 1995), 25.

commensurate with human capital skills and investments.[16] By contrast, ethnic affiliation among nineteenth-century Irish and Polish migrants was protective and defensive, a means of coping with the disadvantages, disabilities and discrimination of the secondary labour market in which most were confined. As Weber suggested, ethnicity exists in direct relationship to its usefulness as a mechanism of group formation and mobilisation. Whereas classes in the Marxian sense must develop their sense of identity, forms of organisation and culture *ab initio*, ethnic groups can call upon their sense of ethnicity and their forms of ethnic bonding as a resource. From the outset, as John Rex notes, they are 'ethnics-for-themselves'. There can be rapid progress from ethnic identity (factors which distinguish one communal group from another) to ethnic identification (consciousness of the significance of these factors). Awareness of ethnic category leads readily through participation in ethnic network and ethnic association to ethnic community. Given this facility, ethnic forms of collective association and mutuality can reach into parts untouched by the class-based movements privileged in conventional labour history.[17] However, there were limits to such inclusion. There was to be no place for Protestants in the Irishness of the diaspora: ethnic and religious identity were increasingly interwoven, a symbiotic relationship which 'made Irish, Catholic, and Catholic, Irish'. Despite their common provenance, Jewish migrants from Poland were excluded from Polonia, the preserve of Catholic migrants.

There are problems in applying functional resource mobilisation theory to nineteenth-century migrants. The necessary components of ethnic affiliation – a common proper name; a myth of common ancestry; shared historical memories; elements of common culture; link with a homeland; and a sense of solidarity – were not all in place, ready for instant activation. Migration may have helped to construct an 'imagined' national identity, to superimpose a wider 'invented' affiliation upon traditional and instinctive sub-national loyalties, but it was a delayed and interactive process within which host labelling was an important factor. As both the Irish and Polish outflows evince, chain – or 'network' – migration replaced local and circular forms to become the dominant migration system in

16] For a critical introduction to the 'enclave-economy hypothesis' of Alejandro Portes and colleagues, see J.M. Sanders and V. Nee, 'Limits of Ethnic Solidarity in the Enclave Economy', *American Sociological Review*, Vol. 52 (1987), 745–67.
17] John Rex, 'Ethnic Mobilisation in Multi-cultural Societies' in *Ethnic Mobilisation in Multi-cultural Europe*, ed. J. Rex and B. Drury (Aldershot, 1994), 3–12.

nineteenth-century Europe, facilitating long-distance movement from densely populated peripheral areas – particularly Ireland, Italy and the Polish provinces – to core industrial and commercial regions.[18] Working through family networks, social connections, village and regional solidarities, chain migration involved social arrangements with people already at destination, who characteristically helped newcomers to find jobs and housing, thereby protecting them from disorientation, dislocation and anomic behaviour. The initial mechanics of chain-migration preserved old sub-ethnic allegiances, functioning along lines of clan, county and regional filiation. Polish peasants limited their identification to the *okolica* or area within which their reputation resided.[19] Irish migrants were no less particularistic. In the paddy camps of Lowell, Massachusetts, workplace loyalties to specific foremen were based upon clan/family/regional ties simply transferred across the briny ocean. Faction fighting, indeed, was transplanted with undiminished vigour: 'Far-ups' and 'Far-downs' adapted the intimidatory tactics of the agrarian secret societies to defend territory and jobs in urban-industrial America. In the shanty camps of canal construction, rivalry between Corkonians and Connaughtmen was the axis around which existence was ordered, subsets which created social solidarity but more profoundly led to dissonance in the canaller community.[20] Such fierce rivalries notwithstanding, combatants were perceived by resident Americans as one and the same: Irish.

To Americans, provincial and village identities were meaningless: migrants were lumped together into ethnonational categories, Irish, Italian, Polish (or more likely, Micks, Wops and Pollaks). Continually labelled in this way, migrants began to take an inverted pride in their 'ethnic' identity. Life in America, Patrick Ford later observed, elevated the Irish out of 'the littleness of countyism into the broad feeling of nationalism'.[21] The development of networks and associations above the region, clan and

18] Leslie Page Moch, *Moving Europeans: Migration in Western Europe since 1650* (Bloomington, 1992).
19] Helena Znaniecka Lopata, *Polish Americans* (2nd edition: New Brunswick, 1994), 3.
20] Brian Mitchell, *The Paddy Camps: The Irish of Lowell 1821–61* (Urbana, 1988). Way, *Common Labor*, 192–99. See also, David Montgomery, 'The Irish and the American Labor Movement' in *America and Ireland, 1776–1976*, ed. D.N. Doyle and O.D. Edwards (Westport, 1980), 206–9; and R.S. Wilentz, 'Industrializing America and the Irish: Towards the New Departure', *Labor History*, Vol. 20 (1979), 582.
21] Quoted in T.N. Brown, *Irish-American Nationalism* (Philadelphia and New York, 1966), 21.

faction, however, depended on a number of factors. As Conzen, Gerber, Morawska, Pozzetta and Vecoli have shown, migrant 'ethnicisation' was a dynamic and contingent historical process, requiring 'constant invention, innovation, negotiation and renegotiation on the part of those seeking to organize identities, patterns of daily life, or the competitive struggle for social resources around ethnic symbols'.[22] For the purposes of comparative analysis, I want briefly to highlight two of the key agencies: middle-class culture-brokers and the Catholic church.

Let us start with American Polonia, an ethnic community embodying what has been called 'institutional completeness'. Built upon interlocking networks of churches, building and loan associations, parochial schools and fraternal associations, Polonia came to offer nearly all the services – religious, educational, political, recreational and economic – which Polish-Americans required without recourse to the host society. Polonia, indeed, proudly regarded itself as the 'fourth province of Poland'.[23] At the found-ation of this super-territorial ethnic community was the local neighbour-hood organised around the parish church, construction of which was the first obligation on migrant earnings. Here was an important element of continuity, preserving essential aspects of the distinctive (and intense) religiosity of the Polish village: solemn services of worship; the high esteem given to sacred objects; and an intensive cult of the Blessed Virgin.[24] An anchor for communal life in the new urban setting – the base upon which new forms of associational culture and collective mutuality were con-structed – the parish represented 'the single most important link with the Old Country and the focal point of the New World ethnic community'.[25] A pervasive spiritual and social influence in the migrant community, the church served to transcend regional divisions and to promote a national consciousness. In the 'occupied' Polish territories, the church was the one national institution spanning the partitions, providing haven and sanctuary

22] K.N Conzen, D.A. Gerber, E. Morawska, G.E. Pozzetta and R.J Vecoli, 'The Invention of Ethnicity: A Perspective from the USA', *Journal of American Ethnic History*, Vol. 12 (1992), 3–41.

23] Lopata, *Polish Americans*, chs 1 and 3.

24] Anna Zarnowska, 'Religion and Politics: Polish workers c.1900', *Social History*, Vol. 16 (1991), 299–316. Marian ideology served both as a 'mechanism of control' and a 'militant engine', see John J. Bukowczyk, 'Mary the Messiah: Polish immigrant heresy and the malleable ideology of the Roman Catholic church, 1880–1930', *Journal of American Ethnic History*, Vol. 4 (1985), 5–32.

25] W. Kruszka, *A History of the Poles in America to 1908. Part One* (Washington DC, 1993), xii.

for Polish language and culture against 'de-nationalising' Kulturkampf attack. Implanted in Polonia, the church was the very symbol of Polish nationality and identity.

The essential aim of the church in Polonia was to construct and maintain this ethnic Catholicism, to prevent contamination by other forms. This single-minded internalising of energies denied the Poles wider influence within American Catholicism – by 1900 there were nearly 900 Polish parishes in the United States, but not one Polish bishop.[26] The Irish experience was very different. Having left Ireland before the 'devotional revolution', many migrants arrived with a nominal Catholicism which, lacking the ritual and ornament of continental European Catholicism, caused less grievous offence in Protestant America. While ensuring against leakage and Protestant proselytisation, Irish clergy assiduously promoted American patriotism, bourgeois values and upward mobility among their congregation (and themselves). Some clerics even demanded that emigrants Anglicise 'unpronounceable' Gaelic names. This readiness to adapt – anathema to Polish Catholics – placed the Irish at the head of the Catholic hierarchy, clerical and lay. Some Irish-Americans, indeed, were to seek a more integrated form of hyphenated identity, placing themselves at the head of other ethnic groups as the leaders of Catholic-America. The Knights of Columbus, which emphasised Catholic and American loyalties over narrowly Irish ones, proved very popular with successful second-generation 'lace-curtain' Irish-Americans.[27]

Ethnicity, then, kept the Poles apart, but enabled the Irish to secure a leading role for themselves in larger formations – not only in the Catholic church but also in the Democratic Party and the American labour movement. The contrast here is not between ethnic persistence and ethnic fade. Irishness, indeed, was to become more pronounced as the 'ethnic' Irish networked their way into American structures. The difference is perhaps best understood by comparative study of middle-class migrants, the culture-brokers of ethnicity.

As expressed in the (occupied) homeland, Polish nationhood was jealously preserved as their own 'property' by the native upper class, gentry and

26] Ibid., xiii.
27] Lawrence J. McCaffrey, *Textures of Irish America* (Syracuse, 1992), 47–88. Kerby A. Miller, *Emigrants and Exiles: Ireland and the Irish Exodus to North America* (New York, 1985), 331–35 and 526–31. See also the local studies in T.J. Meagher (ed.), *From Paddy to Studs: Irish-American Communities in the Turn of the Century Era* (New York, 1986).

urban intelligentsia. Throughout the diaspora, however, it resonated with a much wider constituency, boosted by the presence in Polonia of petty déclassé gentry and émigré lesser intellectuals. In similar manner to other East European émigrés (representing no less than fourteen proudly distinct groups), they articulated a passionate nationalism to symbolise their link with the homeland elite – and to underpin their status within the migrant community where literary and cultured forms were placed above 'folk'.[28] With its exclusive focus on the homeland (and disregard of American political context), their nationalism served to complement rather than to contest that upheld by the Polish church. However, rival super-territorial structures – the Polish National Alliance and the Polish Roman Catholic Union – were in place by the 1880s, both with head-quarters in Chicago. As Kantowicz notes, the religionist-nationalist rivalry among Poles was comparatively mild. Factionalism abounded, but unlike the Bohemians, there was no split into two completely separate cultural communities: 'Nationalists and religionists formed two tendencies within one community of Polish Americans … divisions remained for the most part within the Polish family, which prayed together and stayed together'.[29] Above all, the national cause was extended throughout the migrant community by proud preservation of ethnic culture, a form of cultural-economic autarky – similar to their separate Catholicism – facilitated by members of the professions (who found a sufficient client base and adequate status reward within Polonia) and by ethnic entrepreneurs. Specialist businesses were opened to meet migrant needs, combining language retention (as in the many printshops) with other homeland traditions and delights (remembered and/or invented): the national diet and drink available in Polish saloons; the retail of religious and patriotic goods; and funeral parlours offering the full Polish ceremony.[30] As Poles were enjoined to 'Patronise Your Own', anti-semitism came into force, directed against stores run by Jewish migrants.[31]

As Roy Foster has shown, there were 'Micks on the make' in the Irish

28] See the section on 'Changing Images of the Old Country and the Development of Ethnic Identity among East European Immigrants', in Conzen et al., 'Invention and Ethnicity', 21–26, drawing upon the work of Ewa Morawska.
29] E.R. Kantowicz, 'Polish Chicago: Survival through Solidarity' in *Ethnic Chicago: A Multicultural Portrait*, ed. M.C. Holli and P.d'A. Jones (4th edition: Grand Rapids, 1995), 182.
30] Lopata, *Polish Americans,* 71–72.
31] Pacyga, *Polish Immigrants,* 224.

diaspora, but their ethnicity – at least in the days before the Gaelic revival and Sinn Fein ('Ourselves alone') – was less essentialist and autarkic, indeed more acceptable and marketable to a wider audience.[32] Like the émigrés in Polonia, political refugees enjoyed considerable prestige. As recollected in American exile, 1798 became a legacy of pride, providing the martyrs, myth and mission to inspire immigrant support for the nationalist cause with fervour absent in Ireland itself. In the absence of a language of its own, however, this nationalism was expressed through the public political rhetoric of the new land of residence. Aligned with the American master narrative of republican liberty, and, through its Canadian connections, with the manifest destiny of republican expansionism, Ireland was projected as the privileged site for American aid and intervention. Assertion of Irish nationalism was thus a means of challenging 'Know-Nothing' nativist prejudice, of affirming Irish-American republican credentials within the American body politic.[33]

Similarly, entrepreneurs who identified their best interests (or market niche) in servicing the Irish migrant community did not restrict their customer base on exclusive ethnic lines. This was most famously the case with the Irish saloon-keeper – and with Paddy, the vaudeville artist whose bibulous and genial ethnicity was much enjoyed by otherwise strait-laced Yankee audiences in need of vicarious saturnalian release.[34] Like its Polish counterpart, the Irish saloon provided an alternative and/or complementary base to the parish for ethnic associational culture and collective mutuality. However, where the Polish tavern was ethnocentric and enclosed in victuals and location, Irish pubs were 'universal', catering for a mixed clientele in prime thoroughfare sites.[35] They were the ideal location for wider political networking, for the construction of Democrat machines under the control of Irish ward captains. From such bases, the Irish gained control of a number of cities, henceforth under the grip of 'boss' politicians.

Rehabilitated in filiopietistic Irish-American studies as 'modern urban Robin Hoods', these notorious figures ruled 'miniature welfare states'

32] Roy Foster, 'Marginal Men and Micks on the Make: The Uses of Irish Exile, c.1840–1922', in his *Paddy and Mr Punch* (London, 1995), 281–305.
33] John Belchem, 'Nationalism, Republicanism and Exile: Irish Emigrants and the Revolutions of 1848', *Past and Present*, Vol. 146 (1995), 103–35.
34] W.H.A. Williams, *'Twas Only an Irishman's Dream: The Image of Ireland and the Irish in American Popular Song Lyric, 1800–1920* (Urbana, 1996), ch. 6.
35] P.R. Duis, 'The Ethnic Saloon; a Public Melting Pot' in *Ethnic Chicago*, ed. Holli and Jones, 503–28.

based on corruption, graft and personal loyalty (not least from the disproportionate number of Irish-Americans who gained upward mobility into the secure ranks of the uniformed and pensioned working-class in city employment). Social justice was dispensed through the ward captains who functioned like members of the St Vincent de Paul Society, participating in the daily life of the Irish-American community – attending funerals, club meetings and parties, and helping their constituents with jobs, rents, food, fuel and personal problems. These benefits, apologists like Lawrence McCaffrey argue, were later extended to multi-ethnic neighbourhoods in return for political support.[36] Recent research, however, has questioned the scale and benefits of 'rainbow' politics. Other ethnic groups were paid off at minimal cost to continued Irish control over such (limited) power and patronage at the disposal of the machine.[37] Here, indeed, was one of the main points of contention between Polish and Irish migrants. When middle-class Poles in Chicago sought (somewhat belatedly) to encourage their working-class compatriots to engage in domestic politics, progress was disappointingly slow. Internal factionalism, low levels of naturalised citizenship, and the lack of political experience were principal factors, but it was the Irish who were blamed in the Polish-American press:

> Whoever is familiar with our city politics knows only too well how the Irishmen, the most notorious political tricksters in the entire country since the earliest times, manipulate continually and invariably the divergent ambitions of private groups within the non-Irish nationalities against one another in order to promote thereby their own selfish interest.[38]

By the late nineteenth century, the Irish exercised a similar dominance within the American labour movement. Here again, account must be taken of the role of the Irish-American middle class. An important influence in the community, they encouraged less fortunate fellow countrymen to abandon transience, faction fighting and other behaviour that conformed

36] L.J. McCaffrey, 'Irish-American Politics: Power with or without Purpose' in *The Irish in America: emigration, assimilation and impact*, ed. P.J. Drudy (Cambridge, 1985), 169–90. T.N. Clark, 'The Irish Ethic and the Spirit of Patronage', *Ethnicity*, Vol. 2 (1975), 305–59. See also, T.H. O'Connor, *The Boston Irish: a Political History* (Boston, 1995).
37] S. Erie, *Rainbow's End. Irish Americans and the Dilemma of Urban Political Machines, 1840 to 1985* (Berkeley, 1988), ch.1.
38] *Dziennik Chicagoski* 4 Feb.1922, quoted in Pacyga, *Polish Immigrants*, 198.

to host labelling, and to adopt instead a trans-regional national or ethnic 'Irish' pride in themselves. Once implanted, ethnic associational culture provided a means by which successful Irish-Americans could guard against social and labour radicalism while keeping a check on violent inflexions of nationalism.[39] In alliance with the Catholic church, these middle-class culture-brokers took prompt action to eradicate the 'wild' Irishness displayed in 'primitive' forms of trade unionism, most notably the 'terrorism' of the Molly Maguires in the anthracite region of Pennsylvania. Through sponsorship of formal and respectable types of collective mutuality (including the re-branded Ancient Order of Hibernians, shorn of its former secrecy), the Irish-American middle class imposed its version of Irish ethnic affiliation, promoted in a manner which conformed to the norms and values of the host society.[40] In the process, blue-collar Irish-American workers – the target audience of the proliferation of Irish clubs and societies in the last third of the nineteenth century – acquired useful transferable skills, the organisational and associational know-how that was soon to carry them to leadership positions within the formal trade unionism of the American Federation of Labor. By the end of the century, as David Doyle notes, 'numerically, Irish Americans *dominated* few trades (except plumbers and steam fitters); politically they dominated a majority of the unions of organised trades'.[41] Irish women in garment-making, textiles, steam laundries, shoemaking, meat-packing, restaurants, printing and telephone exchanges were also ardent trade unionists, often to the fore in leadership positions. Like the men, however, only a handful of Irish-American women moved on from trade unionism to a more radical economic analysis.[42]

Extending beyond the labour movement, Irish-American women developed an associational culture of their own, assisted by sisters in the female religious orders. An esteemed alternative to marriage and mother-

39] D.B. Light, Jr, 'The Role of Irish-American Organizations in Assimilation and Community Formation' in *Irish in America*, ed. Drudy, 113–42. Kerby A. Miller, 'Class, Culture and Immigrant Group Identity in the United States: the Case of Irish-American ethnicity' in *Immigration Reconsidered*, ed. Yans-McLaughlin, 96–129.

40] Kevin Kenny, 'The Molly Maguires and the Catholic Church', *Labor History*, Vol. 36 (1995), 345–76.

41] David Doyle, 'The Irish and American Labour 1880–1920', *Soathar*, Vol. 1 (1975), 42–53.

42] Hasia Diner, *Erin's Daughters in America: Irish Immigrant Women in the Nineteenth Century* (Baltimore, 1983), ch. 4.

hood, sisterhood offered considerable fulfilment. The entrepreneurial nun, it has recently been argued, was one of nineteenth-century Ireland's most successful exports,[43] developing the infrastructure which enabled large numbers of single women to prosper in the migrant outflow – with the possible exception of Sweden, Ireland was unique in the gender balance of its emigration. Against the odds, nuns developed a national network of social services in the new lands of residence, providing training schools and employment services, houses of refuge and shelter, medical facilities and day nurseries. While trusting to heighten the spirituality of Irish-American women and their daughters, the Sisters of Mercy helped them to acquire economic self-sufficiency – or at least a sufficient dowry to attract a co-ethnic marriage partner.[44]

By 1900, the Irish were securely located in the mainstream of the working class enjoying the American standard of living, the 'wages of whiteness'.[45] Originally located alongside African-Americans, the Irish had finally become white – a longer, more complex and contested process than Ignatiev suggests[46] – boosted by the 'uplifting effect' of subsequent waves of 'foreign' in-migration. Having learnt trades by on-site experience, the Irish were elevated to supervisory status in steel mills, iron foundries, anthracite mines and railroad yards to take charge of the new unskilled labour force recruited from eastern and southern Europe. Old stereotypes were abandoned along with pseudo-scientific taxonomies. No longer portrayed as physically different, Paddy and Bridget were recast as Maggie and Jiggs in a comedy of suburban middle-class manners where Irish-Americans were applauded as role models, as suitable intermediaries to acculturate the new wave of European in-migrants.[47] As union leaders (and urban political bosses), Irish-Americans may have constructed some inter-ethnic solidarity among the Poles and other 'not-yet-white ethnics'. As workplace culture-brokers (and boundary-markers) for the white

43] See the editors' introduction in R. Swift and S. Gilley, *The Irish in Victorian Britain: the Local Dimension* (Dublin, 1999), 9.
44] Diner, *Erin's Daughters*, ch. 6.
45] David R. Roediger, *The Wages of Whiteness: Race and the Remaking of the American Working Class* (London, 1991), ch. 7.
46] Noel Ignatiev, *How the Irish became White* (New York, 1995).
47] K. Donovan, 'Good old Pat: an Irish-American Stereotype in Decline', *Éire-Ireland*, Vol. 15 (1980), 6–14; and J.J. Appel, 'From Shanties to Lace Curtains: the Irish Image in *Puck*, 1876–1910', *Comparative Studies in Society and History*, Vol. 13 (1971), 365–75. See also, Dale T. Knobel, *Paddy and the Republic* (Middletown, 1986).

American mainstream, however, they implanted dominant attitudes, thereby ensuring the spread of racist stereotyping and prejudice (delayed amongst the Poles, however, until the inter-war years). Originally an ethnic minority, the Irish were to contribute much to 'Americanization from the bottom up'.[48]

The contrast sketched here between Polish ethnic isolationism and Irish ethnic networking into the mainstream is crude, but I hope it provides a useful starting point for comparative analysis. Some qualifications must be entered straight away. For women, there was little difference in ethnic inflexion. Whether in Irish or Polish form, ethnic associational culture (and the preference for intra-marriage) tended to reinforce patriarchy and traditional gender roles, but it allowed women considerable space. Catholic sodalities and the like served to complement the two key components of the ethnic community: kinship ties (which in the migrant context more nearly resembled peer groups than lineages); and neighbourliness. Constructed in this way, ethnic communities should not be studied in terms of the conventional distinction between private and public. Ethnic associational culture operated within an enlarged private space shared by men and women: the public sphere was further off, beyond a boundary that some married women were perhaps never to cross. Newspapers published by Polish women's organisations emphasised the domestic origins of communal responsibility through the socialisation of children into ethnic consciousness, the maintenance of ethnic institutions and the proscription of materialist Protestant-American alternatives. Admittedly, the Polish Women's Alliance took an interest in the struggle for women's rights, but it kept apart from American feminist associations and activists.[49] Middle-class women in the ethnic community acted as 'social housekeepers': class status, female activism and mutual aid were interwoven, Donna Gabaccia notes, as they 'used their "brooms" simultaneously to sweep away native-born competitors, to guarantee their own status, and to promote ethnic group survival'. Significantly, once the public associational framework began to decline (along with patterns of neighbourhood residence), the

48] J.R. Barrett, 'Americanization from the Bottom Up: Immigration and the Remaking of the Working Class in the United States, 1880–1930', *Journal of American History*, Vol. 79 (1992), 996–1020.

49] Pien Versteegh, 'Survival Strategies? The Role of Family and Ethnic Networks in Migration and Settlement of Polish Migrants in Pennsylvania 1890–1940', paper presented to the European Social Science History Conference, Noordwijkerhout, May 1996, 12–14.

maintenance of 'symbolic' ethnicity came to depend more on women. An optional lifestyle, ethnicity became domesticated, a residual matter of family festivals, stories, tales and the socialisation of children. [50]

This brief portrayal of Irish and Polish ethnicity in America has taken insufficient account of internal contestation, contradiction and confusion. 'Irishness' was not always articulated in conformity with the norms and mores of the middle-class culture-brokers. Lower down the socio-economic scale, the 'Gaelic-Catholic-disability variable', to use Don Akenson's terminology, came into play.[51] In a dependency culture of inverted pride, poverty was valorised by the conflation of religious adherence and ethnic affiliation. Sanctified by Catholicism, the holy virtue of poverty became the hallmark of being genuinely Irish, exiled from the 'martyr nation' which had suffered seven centuries of British oppression for its faith.[52] This 'culture of poverty' – and the dependency it engendered – was replicated throughout the Irish diaspora, even where Irish migrants were quick to acquire socio-economic parity, as in Australia.

The Irish were by far the largest 'ethnic' group in Australia, constituting about 25 per cent of all immigrants from 1788 to the early twentieth century. Significantly, middle-class migrants held back from 'Irish' mobilisation until prompted into action by the Catholic church. Originally in the control of English Benedictines, the church underwent 'hibernicisation' to cater for the Irish influx, a process hastened by Cardinal Moran's championing of Irish home rule – its attainment, he trusted, would greatly improve the status and standing of Catholic Australians. Once blessed by the hierarchy, Irish associational culture emerged from relative obscurity to attract the temporal resources (and secular aspirations) of successful Irish immigrants. At this level, ideals of colonial success and loyalty readily harmonised with hopes for Ireland (as for Australia) as an independent dominion within the British empire.[53]

50] Donna Gabaccia, *From the Other Side: Women, Gender and Immigrant Life in the U.S. 1820–1990* (Bloomington, 1994), 92 and 121–23. For the public aspect, see Colleen McDannell, 'Going to the Ladies' Fair: Irish Catholics in New York City, 1870–1900' in *The New York Irish*, ed. R.H. Bayor and T.J. Meagher (Baltimore, 1996), 234–51.
51] D.H. Akenson, *The Irish Diaspora* (Belfast, 1996), 237–42.
52] Miller, *Emigrants and Exiles*, 333 and passim.
53] As well as the classic study, Patrick O'Farrell, *The Irish in Australia* (Kensington, NSW, 1986), see also C. McConville, 'Emigrant Irish and Suburban Catholics: Faith and Nation in Melbourne and Sydney', unpublished PhD thesis, University of Melbourne, 1984, 301–19.

Despite its exclusive and integrative beginnings, Catholic-led ethnic culture soon developed in a radical direction. Dismayed by Protestant conservative reaction against Catholic claims at the time of federation, Moran gave his blessing to the Australian Labor Party. Sectarian strife was not long delayed, provoked by Archbishop Mannix's radical advocacy of Catholic (and workers') claims during the frenzied atmosphere of the First World War. Mannix became the hero of working-class Catholics – and the arch-villain of patriotic established Protestants (in whose ranks Irish Protestant migrants were well represented) – as he led the successful anti-conscription campaign of 1916, upholding the cause of the Irish rebellion while he condemned the capitalist war, Australian society and anti-Catholic discrimination.

Under Mannix, Irishness became a characteristic not of the Irish-born but of the Catholic worker, of those who fared least well in the Australian narrative of material advance. For all their 'ordinariness and normality' as Australians, Irish Catholics lagged behind others in reaping the socio-economic rewards. Stirred into recognition of their relative deprivation by Mannix's rhetoric, the Irish Catholic working class were drawn into a rich and overlapping pattern of assertive associational culture, embracing the Labor Party branch and parish-based sporting and welfare societies. Mannix, indeed, succeeded in fusing religious, ethnic and class identities, but in a manner detrimental to the wider projection of the Australian labour movement, subverting its carefully constructed non-sectarian image. In a potent sectarian backlash, the Labor Party was stigmatised as Irish and Catholic, and hence un-Australian, a stigma which was to persist well into the 1920s. By this time, however, nationalist associational culture had reverted to its low Australian norm as the Irish cause lost direction and identity.[54] Henceforth, Irishness was expressed in informal and domestic manner: while eschewing specific ethnic associations in the public sphere, Irish-Australians delighted in giving Irish names to their homes. In the inter-war Australian city, identity and affiliation tended to be determined by locality – the symbols of local pride were as likely to be the local football ground, town-hall steeple, pub or bookie as the Catholic church – but the incidence of intra-marriage, street crime and gang

---

54] Frank Farrell, 'J.H. Scullin, the Irish Question and the Australian Labor Party' in *Australia and Ireland 1788–1988*, ed. C. Kiernan (Dublin, 1986), 156–69.
55] S. Alomes, 'Culture, Ethnicity and Class in Australia's Dominion Period, 1900–39' in *Australia and Ireland*, ed. Kiernan, 189–90. McConville, 'Emigrant Irish', ch. 7.

behaviour (the 'larrikin push') suggested an Irish 'apartness'.[55] Some Irish-Australians played up to the image by constructing a 'culture of poverty' which eschewed the Australian ethic of individual material advancement in favour of the communality and solidarity available only at the bottom of the social (but not spiritual) scale.[56]

As Australia evinces, middle-class ethnic hegemony was by no means assured. In the United States, Irish working-class voters turned to local labour parties, unions and nationalist formations when urban party bosses, conscious of the maintenance needs of the machine and its limited tax base, abandoned radical ventures (and ethnic largesse) in favour of fiscal conservatism.[57] At the time of the Land League, as Eric Foner has shown, Irish nationalism carried workers forward into a class-based social radicalism deeply critical of Gilded Age America. Patrick Ford's aptly titled *Irish World and Industrial Liberator* promoted Irish nationalism, Georgeite land reform and the labour movement in unison. The same conjuncture was personified in the career of Terence Powderly, prominent member of the Clan-na-Gael, the Land League and the Knights of Labor.[58] Under Powderly's leadership, the Knights acted in defiance of the racism associated with the Irish: in the South, some 60 000 African-American men and women were recruited into its ranks. Out in the western states, however, the Irish-led Knights spearheaded the 'abatement' campaign to drive Chinese workers out of lumber and mining camps.[59] The social thought of New York Irish nationalists, David Brundage has shown, was characterised by ideological incoherence and inconsistency. Although hostile to labour radicalism and militant working-class activity, middle-class advocates of home rule continued to uphold the radical stance of the Land League towards religious, class and gender equality while revolutionary separatists, a male-dominated approach, became increasingly conservative and exclusively Catholic in their republican Irish nationalism.[60]

56] O'Farrell, *Irish in America*, 299.
57] Erie, chs 2 and 3.
58] Eric Foner, 'Class, Ethnicity and Radicalism in the Gilded Age: Land League and Irish America', *Marxist Perspectives*, Vol. 1 (1978), 6–55.
59] David Brundage, '"Green over Black" Revisited: Ireland and Irish-Americans in the New Histories of American Working-class "Whiteness"', paper presented to 'Racializing Class, Classifying Race' conference, St Antony's College, Oxford, 11–13 July 1997.
60] David Brundage, '"In Time of Peace, Prepare for War": Key Themes in the Social Thought of New York's Irish Nationalists, 1890–1916' in *New York Irish*, ed. Bayor and Meagher, 321–34.

Generational tensions added to the confusion and complexity. In Butte, Montana, indeed, they pulled the Irish 'community' apart, weakening their control of this high-wage hard-rock mining town. Through manipulation of Irish organisations (most notably the Ancient Order of Hibernians, the Clan-na-Gael, and the Irish-dominated Miners Union), the key underground workers, an 'ethno-occupational aristocracy', safeguarded their privileges and security, rigorously excluding transient fellow countrymen who showed no interest in steady employment and home-ownership. The next generation, however, aspired higher: sons preferred to cross the collar gap, abandoning the mines and exclusively Irish forms of associational culture. Wages and security were later put at risk when Butte's disposable labour force was swollen by the arrival of a new generation of Irish in-migrants. Imbued with Larkinite social radicalism, they joined together in class alliance with disadvantaged ethnic groups to mount a fundamental challenge to the cosy ethnic/corporate/union world of the settled Irish workers. [61]

Such tensions were less evident in Polonia. Although its internalised 'status competition' took no heed of the status-gaining resources of the dominant society, it proved sufficiently robust, Lopata contends, to 'motivate even second, third, fourth and fifth generations of Polish Americans to concentrate their energies and concerns in its direction'.[62] There were increasing differences of emphasis, however. Members of the Polish National Alliance sought to refine ethnic purity prior to return to an independent Poland – a dream largely dispelled in the years after the First World War – while the Polish Roman Catholic Union wished to maintain an ethnic identity in the new (and permanent) land of residence. The Polish Falcons, established as a private army to fight for Polish freedom, soon developed into a welfare and education association, offering education in English along with other increasingly bilingual means to help Polish workers to overcome workplace discrimination.[63]

Although the project of middle-class culture-brokers, ethnicisation did not preclude proletarianisation. In industrial South Side Chicago, ethnic communality facilitated wider mobilisation through pan-ethnic federation of unions and locals in the stockyards and steelworks, a strategy promoted

61] D.M. Emmons, *The Butte Irish: Class and Ethnicity in an American Mining Town, 1875–1925* (Urbana, 1989), chs 3–7, and 'Faction Fights: the Irish Worlds of Butte, Montana, 1875–1917' in *The Irish World Wide Volume 2: The Irish in the New Communities*, ed. P. O'Sullivan (Leicester, 1992), 82–98.
62] Lopata, *Polish Americans*, 11–13.
63] Versteegh, 'Survival Strategies', 10–12.

by John Kikulski. In the tense aftermath of the First World War, however, labour advance was reversed by race riots and inter-union civil war – Kikulski was murdered, allegedly by the Irish – as employers imported increasing numbers of African-American labour. The Poles continued to advocate the widest working-class unity – they took particular exception to criticism of the anti-semitism practised in their newly independent homeland from hypocritical racist Americans. As nativist sentiment and economic pressures intensified, the entire Polish community – including priests, professionals and business owners – rallied to support their striking compatriots in the packing-house strike of 1921–22. Ethnicity and class proved mutually reinforcing, but the strike ended in disastrous failure, much to the detriment of organised labour and race relations in Chicago. Through this painful process, Polish-American workers were finally acculturated into the white American working class.[64]

Turning briefly to Europe, it would seem that the contrast between isolationism and networking might need to be inverted. It was the Poles, not the Irish, who were more adept at mobilising ethnic resources to gain recognition and inclusion. Murphy's study of the Poles in Bottrop, an 'ideal type' exercise in Milton Gordon's assimilation model, recounts a pluralist 'success story of American dimensions'. The Poles did not confuse the preservation of a distinct ethnic community with the creation of an autonomous 'Little Poland'. From their ethnic associational base, they were able to negotiate a secure place for themselves within the new urban culture of the Ruhrgebiet.[65] Furthermore, as John Kulczycki's masterly study of the Zjednoczenie Zawodowe Polskie (ZZP) has shown, linguistic, cultural and ethnic divisions did not preclude class solidarity and industrial militancy. Uprooted from a rural homeland, Polish migrants sought mutual protection by borrowing and adapting the associational culture of the Catholic German miners. Once established, these mutual aid societies – different in origin and form from those implanted in American Polonia – acquired a class dynamic which was to distance and emancipate Polish workers from conservative ethnic interests: church leadership and the influence of the middle-class intelligentsia at the head of Polish nationalist organisations. Thenceforth, it was but a short step to institute a formal trade union specifically for Polish-speaking migrants. Avowedly Christian itself, the militant ZZP rejected the industrial conciliation of the

64] Pacyga, *Polish Imigrants*, ch. 6.
65] Murphy, *Guestworkers*, passim.

Gewerkverein, while distinguishing itself from the international socialist image promoted by the Alter Verband. Union officials remained lowly-paid and close to their roots, aiding the ZZP in its dual mission to express and support the class grievances of the miners while identifying with the cultural characteristics that differentiated Polish-speaking miners from native workers. Before the First World War, the ZZP had integrated itself into the German labour movement and succeeded in equating the interests of the Polish nation with those of the Polish working class. In the pre-war Ruhr, Polish ethnicity was a proactive force, an essential preliminary to the construction of wider class-based attitudes and structures.[66]

By contrast, the Irish in Britain – at least as portrayed in current historiographical orthodoxy – were not an ethnic community. Coming from a range of backgrounds, they took up a number of occupational and residential opportunities without the need for distinctive 'Irish' cultural and associational forms. Migrants readily identified, affiliated and integrated with host members of their particular class.[67] However, despite this purported 'ethnic fade', anti-Irishness was to persist in British culture. Although technically internal migrants within the United Kingdom, the Irish continued to be labelled in popular stereotype as alien and 'outsiders'. They remained apart, occupying 'a curious middle place' without the 'ethnic' (and other) resources to effect either full assimilation or complete separation.[68] There was not even the possibility of a hyphenated identity as Irish-British.

There was one exception: Liverpool. Disparaged by historians as a sectarian redoubt, 'marginal to the cultural and political life of the nation',[69] Liverpool contained an Irish 'colony' of sufficient dimensions to merit comparison with ethnic enclaves across the Atlantic. In pluralist fashion, middle-class Irish Catholics – Micks on the make on the Mersey – stood forward as ethnic culture-brokers. Under their patronage and sponsorship, Irish nationalism was projected in constitutional terms, hence its blessing

66] John J. Kulczycki, *The Polish Coal Miners' Union and the German Labor Movement in the Ruhr, 1902–1934* (Oxford, 1997), chs1–4.
67] For critical perspectives (other than my own) on the current socio-economic orthodoxy, see Mary J. Hickman, 'Alternative Historiographies of the Irish in Britain: a Critique of the Segregation/Assimilation Model' in *The Irish in Victorian Britain: The Local Dimension*, ed. R. Swift and S. Gilley (Dublin, 1999), 236–53; and D.M. MacRaild, *Irish Migrants in Modern Britain, 1750–1922* (Basingstoke, 1999), 2–8.
68] D. Fitzpatrick, 'A Curious Middle Place: the Irish in Britain, 1871–1921' in *The Irish in Britain 1815–1939*, ed. R. Swift and S. Gilley (London, 1989), 10–59.
69] Steven Fielding, *Class and Ethnicity: Irish Catholics in England 1880–1939* (Buckingham, 1993), 5.

by the Catholic church, quick to adjust to the hibernicisation of its congregation. Violence was excluded, socialist radicalism was marginalised – hence Liverpool's backwardness in the forward march of Labour – while the Irish poor were instructed in respectability and citizenship. However, in taking such active charge of migrant adjustment, the ethnic leaders (nationalist and clerical) constructed a self-enclosed, self-sufficient network which, viewed from outside, emphasised Irish-Catholic apartness. Ironically, the bid for inclusion served to confirm Irish 'difference': they remained the internal 'other' against whom the otherwise 'non-ethnic' English defined themselves. The Liverpool-Irish continued to suffer the prejudice and negative reputation which, in the late twentieth century, came to blight the city itself.[70]

The Liverpool-Irish were the last to transfer political allegiance to Labour. Considerable tensions remained. Working-class Irish Catholics throughout Britain believed that Labour had no place taking political positions outside the industrial domain, certainly not to interfere with their 'way of life' in such family matters as birth control and education. Equally, they believed the Catholic church should respect its boundaries of competence and refrain from ideological and political intervention.[71] This is a timely reminder that identities seldom conform to the neat programmatic prescriptions of ethnic or class-based associations. As post-modernist deconstruction has confirmed, people are eclectic in selection and fusion of ideologies, languages and narratives. As comparative study of Irish and Polish migrants will surely confirm, ethnicity and class are neither discrete nor mutually exclusive, but form a complex, often bewildering, continuum. However, it may be significant to note by way of conclusion that among the elderly Poles in Britain today – exiles who remained as post-war political settlements made return to Poland unacceptable – good mental health depends on two factors: involvement in ethnic associational culture, and the opportunity to relate a national narrative of the past.[72]

70] See the essay 'Micks on the make on the Mersey' in this volume.

71] There has been much debate on these issues with relation to the Irish and 'Red Clydeside'. See J.F. McCaffrey, 'Irish Issues in the Nineteenth and Twentieth Century: Radicalism in a Scottish Context' in *Irish Immigrants and Scottish Society in the Nineteenth and Twentieth Centuries*, ed. T.M. Devine, (Edinburgh, 1991),116–37.

72] M. Winslow, 'Polish Migration to Britain: War, Exile and Mental Health', *Oral History*, Vol. 27 (1999), 57–64. For an earlier study of their 'accommodation', see J. Zubrzycki, *Polish Immigrants in Britain: a Study of Adjustment* (The Hague, 1956).

8

'Grandes villes': Liverpool, Lyon and Munich*

D espite their remarkable demographic growth, large provincial cities do not feature prominently in early labour history. Given their increasing complexity, large cities (with half a million inhabitants or more by the late nineteenth century) seemed unsuited for united endeavour: such 'grandes villes' lacked the structural foundations for collective action found in small and single-industry townships where communal loyalty reinforced occupational solidarity. As this essay shows, however, the size and complexity of large cities did not necessarily impede trade union development. Indeed, workers could take advantage of the metropolitan atmosphere, utilising the facilities of an agitational infrastructure – public venues, the press, the presence of intellectuals, speakers and activists – to coordinate and enhance local neighbourhood and workplace networks. (This metropolitan public political space was also open to the advocates of female emancipation, a cause which attracted considerable early support in large cities.) Furthermore, large cities were keen to assert their own identity and their provincial pre-eminence, a double-aspect cultural process which awaits adequate historical deconstruction. While distinguishing themselves from the capital, 'grandes villes' placed themselves at the forefront of wider, more representative national trends. As this essay suggests, in such proud 'second capitals' as Liverpool, Lyon and Munich, the development of the labour movement tended both to prefigure and accentuate the respective national 'model'.

* This essay, prepared with the assistance of Karl Heinrich Pohl and Vincent Robert, was presented to the conference , 'L'Invention des syndicalismes en Europe à la fin du XIXe siècle', Paris, 12–14 Oct. 1995. It has been published in French in *L'Invention des syndicalismes. Le syndicalisme en Europe occidentale à la fin du XIXe siècle*, ed. J.L. Robert, F. Boll and A. Prost, (Paris, 1997), 181–95.

Although entirely arbitrary, the selection of Liverpool, Lyon and Munich as the 'grandes villes' has proved a fortunate choice for comparative labour history. Any other group of cities, it must be admitted, might have produced very different findings. At first sight, the chosen cities seem outside the scope of conventional labour history. None of the three was essentially industrial or 'proletarian': there was an absence of huge factories and large employers. Each city was multi-functional, a pattern emphasised by the inexorable (and complementary) growth of the 'white collar' lower middle class and of the 'uniformed' working class ('semi-skilled' workers in public transport and utilities). Traditional urban dwellers, whether artisan craft workers or the bourgeois professions and patriciate, were steadily outnumbered and/or displaced. In these (and other) respects Liverpool, Lyon and Munich were altogether more 'modern' and complex than the mono-industrial towns and medium-sized 'polyactive' towns privileged in most accounts of 'labour's turning-point'. As pointers to the future, they surely merit special attention.

This essay is divided into three sections: first, an introductory analysis of the socio-economic character and political and cultural identity of each city; second, a brief survey of trade union development within them between 1880 and 1900, focusing on the role of local coordination and inter-trade union bodies; and third, a case study of railway workers and tramway workers, occupations of particular significance to large cities.

THE CITIES: STRUCTURE AND IDENTITY

Population

By the end of the nineteenth century, Liverpool, Lyon and Munich were substantial cities: the 1901 census listed Liverpool Borough as 684 958 inhabitants, while calculations for the greater Lyon area and Munich in 1900 have produced figures of 507 000 and 490 000 respectively. The pace and pattern of demographic growth of each city, however, differed significantly. Liverpool grew inexorably, although by 1880–1900 there was considerable out-migration from increasingly unattractive inner residential areas. The most rapid growth, indeed, was outside the recently-enlarged borough boundary: the wider Merseyside conurbation (the whole of Liverpool, West Derby, Birkenhead and Wirral registration districts along with the Huyton, Much Woolton and Hale sub-districts of the Prescot registration district) grew from 817 821 in 1881 to 1 022 748 in 1901. In Lyon, there was a similar expansion and annexation of the built-up area – la Guillo-tière, la Croix Rousse and Vaise were annexed in 1851 – but the growth rate began to level off towards the end of the century. Population growth (along with modern factory development) was restricted to the outer sub-urbs and unannexed townships, such as Villeurbanne where the popula-tion doubled from around 20 000 in 1896 to about 40 000 in 1911. In Munich, by contrast, long-term population growth accelerated dramatically at this stage: the population more than doubled between 1882 (240 000) and 1900 (490 000), a faster rate than in comparable German cities. There-after, there was a marked deceleration until after the First World War.

In-migration was the main factor of growth in all three cases, but Liverpool, a major port of entry for migrants and a human entrepôt for trans-continental emigration, was a case apart. In Lyon and Munich, in-migration was preponderantly short-distance, essentially from adjacent rural and out-working areas, from a hinterland of shared culture, religion and regional identity. Figures for newly-married members of the working class in Lyon in 1911 show that only four per cent of the women and 4.7 per cent of the men were born outside France. However, there was a significant Italian presence in small shops and businesses in working-class areas. Among the working class, in fact, there was a certain reticence towards Italians, even in trade unions. In Munich, where two-thirds of the workforce in 1907 had been born outside the city, some 90 per cent of in-migrants came from Bavaria. Liverpool, by contrast, attracted long-distance migrants, primarily the Irish (22.3 per cent of the population in 1851 was Irish-born), but also significant numbers of Welsh and Scots. Where rural in-migration into Lyon and Munich served to reinforce their culture, character and status as regional capitals, the multi-ethnic, mainly celtic inflow transformed Liverpool, setting it apart from surrounding Lancashire (and from the rest of England). The 'melting-pot' of in-migration gave Liverpool its unique identity, a construction riven with considerable cultural, sectarian and political division.

Social and economic structure
In-migration also accounts for the pronounced pattern of spatial segre-gation which emerged earlier in Liverpool than in other cities. Residential location was a compromise between proximity to work and a suitable residential area in terms of cost (often linked to position in the family life cycle), social status and ethnic affiliation. The skilled working population,

located in inner residential suburbs, was associated with Welsh and Scottish minority groups, while a large proportion of the unskilled and semi-skilled working class, clustered close to casual labour markets of the city centre and the waterfront, were of Irish origin.

While there were significant changes in the topography of Munich with the development of a commercial and industrial belt to the south and west of the city centre, the extent of spatial segregation was less evident. Unlike Berlin or Hamburg, Munich lacked specific working-class areas with high indices of segregation. With its four-storey 'workers' barracks', rapidly-expanding Westend was the most working-class part of the city, separated from the centre by railway lines and industrial development, but even here there was a considerable lower middle-class presence (mainly white-collar workers and state employees) alongside manufacturing, transport, postal and other workers. Commercial development and industrial relocation transformed the topography of Lyon, forcing the working class out of the old central areas into the new industrial areas along the left bank of the Rhone and into outlying districts. The city centre was transformed by commercialisation between 1850 and 1870 as banks, department stores, newspaper and other offices displaced working-class inhabitants. Mechanisation of silk production led to its relocation on the right bank of the Rhone, along with its associated finishing industries, and a variety of metal-working, chemical and glass-making factories. La Croix Rousse, the original centre of Jacquard hand production, became an area inhabited by office workers and self-employed artisans. Lyon was metamorphosed into a largely commercial metropolis with 33 per cent of its workforce in the service and white-collar sectors and its new proletariat dispersed into outlying suburbs. Such structural change, Lequin has argued, accounted for the 'lull' in militancy in the 1870s as the radical culture of the *canuts* was undermined.

Despite the rapid growth of the white-collar sector – the numbers rose from 10 per cent in 1851 to some 30 per cent of the newly-married in 1911 – Lyon remained a working-class city, although different in character from the heavy industrial districts of France. There were few large industrial establishments. Small firms flourished in symbiotic relationship with the needs of large primary concerns. Some firms in mechanised silk production and dyeing employed over 100, but most establishments in the textile industry had a workforce of between 25 and 100. Similarly, in metal-working and engineering, there were one or two large concerns, but small to middling firms remained preponderant. As a result of technological change, the number of male workers in silk fell dramatically, from 41.5 per cent of the male working-class population in 1876 to 15.4 per cent in 1891. By this time, building accounted for 31 per cent, the largest occupation for working-class males, but here units were small-scale, scattered and transient. In general, most workers in the city worked in medium-sized establishments or small workshops.

In Munich there was greater economic diversification. As a multifunctional city with a weakly developed industrial sector, Munich exemplified the 'South German model'. There were significant numbers in public administration (in 1907, 20 per cent of income was earned in the public services), as well as many scientists, artists, pensioners (rich and poor), and workers associated with tourism. By 1907, only 40 per cent of the working population was employed in industry (most notably in metalworking and engineering, building, clothing, woodworking, printing and brewing), and some 20 per cent in commerce and transport. Even so, Munich was the largest industrial city in Bavaria. Unlike other parts of industrial Germany, however, establishments tended to be small to medium in size. There were 15 firms employing more than 500 workers in 1907, but taken together these accounted for only 6.5 per cent of the working population. About 70 per cent worked in small to medium-sized establishments – in fact 26.4 per cent worked in units employing between one and five workers. Within this industrial structure, skilled male workers and the self-employed retained considerable significance. In social terms, Munich was weighted towards the middle class – in 1906, the upper class comprised 10 per cent of the population, the middle class 45.1 per cent, and the lower class 44.1 per cent – but many of the lower middle class were financially insecure, often on similar incomes to skilled workers.

Liverpool was dominated by the docks and a vast casual labour market, the 'mecca of all British jetsam'. General labour and dock and warehouse labour – in which there was a high proportion of Irish migrant labour – together accounted for 22.3 per cent of all males over 20 in the 1871 census. Not all waterfront labour, however, was casual and unskilled. Alongside labouring work on the docks and in the adjacent processing and refining plants, there was a substantial 'manufacturing' sector associated with iron founding, ship repairing (ship-building had crossed the Mersey to Birkenhead) and marine engineering, comprising some 10.3 per cent of all males aged over 20 in the 1871 census. These trades, with their regular high wages, attracted skilled migrants from Scotland, Wales and the Black Country. Of particular importance for the growth of the labour movement was the development of the railway sector, which provided regular employment for less skilled workers, the 'uniformed' working class.

Given the prominence of casualism and the 'macho' culture of the docks (where employment was exclusively male), the sexual division of labour was particularly pronounced in Liverpool, more so than in Lyon where gender marked the boundary between skilled and unskilled labour in textiles and other industries. In Liverpool there was no textile employment: female factory and warehouse employment was restricted to the lowliest tasks in food and tobacco, sack-making and mending, rag and cotton picking. A few apprenticeships were available in printing and related trades, but in the workshop sector most women were confined to the sweated clothing trades. Restructuring and mechanisation undermined the few areas of skilled and apprenticed women's trades in the factories: even in the tobacco factories, where nimble-fingered women cigar-makers had once been a skilled elite, women's work soon became equated with unskilled work. Along with the retail sector, the expanding office sector offered an alternative for the daughters of the lower middle class, but within the overall de-skilling of clerical work, male clerks succeeded in upholding a superior status. By far the largest category of female employment was domestic service.

Identity
From the construction of its innovatory wet-docks system in the early eighteenth century, Liverpool identified its prosperity with commerce, not with manufacture. Not just a great seaport, Liverpool was the leading financial and commercial centre outside London, the northern outpost of 'gentlemanly capitalism'. Aspiring to the status of 'second metropolis', commercial Liverpool defined itself against industrial Manchester and in rivalry with London. The ethos was to endure, preventing a wider and much-needed industrial diversification. Eschewing the 'second industrial revolution', Liverpool entered the twentieth century with a distinct (and distorted) economic structure. In the 1920s, when only 37 per cent of Liverpool workers were engaged in production compared with the national average of 67 per cent, the Corporation still expressed satisfaction in the absence of manufacturing and industrial blight.

Proud of its heritage in the Kingdom of Bavaria, Munich regarded itself as the capital of the liberal south in rivalry with Berlin and the conservative north. Its famous beergardens symbolised social harmony and a democratic culture, providing the context in which progressive reformism could develop in advance of the rest of Germany, aided by the presence of a significant number of intellectuals, writers and artists. Although there were signs of growing social and political conflict, it was the one city where there was substantial Catholic (and middle-class) support for the SPD.

Lyon regarded itself as the guardian or 'capital' of *republican* France, proudly in advance of the rest of the country. As the May Day demonstration of 1891 evinced, the workers took great pride in the city's republican credentials and its primacy in earlier workers' revolutionary struggles (as in 1831 and 1834). It is this proud republican heritage which probably explains why the government regarded the Lyonnais socialists and anarchists with a fear disproportionate to their actual numbers or influence. While socio-economic differences between Lyon and other parts of France steadily diminished, the city continued to uphold its political heritage and mission, regarding itself as a rival to Paris.

TRADE UNION DEVELOPMENT

This section begins with a summary overview of developments in each city, pointing to conformity with national models and characteristics. This is followed by more detailed comparative analysis focused on the role of local coordinating bodies, the Liverpool Trades Council, the Lyon Bourse du travail and the Conseil de la Fédération des syndicats, and the Munich Gewerkschaftskartell (Union Cartel).

Liverpool exemplifies many of the key features of British 'new unionism'. In the favourable economic climate of 1889–91, labour turbulence was prolonged and severe, more so than in London. There was a major explosion of militancy and union organisation, a classic British 'strike wave' (similar to subsequent events in 1911–13 and 1919–20) which registered a shift towards more inclusive organisation of less skilled workers, a rejection of the cautious advice of established officials, and a renewed emphasis on the efficacy of strike activity. Despite the socialist revival of the 1880s, ideological developments accounted for little in this militant tenor, prompted for the most part by cyclical fluctuations and adverse changes in the labour process – dockers, seamen and other workers fiercely contested employer prerogative as they sought job regulation. Unlike previous attempts to organise the semi-skilled and unskilled, the new unionism of

the late 1880s and early 1890s was to endure, although survival was dependent upon amalgamation and/or the abandonment of some distinctive
'new' features. Without supplanting the old craft unions, new unionism
broadened the base of organised labour in Liverpool, as reflected in the list
of 79 unions operative in the city in 1911.

The leading organisers and activists of new unionism in Liverpool came
from a bewildering variety of political backgrounds – J.G. Taggart, a former
labourer at Tate's sugar refinery and the first secretary of the Mersey
District of the National Union of Gasworkers and General Labourers, was
an Irish Nationalist; the cotton porters and carters (occupations traditionally dominated by Protestants) were led by Tories. As the great western
seaport, Liverpool was particularly receptive to American (and Irish)
influences. From its branch in Bootle, the Knights of Labour pointed the
way towards broad and inclusive structures, but rejected strikes in favour
of harmony, arbitration and boycotts, tactics which the Catholic church
was prepared to endorse. Within a few months, however, the Knights were
ousted from influence by the arrival of a more militant body on the Liverpool waterfront, the National Union of Dock Labourers, whose leaders
were not socialists, but radical supporters of the great American radical
and land reformer, Henry George.

The dockers' strike and its settlement introduced a new structural
dimension to industrial relations with a movement away from autonomous
and fragmentary regulation by small groups of employees and individual
employers towards a wider coverage of the unit of regulation – one which
would be subject to approval of external authority as represented by the
union on the one side and the employers' association on the other. Both
organisations were to become permanent, but each had teething problems:
the union had to restrain and control its members' actions in the union's
own long-term interests; employers were not entirely united in response to
the challenge of the union as some still refused to join the Employers
Labour Association, to relinquish their self-sufficiency in labour matters.

Limited as it was, socialist influence was more notable among women
workers. Assisted by socialists and middle-class critics of the sweating
system, such as Jeannie Mole, a Fabian socialist and wife of a wealthy local
fruit merchant, women workers were encouraged to form all-female
unions. Unlike the men, female unionists were ready to accept middle-
class organisers: other women were frequently more sympathetic to their
demands than were the unionised menfolk of their own class. In the height

of the fervour for new unions, female unions were established (if only briefly) among cigar-makers, book-folders, upholstresses, marine-sorters, coat-makers, laundresses and sack and bag makers. Joseph Goodman of the Social Democratic Federation was joint organiser of the Liverpool Tailoresses and Coatmakers Union and chairman of its strike committee, which also received financial support from the Liverpool Socialist Society. The successful outcome of the strike in 1890 sparked off a general recognition of the plight of exploited women in the city. Once the reduction in hours was secured, however, the number of women in the union began to diminish – by 1894 only 100 members remained. More than their male counterparts, female new unions in Liverpool tended to be episodic: women seemed to have joined unions for short-term goals, moving out either when these were achieved or once it became apparent that they were not immediately to be granted.

Trade union development in Lyon in the late nineteenth century exemplifies what have subsequently been considered as national trends in France: numerical and financial weakness; intense ideological and political division – finally resolved at Lyon when the 'apolitical' *blanquistes* and anarchists supplanted the *guesdistes*; and the use of strikes and mass demonstrations, such as May Day. Lyon, however, already had a strong trade union tradition with substantial participation. But towards the end of the century, unions were fragile and membership fluctuated wildly, even among craft workers: the leather-tawers went from 12 members in 1892 to 340 in 1893, then down to six in 1897 and back up to 140 in 1898; the powerful union of glassworkers of Lyon and Oullins, capable of exercising considerable control over the trade, collapsed from a peak of 500 members at the time of a major strike in 1887, and was rendered almost lifeless by defeat in an eight-month strike in 1891 – by 1895 it counted just 56 members. Following the defeats, however, several glassworkers moved elsewhere in the region to swell the numbers of other unions – at Rive de Gier, some 40 kilometres from Lyon, the union grew from 400 members in 1891 to 1100 in 1894, before itself collapsing in a hard-fought strike.

Organised workers in Lyon were to the fore in proposing and promoting a number of national federations in the 1890s – glassworkers, masons, builders, leatherworkers, and weavers – but none secured institutional permanence. By British and German standards, the degree of organisational mobilisation was low. However, there were high levels of militancy and ideological awareness among the mobilised minority, another 'national' characteristic. The glassworkers were *blanquiste*, while metalworkers and builders were *guesdiste*. Traditionally, weavers' unions were radical-socialist strongholds, but the *guesdistes* were to the fore in attempts to organise weavers and dyers in the mechanised sector. There was also a Catholic union among the silk-weavers, with some 500 members throughout the 1890s, the only 'independent' union in Lyon prior to the later expansion of 'yellow' unionism. The one exclusively female union in Lyon, comprising office workers, the needlework trades and silk-workers, was also organised by the Catholics between 1899 and 1903.

Among the socialists, the *blanquistes* were less numerous but better organised: there were some 200 activists, almost all of whom were based in the city itself. The *guesdistes* had between 250 and 300 activists, mainly located in the suburbs and surrounding industrial areas. Within the Bourse du travail, as will be shown below, ideological affiliation was of crucial importance. In other arenas, however, socialism proved less schismatic. Both groups cooperated in upholding May Day as a day of socialist protest and demonstration in contradistinction to anarchist aspirations to trigger revolution. Both groups, too, aligned themselves within the large coalition of the left upon which the dominant Republican regime could generally rely – in 1898, an independent socialist in la Croix Rousse and two *blanquistes* in la Guillotière gained election thanks to an accord with the moderate Republicans. Furthermore, they worked together in the Fédération Lyonnaise des Syndicats, a pioneer attempt at local trade union coordination established in 1881, from which, however, the main textile manufacturing unions kept apart. Having suggested the formation of a national federation, the Fédération Lyonnaise was reconstituted as the Conseil local de la Fédération Nationale des syndicats in 1887, at which point militant *guesdistes*, already in control of the Bourse du travail, asserted their dominance.

Little influenced by strike waves or ideological division, trade union growth in Munich, as throughout Germany, was steady and secure. In the formative decades at the end of the nineteenth century, Munich set the pace in Germany, with high membership levels, close cooperation between unions and political party, and the extension of institutionalised collective bargaining. The percentage of the workforce in 'free' or social democratic unions rose from 12.7 per cent in 1894 to 24.7 per cent in 1899 to around 70 per cent in 1907, by which time some 77 different trades were organised, usually linked in centralised manner to the Generalkommission in Berlin.

There were also a number of Christian Unions, mainly formed where socialist unions were not allowed, as was the case with the railway workers discussed below. This remarkable expansion can be attributed to two related factors: the crucial role of the Munich Gewerkschaftskartell in co-ordinating industrial, political and cultural activity (discussed below); and the extension of institutionalised collective bargaining. Here Munich was in advance of the rest of Germany, setting a pattern of reformist progress-ivism based on union recognition, state involvement and conciliation. Such collective bargaining agreements extended to 75 per cent of the male workforce (60 per cent of the combined male and female workforce) in 1912, when only 12 per cent of workers elsewhere in Germany were covered by similar arrangements. It should be noted too that the SPD enjoyed con-siderable political influence. At state level, Bavaria prided itself on being open to reform. The Bavarian government, confident that the socialists would not acquire majority status, saw no risk in liberal and democratic policies, prompting the socialists to move further in a reformist direction. At community level in Munich itself, the SPD enjoyed greater active parti-cipation and strength in the bi-cameral system, the restrictions of the franchise and the large number of Catholic and middle-class voters notwith-standing. On educational and cultural issues, the SPD cooperated with the Liberals against the Catholic Centre Party, while in matters concerning workers' rights and status the SPD cooperated with the Catholics against the right wing of the Liberals. By 1911, the SPD emerged as the largest single party, with 37.9 per cent of the vote and most of the seats in one of the chambers. In no other German city had the socialists yet achieved such political integration. The presence and involvement of middle-class intellectuals and activists (including Hope Bridges Adams Lehmann, the British wife of the socialist Dr Karl Lehmann, and a leading campaigner for the emancipation of women) ensured against a class-exclusive 'prole-tarian' image, and encouraged Munich social democracy along the path of social liberalism, a 'modernising' course followed throughout Germany some decades later.

In each city, the character and shape of trade union development was much influenced by the local coordinating body. The Liverpool Trades Council (LTC), established in 1848, was among the first in the country, but membership was restricted to well-established craft organisations in the building industry and waterfront trades. By 1887, the LTC had an affiliated membership of only 3000 and an annual income of just £10 from affiliated trade unions of engineers, printers, tailors, saddlers, bookbinders, railwaymen, gilders, cabinet-makers, sawyers, brushmakers, bootmakers, mast-block makers and upholsterers. By 1891, with the advent of new unionism, the fortunes of the LTC had been transformed: with 47 affiliated trades and over 46 000 members, the LTC was the largest and most important provincial Trades Council.

Throughout the 1890s, there was considerable tension between the National Union of Dock Labourers, the most significant of the new unions, and the LTC. Although aggravated by the personality of Sexton, the new leader of the dockers, these tense relations exposed the social and cultural gulf between the regularly-employed, relatively well-paid and time-served craft workers who still dominated the LTC – 'would be aristocratic artisans', to use Sexton's terminology – and the low-paid, casually-employed water-front workers in the surviving new unions. (There were gender tensions as well: when the LTC reluctantly admitted its first woman delegate in 1890, it decided to transfer meetings from the usual pub to a more 'respectable' venue.) The LTC continued to be dominated by skilled craft workers: in 1905, most delegates to the LTC lived in wards near the city centre but some distance uphill from the river, well away from unskilled, Catholic waterfront wards.

Given these divisions in the labour movement, and the strength of sectarian political formations, it is not surprising that Liverpool played a backward role in the next stage of 'labour's turning-point', the slow and pragmatic development from trade unionism to independent (and parliamentary) labour politics. Given the entrenched strength of the city's ethnic-sectarian political formations, there was neither space nor need for independent Labour. There was no working-class Conservative councillor before 1914, but through the interlocking associational network – party, sectarian and popular – local Tory notables were forcibly reminded of the need to protect the 'marginal privilege' of the Protestant worker. As the Irish National Party passed into the hands of second-generation (i.e. Liverpool-born) Irish, it displayed less interest in the fate of Ireland than in the immediate needs of the local Catholic community in housing and employment. While the extent of political patronage and welfare benefits at the disposal of these sectarian machines is open to question, both reached deep into their respective constituencies, assisted by pub- and parish-based networks of associational culture and collective mutuality.

Despite valiant efforts to provide a vibrant, non-sectarian counter culture, socialists secured little influence within the Liverpool labour movement. The LTC resisted proposals for a new political alignment put forward by socialists and others involved in agitation among the unemployed: in 1893, for example, Sexton's attempt to federate the LTC with the Independent Labour Party was rejected. But pressure for labour representation steadily increased. Resolutions in favour of independent labour representation (as well as 'fair-wage' clauses in corporation contracts and an eight-hour day) were a key feature of May Day demonstrations, the first of which was held in Liverpool on 2 May 1891 – May Day in Liverpool, however, was traditionally the occasion of the horse parade by the carters, an exclusively Protestant occupation. In 1900, the LTC eventually joined with the socialist groups – the ILP (Independent Labour Party), Fabians, and the Social Democratic Federation – and the Edge Hill and Garston Labour Clubs (wards with large numbers of railway workers) to form what became by 1903 the Liverpool Labour Representation Committee, which in turn affiliated to the national Labour party in 1907. However, there was limited advance until inter-war slum clearance gradually destroyed the community base of the old sectarian politics. It was not until 1955 that Labour gained control of the municipal council, a generation later than equivalent triumphs in other major conurbations. In its combination of political and ideological weakness with workplace industrial militancy, a pattern established in the formative decades at the end of the nineteenth century, Liverpool labour history provides an accentuated inflexion of British national characteristics.

During the next great strike wave (1911–13), when Liverpool was 'close to revolution', syndicalists were able to exploit the structural tensions not only between old craft unions and new unions but within the new unions themselves. As casual labourers lacked the guaranteed time, relevant experience or financial resources for regular involvement, new unions were perforce dominated by full-time officials. These bureaucrats soon sought union incorporation in national agreements with employers, to which end they were prepared both to discipline and decasualise the membership. In so doing, they offended against the independence and pride of the Liverpool labourers. For all its ills, casualism was a cherished symbol of independence, the best guarantee of freedom from irksome work-discipline, from the tyranny of the factory bell. In protesting against decasualisation, the workers were championed by syndicalist advocates of direct action, but the incidence of subsequent rank-and-file militancy seems to have been determined less by theory and praxis than by specific grievances and traditional attitudes. Long after the decline of the docks, shipping and casualism, Liverpool workers continued to protest against *workplace* impositions and innovations – national agreements, bureaucratic structures and new work practices – which denied their residual independence and democratic local autonomy. To unsympathetic observers, 'militant' Merseyside represented the 'British disease' at its worst.

In Lyon, local attempts at coordination foundered on ideological division rather than structural tensions. The Conseil local de la Fédération nationale des syndicats secured a temporary dominance of the labour movement from 1889–90, when it assumed responsibility for May Day and other major demonstrations. By 1890, 45 Lyon-based unions were affiliated – building workers and metalworkers were strongly represented, along with glassworkers, leatherworkers and shoemakers – as were 33 weavers' unions in the adjacent Beaujolais region. In Lyon itself, the old weavers' unions, still dominated by radicals, kept apart, but unions in mechanised weaving and dyeing sectors were quick to affiliate. Such coordination, however, did not endure. At the second May Day demonstration, more revolutionary elements came to the fore. Rioting led to repression which in turn prompted the more politically-minded, notably the *guesdistes*, to seek some accommodation with the authorities. This sequence of events led to disillusion and apathy, to the point at which the purpose of the ailing Conseil local was called into question. There seemed no prospect of its calling a general strike, while more routine administrative matters of local coordination were increasingly undertaken by the Bourse du travail.

There was no equivalent in Liverpool or Munich of the Bourse du travail, where workers from different industries could meet in premises provided by the local authorities. At Lyon, the local authority operated a separate employment exchange for women workers, but some women workers in the organised weaving, dyeing and tobacco trades were represented at the local Bourse du travail, housed in the former théâtre de variétés. Sponsored by Republican municipalities throughout France in the hope of coopting a tame labour movement, the Bourses du travail soon engendered a syndicalist mentalité, a general 'workerist' mistrust of both Republican reform and socialist sectarianism. In Lyon, the latter was much in evidence. Ideological divisions were particularly pronounced as the dominant *guesdistes* seemed intent on eradicating any *blanquiste* influence within the Bourse. Indeed, it was this determination which created the impression of fundamental polarisation in Lyon between moderates and revolutionaries, whether *blanquiste*, anarchist or independent. As events turned out, the *guesdistes* were unable to impose control. They gradually lost influence within the Bourse du travail. Furthermore, they were excluded by *blanquistes* and anarchists from the new committee for May Day which appeared in 1897, along with a new local federation which was ultimately to adhere to the CGT (the general confederation of French labour).

The Munich Gewerkschaftskartell secured a much higher degree of integration and coordination, in both the industrial and political aspects of the local labour movement. A clearing house for all social, cultural and economic questions, the cartel provided the organisational and financial infrastructure – and the overlap of personnel – for coordinated reformist practice by unions and party. The cartel, however, did not construct a workers' counter-culture as was the case elsewhere in Germany. In Munich this was unnecessary: by no means proletarian in image and identity, the labour movement developed within the wider framework of Bavarian democratic and 'social-liberal' culture.

OCCUPATIONAL CASE STUDIES

Given the multifarious nature of economic activity within the cities, it is difficult to select representative occupations for case-study. In the city centres, office work and shop work expanded rapidly, but judging by the Liverpool experience, powerful barriers of status, work practice and culture – a veritable 'collar gap' – kept these white-collar workers apart from the wider labour movement and the working class in general. The development of 'professional' organisations attested to insecurity as the rapid expansion of numbers (and the introduction of new office technology) threatened to reduce traditional status and gender differentials. While work in small shops was long, poorly-paid and ill-regarded, the new multiple and department stores in the city centres were altogether more prestigious. Educational requirements were high, beyond the reach of most working-class young women.

White-collar workers kept distant from organised labour. As commercial centres, large cities required efficient transport networks to link with the rest of the country and to serve their own rapidly expanding built-up area – not least to carry clerks and shop assistants from respectable suburbs to central workplaces. Preliminary comparative research has revealed important differences in the organisation of railway workers and tramway workers in the three cities.

Railway workers

As members of the uniformed working class with job security and a regular wage, railway workers occupied an important position in Liverpool labour history. In the 'false dawn' of new unionism in 1871–73, the railwaymen alone managed to secure a permanent form of organisation with the establishment of a Liverpool branch of the Amalgamated Society of Railway Servants. Not dependent on the casual labour market, railwaymen were the one group of non-craft workers with the time and means to devote to trade unionism; to the cooperative movement (in 1891–92, 43 per cent of new male members of the Liverpool Cooperative Society were railway workers); and to the development of independent labour politics. Where most workers moved within the sphere of sectarian associational culture, Liverpool railwaymen developed a more proletarian style and culture.

In Lyon, some 350 railway workers were unionised in 1891. The real strength of the union, however, was outside the city in railway workshops in Oullins where 1000 of the 1500 workers were organised. Like the local metalworkers, they kept apart from the labour movement in Lyon itself. They used a different Bourse du travail and concentrated their efforts less on local coordination than in spreading unionisation along the Paris–Lyon–Marseille line.

Despite the consensual political atmosphere, railway workers in Munich were prohibited from joining socialist trade unions. There were no such restrictions, however, on membership of the Christian (or Catholic) unions. In 1897, 1500 railway workers belonged to the Christian union, comprising more than 60 per cent of the total membership of all such unions in Munich.

Tramway workers

Efficient local transport was very important for large cities. Tramway workers were constrained in their options for militant action, however, by a complex framework of industrial relations, which included the general public as well as employers and local authorities.

The lengthy tramwaymen's agitation in Liverpool (late June 1889–January 1890) has been described as an abject failure. The United Tramways Company was notorious as a tyrannical employer, but the tramwaymen decided against militant strike action for a number of reasons. Previous attempts at unionisation and strike action in the 1870s had ended in disaster and fiasco. This time it was the Knights of Labour who organised the men into the Liverpool Amalgamated Tramway and Hackney Carriage Employees' Association and advised them not to strike but to rely on public opinion and conciliation. Those activists who favoured a more militant policy lacked support among the workforce, most of whom were reluctant to jeopardise regular employment within the uniformed working class. Take-home pay fluctuated as a result of petty fines imposed by the employer, but the advantage of regular work and a regular income, particularly within the context of Liverpool's predominantly casual labour market, was a benefit not lightly to be discarded. As late as the great Liverpool transport strike of 1911, tramwaymen remained weak, apathetic and abused by their employers, municipalisation of the service notwithstanding.

In Lyon, where a private company operated the network under a concession from the local authority, tramway drivers and conductors were not organised until 1896 when Victor Darme, a *guesdiste*, took the lead. Tactical considerations, rather than ideology, accounted for their moderate stance in industrial relations. Given their prominent visibility to the general public, tramway workers sought above all to project an image of moderation and respectability. When they took strike action in 1900, they marched silently through the town centre in neat columns, all dressed in uniform, behind the tricolour, not the red flag. The union officials were at the head, followed by the workers ranked according to age and seniority. Similarly in Munich, tramway workers were well organised, but were reluctant to take militant action for fear of jeopardising their job security, particularly as many were elderly and thus unlikely to find alternative employment. Within the Gewerkschaftskartell, the tramway workers were a moderating influence, seeking to pacify more militant workers.

For the uniformed working class, large cities held out the prospect of an early advance into 'public service' or 'municipal' socialism. However, they were often restrained in their industrial tactics, fearful of jeopardising their relative security or of offending public opinion within the city. As providers of essential services, unionised manual workers were conditioned by the discourse of civic pride. The interests of the city could take precedence over those of labour.

The predicament of the tramway workers is an appropriate reminder of the ambivalent identities (complementary, overlapping or competing) on option to workers. Pride in the city did not preclude commitment to wider affiliation, particularly if the city took the lead in constructing national, occupational, confessional, class or gender-based associations. At times of industrial dispute, however, workers faced the charge of civic disloyalty, alienating public opinion by bringing city services to a halt. To understand the origins of this complex (and increasingly familiar) pattern of industrial relations, more research is urgently required on the 'grandes villes' of the late nineteenth century.

Also of relevance to the theme of this essay are: J. Belchem (ed.), *Popular Politics, Riot and Labour: Essays in Liverpool History 1790–1940*, Liverpool, 1992; H. Hikins (ed.), *Building the Union: Studies on the Growth of the Workers' Movement: Merseyside, 1756–1967*, Liverpool, 1973; Y. Lequin, *Les Ouvriers de la région lyonnaise*, 2 vols, Lyon, 1977; K.H. Pohl, *Die Münchener Arbeiterbewegung. Sozialdemokratische Partei, Freie Gewerkschaften, Staat und Gesellschaft in München 1890–1914*, Munich, 1992; and G. Neumeier, *München um 1900. Wohnen und Arbeiten, Familie und Haushalt, Stadtteile und Sozialstrukturen*, Frankfurt, 1995.

Index